Learn Microsoft Visual Studio App Center

With Xamarin Forms

Sunny Mukherjee

Apress®

Learn Microsoft Visual Studio App Center: With Xamarin Forms

Sunny Mukherjee
Tampa, FL, USA

ISBN-13 (pbk): 978-1-4842-4381-7   ISBN-13 (electronic): 978-1-4842-4382-4
https://doi.org/10.1007/978-1-4842-4382-4

Managing Director, Apress Media LLC: Welmoed Spahr
Acquisitions Editor: Smriti Srivastava
Development Editor: Matthew Moodie
Coordinating Editor: Shrikant Vishwakarma

Cover designed by eStudioCalamar

Cover image designed by Freepik (www.freepik.com)

Distributed to the book trade worldwide by Springer Science+Business Media New York, 233 Spring Street, 6th Floor, New York, NY 10013. Phone 1-800-SPRINGER, fax (201) 348-4505, e-mail orders-ny@springer-sbm.com, or visit www.springeronline.com. Apress Media, LLC is a California LLC and the sole member (owner) is Springer Science + Business Media Finance Inc (SSBM Finance Inc). SSBM Finance Inc is a **Delaware** corporation.

For information on translations, please e-mail rights@apress.com, or visit www.apress.com/rights-permissions.

Apress titles may be purchased in bulk for academic, corporate, or promotional use. eBook versions and licenses are also available for most titles. For more information, reference our Print and eBook Bulk Sales web page at www.apress.com/bulk-sales.

Any source code or other supplementary material referenced by the author in this book is available to readers on GitHub via the book's product page, located at www.apress.com/978-1-4842-4381-7. For more detailed information, please visit www.apress.com/source-code.

Printed on acid-free paper

Dedicated to my late father, Dr. Arup Mukherjee

My father, Dr. Arup Kumar Mukherjee
12/02/1953 – 12/17/2018

*I am dedicating my first book to my dear and late father,
Dr. Arup Kumar Mukherjee. I started writing this book in mid-2018 as
part of a bigger project. My father knew about this project from the
beginning, gave me solid advice, and encouraged me from start to
finish. He passed away just a day after I finished writing this book, on
December 17, 2018. It will be my life-long regret that I could not tell
him that I finally finished this book. And I regret that I could not give
him the happiness he deserved because, to my mother and me, he left
this life at a young age before he could enjoy it with us fully.*

*I want to share a few things about my father. Naturally, every son
will say that their father is the greatest. As a father, he taught me
mathematics and science, fought for me whenever I ran into trouble
in life, helped me win multiple spelling bee competitions at school,
helped me attain full-tuition scholarships, and taught me solid
principles and ethics to be a good human being later in life.
But I know objectively my father is an incredible soul, not from
my experience, but from the words and experiences of those he
touched in his life. He started his education at the Indian Institute
of Technology in Kanpur, India. He completed his studies with the
highest honors while fighting for student rights. He even spoke to the*

Prime Minister of India, Indira Gandhi, on behalf of student welfare at IIT. He married my mother when he was only 25. He moved to the U.S. soon after. With only a few dollars in his pocket, he started our lives in Knoxville, Tennessee where he was allowed to skip his Masters and begin his Ph.D in Management Science from the University of Tennessee. Later, our family moved throughout the country and eventually settled in Pensacola, Florida. I grew up in Pensacola and saw my father's biggest impact when he became a full professor and the Chairperson of the Management Information Systems department at the University of West Florida. He wrote several journals and research articles on topics like Management Science and Decision Support Systems. He continued the practice of his youth, that of fighting for others, by inspiring his students to stand on their own two feet, utilize their talents, and pursue their dreams.

Unfortunately, both my mother and my father struggled during the last few years of his life due to his multiple health problems; my mother was his constant caretaker. He lost his ability to see and take care of himself, so he fell back on using his mind the most during this time. It was during this time also that I finished my MBA and I was brainstorming multiple ideas and projects. I shared some of those ideas with my father. He brainstormed with me, steered me in the right direction, gave me words of wisdom and constructive criticism, and helped me grow my mind. He started seeing himself within me. I would eventually go on to write my first book based on the knowledge I learned on my own in mobile development, DevOps, and cloud services. Even though I could not give him all the joy he deserved at a late age, I hope to keep his name alive in this book and in future projects to come.

My late father was more than just a father. He was my mentor, my friend, and my confidant. Words cannot express how much I love him and how much I will miss his advice and his jokes. Consequently, I dedicate this book to the most intelligent, wisest, most compassionate, and most patient man I have ever known, my late father, Dr. Arup Mukherjee.

Table of Contents

About the Author

Sunny Mukherjee currently works as a lead developer. He has close to 15 years of experience in IT where he has worked on multiple platforms, including web, desktop, mobile, and cloud. He has worked in multiple industries, including healthcare, finance, retail, and defense. His other expertise includes software architecture, business plans and presentations, idea brainstorming and pitching, and fictional works. In his free time, he loves reading about astronomy, following the latest science and technology news, riding his bike, traveling to the beach, taking photographs, cooking, meditating, working out, and watching movies. He routinely shares important articles on his LinkedIn profile about .NET, new technologies, new discoveries, and career tips.

About the Technical Reviewer

 **Afzaal Ahmad Zeeshan** is a computer programmer from Rabwah, Pakistan. He likes .NET Core for regular day development and has experience with cloud, mobile, and API development. Afzaal Ahmad has experience with the Azure platform and likes to build cross-platform libraries and software with .NET Core. He has been recognized as a Microsoft MVP for his work in the field of software development and has been named a CodeProject MVP and C# Corner MVP for technical writing and mentoring.

Introduction

Welcome! I would like to express my sincerest appreciation to you for picking up this book. Have you read about Visual Studio App Center in articles lately? Have you been working on mobile development technologies for a while? Are you interested in a single cloud solution and saving money? If so, you are holding the right book. Visual Studio App Center is Microsoft's all-in-one, holistic DevOps cloud solution for mobile development, including building your app, distributing it, collecting crash data and events, sending notifications to your users, and testing your app in the cloud. *Learn Visual Studio with Xamarin Forms* is a practical, step-by-step exercise in reaping the full benefits of Visual Studio App Center. You will get access to a real Xamarin Forms mobile app so you can integrate directly into Visual Studio App Center. Here is what you can expect from this book.

What You'll Learn

You'll learn the following from this book:

- How to set up continuous builds on iOS and Android

- How to set up continuous delivery to your developers and testers

- How to collect crash events from your users to improve your app

- How to collect analytics to understand your users better

- How to communicate with your users with push notifications on both iOS and Android

- How to handle push notifications in your code in real time

- How to save money on development by testing your app against hundreds of different devices, operating systems, and form factors in the cloud

Microsoft has invested a lot of time and money into the Xamarin platform. It acquired Xamarin and aggregated its many individual applications into a new cloud service, App Center. At around the same time, Microsoft announced its intention to acquire GitHub too. I came up with the idea to write this book because all these major changes and acquisitions were taking place and no single resource existed with step-by-step examples, except for a few technical articles from Microsoft. As a result, I wanted to write a book to help other mobile developers like myself learn how App Center (with a sprinkle of Xamarin Forms, GitHub, and Azure DevOps) can make their lives easier.

I have spent most of my career in multiple software areas from web to desktop to mobile to cloud. My motivation for writing this book was not simply to create a mobile application and integrate it with App Center. I am an avid reader myself in various areas, ranging from astronomy to spirituality to cooking to programming. I have read plenty of good and bad writing. And I appreciate books that show me practical applications and not simply theoretical knowledge.

Therefore, this book will teach you practical, real-life examples of each feature from App Center and will show you how to use each feature in a real mobile application designed in Xamarin Forms. After going through the exercises, you can go back to your office or your team, crush your mobile project, and shine in your next professional review! Without further ado, let's begin the journey.

Who Is the Intended Audience?

This book is clearly for a person with a technical mindset and/or background, meaning the reader may be software developer, architect, tester, or a technical manager. Chapter 1 explains the cloud service and the benefits. The later chapters dive into great technical detail about each feature. Therefore, this book is meant for a reader who can follow along with the code, the settings, and the configuration of various services. It is not intended for a casual reader. It was written for technical users by a technical user.

Furthermore, most of the book is devoted to integrating, configuring, and using Visual Studio App Center in your app. As a result, if you are coming from a mobile development background in Xamarin.iOS, Xamarin.Android, Xamarin.Forms, Objective-C/Swift, React Native, Cordova, or Unity, you will learn how to use App Center because most of the customization is agnostic to the technology. But since I needed to make App Center work with an actual app, I chose Xamarin.Forms because my mobile development background is in Xamarin. Therefore, even if you do not know

C# or Xamarin.Forms, you can learn from the concepts and tailor it to your preferred technology because only the syntax will be different.

But if you are coming from a Xamarin.Forms background, I do make a few assumptions. First, I assume you can program in C# and the .NET Framework. Second, I assume you can program in the Xamarin.Forms framework. This book is not about teaching you either C# or Xamarin.Forms. It is about teaching you Visual Studio App Center and making it work with a sample Xamarin.Forms mobile app.

CHAPTER 1

Getting Started

In order to get a true appreciation for any technology, I personally feel that it is important to understand where a certain technology originated and how it evolved over time.

In 2016, Microsoft unveiled a public preview of Visual Studio Mobile Center as a "mission control" service for mobile apps. In the last few months of 2017, Microsoft rebranded the product offering because it is not just about mobile. It is more about apps on all platforms and form factors, including iOS, Android, macOS, and Windows. Today, it is called Visual Studio App Center.

Visual Studio App Center is a number of solutions for your mobile applications under a single ecosystem or umbrella. Microsoft acquired a number of preexisting products that it saw as essential to its business strategy. And it built several new features into the ecosystem to make the experience smooth and seamless for its customers.

I cover the history of the different products in the coming sections. Not only will you see how Microsoft consolidated the different products, but you will come to appreciate the business strategy and direction of Xamarin and App Center.

HockeyApp

HockeyApp was one of Microsoft's notable acquisitions back in December, 2014. If you have used HockeyApp for your mobile solution, then you are familiar with its benefits, including crash reporting, distribution, analytics, and cross-platform support for iOS, Android, and Windows Phone.

But keep in mind that after the acquisition of HockeyApp, Microsoft integrated its features into Visual Studio App Center and continues growing its list of features in App Center only. At the time of this writing, Microsoft announced that it will retire HockeyApp on November 16, 2019, meaning the service will no longer be available.

1

© Sunny Mukherjee 2019
S. Mukherjee, *Learn Microsoft Visual Studio App Center*, https://doi.org/10.1007/978-1-4842-4382-4_1

If your organization or team has been using HockeyApp as its mobile solution, you can keep using it for now, but Microsoft gives you the option to sync your apps to App Center simultaneously. After your apps are synced, you will be able to view your apps side by side in both HockeyApp and App Center. For example, if you distribute releases to your team members in HockeyApp, you will see the same releases in App Center. If you are collecting analytics using the HockeyApp SDK, the same analytics will be forwarded to App Center and available for viewing on its dashboards. The data that your apps accumulated in HockeyApp are streamed and available in App Center.

The side-by-side experience between HockeyApp and App Center has its benefits and limitations. Although you can view the settings from HockeyApp in App Center, you can only edit them within HockeyApp. These settings include management of the following in HockeyApp:

- Managing app collaborators and testers

- Managing organization owners

- Editing app settings such as the app name

- Managing notification settings

You can find more information at `https://docs.microsoft.com/en-us/appcenter/migration/hockeyapp/side-by-side`.

If you are member of an organization considering App Center as your solution in the future, you can find more information about Microsoft's transition plan for HockeyApp to App Center at `www.hockeyapp.net/appcenter/transition/`. I am not including the roadmap in the book because it is a dynamic roadmap and is thus constantly changing.

Please use the above resources to schedule the migration of your apps from HockeyApp to App Center at an appropriate time for your organization or team. The rest of this book will explain App Center and its benefits.

Xamarin

Now it's time to talk about the big gorilla in the room! The largest acquisition in February, 2016 from Microsoft in the mobile space was Xamarin, the ultimate cross-platform mobile development platform for .NET developers. The companies had a partnership for a number of years to incorporate Xamarin more and more into the Visual

Studio IDE and Azure. The acquisition did not come as a surprise to the development community. But the Xamarin company before the acquisition managed multiple products at the time, including the Xamarin Test Cloud, Xamarin Insights, Xamarin Profiler, and Xamarin Studio. After the acquisition, Microsoft eventually retired Xamarin Studio and incorporated its features into Visual Studio for Mac. And it incorporated Xamarin Profiler into the Visual Studio IDE.

Let's briefly talk about Xamarin Test Cloud and Xamarin Insights. If you were an active paying subscriber of the Test Cloud service, Microsoft automatically upgraded you to a user of App Center. In addition, Microsoft imported teams, organizations, and your apps and test reports into App Center in March, 2018. Microsoft then deprecated the Test Cloud CLI, requiring users to make calls to the App Center CLI. Around the same time, Microsoft retired the Xamarin Insights SDK and required you to use the App Center SDK. These powerful products from Xamarin now fully live on within App Center and Visual Studio.

Understanding DevOps

If you are a team member who wears all hats in a small, nimble team of a startup or a member from a large, multi-national enterprise curious about the value of App Center, you cannot deny the fact that we live in a world where speed to market is an essential business strategy in the software world. The software world has changed and we must adapt.

Why is speed to market so important in this business world? It gives us the ability to deliver promised changes or releases to our customers at a faster rate. Increased speed to market gives organizations the ability to respond faster to new or changing customer requirements, market forces, and competition. For example, if customers report a bug or request a new feature in your product, you can adapt and release. If you discover that a new customer demographic has growing interest in your product, you can prioritize certain features and release. If a new company releases a similar app with similar features for free, you can add in-app purchases for premium features in your app and make the base app free. The list goes on and on, but the common point is a need for speed to market.

This is where DevOps comes in. DevOps stands for Development + Operations. The ultimate purpose of DevOps is to release product changes on short time scales. This section is by no means a complete explanation of DevOps because the subject matter is an entire area of study and discipline in its own right. And multiple implementations of DevOps exist in different technologies, toolkits, and languages. But in order to appreciate how App Center fits into DevOps, it is important at first to understand the core principles of DevOps. Please refer to Figure 1-1 for the explanations that follow.

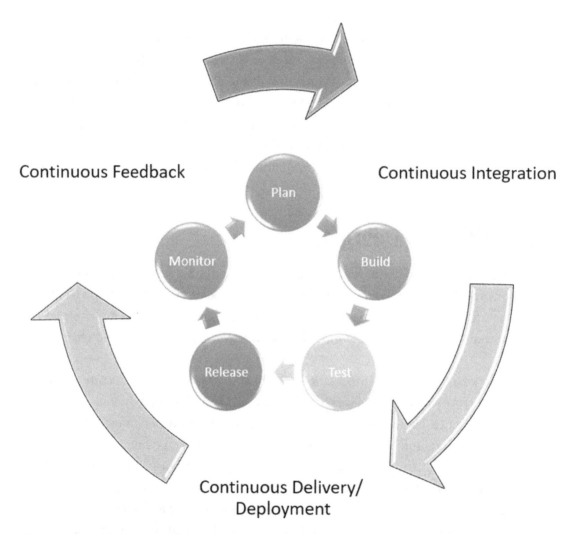

Figure 1-1. DevOps cycle

Let's go through the above concepts one by one.

Continuous integration is the first concept. It is the practice of merging or integrating a developer's code to the code repository on a frequent basis. This practice also involves triggering a code build immediately after the code is merged to the repository. In this way, you and every person on your team knows the status of the build at all times. When a build fails, everyone knows what changes caused the failure. And everyone can download the latest copy of the code at any time. In Figure 1-1, the steps for Plan, Build, and Test fall into this category because you plan your changes, code and build the changes, and test the changes. For example, the developers on a team may be coding and pushing changes into a Development branch of the code repository. Keep in mind that the Test step in the Continuous Integration segment usually means unit tests and not UI tests since developers typically write unit tests in order to test specific API methods or business functions.

This brings us to the second phase of DevOps: Continuous Delivery/Deployment. Both are distinct concepts and have different meanings but are easily confused. Continuous delivery is an absolute requirement of DevOps but continuous deployment is optional. Let me explain.

Continuous delivery means that software is released in short and frequent cycles. But continuous delivery does not necessarily mean delivery into the hands of your customers. Delivery may mean distribution into the hands of internal developers and testers. Continuous deployment means that after you pass continuous delivery, your software must pass a battery of automated tests, such as unit and/or UI tests, before it is deployed to production. Continuous deployment ensures you pass your tests; the code is in a releasable, production-quality state; and the software is released to your customers. Deployment to production in either continuous delivery or continuous deployment depends on the technologies that are used. For example, if the application is a website, it involves shutting down the application pool, deploying the website to the folder specified on the web server, and restarting the application pool. If the application is a desktop application, it involves creating a deployment artifact, such as an InstallShield application, that installs the components for you on your local system. In your case for this book, the deployment artifact will be a native artifact on your iOS or Android device. I am leaving out the technical details until later in the book.

Keep in mind that just because you can delivery software in shorter cycles does not mean that your organization may want to release to the public so frequently. Continuous deployment ensures your changes honor a minimum standard of quality before being released to the public. In Figure 1-1, the steps for Test and Release fall into this category. For example, after developers commit their changes into the Development branch, you may want to create a QA and/or Staging branch to merge your code on a scheduled basis and run your tests. If the tests fail, your code is not safe to release. If they succeed, the branch is in a releasable state.

The last concept is continuous feedback. After your product changes are released to the public, you want to monitor how your users are using the product, what bugs and other feedback they are reporting, and what crashes they are experiencing. This feedback cycle brings you back to the start of the DevOps cycle where you can gather the feedback, make new requirements, and plan new changes.

What Is App Center?

Hopefully, the previous section gave you a high-level idea of what DevOps is about and how it works if you are new to the methodology. If you are an active DevOps user in your organization, then you will see the benefits of App Center immediately as you go forward in this chapter.

Please refer to Figure 1-2 to understand the core features of App Center.

Figure 1-2. *Visual Studio App Center features*

App Center provides you with the core features shown in Figure 1-2 as part of the DevOps mobile solution. I'll give you a glimpse of each feature because the rest of the book goes into great detail and explains how to set up and use each feature.

- **Build**: This feature gives you the ability to set up automated or manual builds in the cloud. It lets you connect to source controls systems like Azure DevOps, BitBucket, or GitHub; select the repository where your app resides; and set up the branch that you want to build in the cloud.

- **Test**: This is a test automation service that allows you to set up UI tests on a number of supported test frameworks and run those tests on hundreds of real, physical devices and operating system configurations on Microsoft data centers.

- **Distribute**: This feature allows you to set up distribution groups or app store connections to which you can release your applications to end user devices. End user devices may be devices belonging to internal testers or to your target market who downloads the app from public app stores.

- **Diagnostics**: This feature allows you to monitor the health of an app in the public. It can upload crash events or error messages automatically so your development team can monitor from App Center and fix the issues in future versions of the app.

- **Analytics**: This feature gathers information about your app users or your target market, such as the number of active users over multiple days, where your users are located, the number of users per version of your app, how much time your users spend using your app, what top devices are used to run your app, and so on.

- **Push**: This feature allows you to send targeted push notifications to users of your app, regardless of the platform, by setting up the connection once for each notification service, such as Apple Notifications Service for iOS, Firebase Cloud Messaging for Android, or Windows Notifications Service for UWP.

- **Settings**: This feature allows you to control the settings and configuration of your apps, groups, connections, etc.

Why Is App Center the Solution?

The above explanations simply highlight each feature but do not explain how or why they benefit you or your team. Take a look at Figure 1-3 to understand the basic workflow of a mobile app from design to distribution and how it fits into the DevOps workflow explained above.

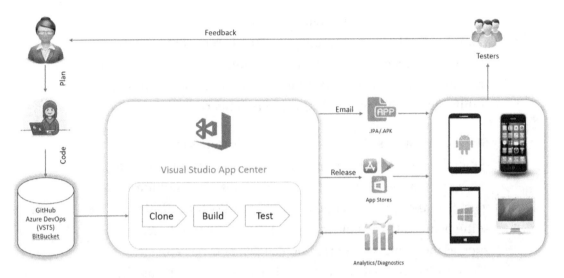

Figure 1-3. *Visual Studio App Center workflow*

Keep in mind the workflow may be different for each organization or team based on your team size, speed-to-market needs, or other requirements. But this workflow is a typical, generic workflow of an organization using App Center.

Let me explain the workflow now.

> **Step 1**: This step begins with a typical software change such as a feature, customer request, or a bug fix from the business in the top-left icon. At this step, the business gathers the requirements and plans the specifications of the change. This is part of the Planning step in the DevOps process.
>
> **Step 2**: This step is where the business transfers the planned changes to the development team to design and code the changes. This step is part of the Build step in DevOps.
>
> **Step 3**: This step is where the development team commits their changes to the source control system of their choice, such as GitHub, Azure DevOps (formerly Visual Studio Team Services), or BitBucket.
>
> **Step 4**: This step involves a set of actions on the App Center server. This step may be manual or automated, depending on the

needs of the team. In this step, the code is cloned into the App Center server from the remote source code repository, the code is built on the server, the code runs through a suite of tests, and the build produces an artifact for distribution. The fourth step fulfills the requirements of continuous delivery.

Step 5: This step is about distribution. This step is entirely dependent on the needs of the organization. If the organization has an internal testing team, they may choose to distribute a test version of the app to internal testers. But every organization at some point will distribute the app to the different app stores, such as the Apple App Store, Google Play, or the Microsoft Store. The fifth step is the Release step in DevOps and completes the Continuous Delivery/Deployment segment.

Step 6: This step shows how analytics and diagnostics are collected from physical devices and sent back to App Center for reporting purposes. This step helps you learn more about your app users and fulfills the Monitor step and the Continuous Feedback segment in the DevOps workflow.

As mentioned, the above workflow is more or less a common workflow most organizations may utilize. Feel free to think about custom workflows that suit the needs of your organization because some steps may be optional. Regardless of your organization's DevOps workflow, hopefully you can now see how the App Center suite of features fulfills each of the segments in the DevOps cycle.

Pricing

If you are considering seriously investing in the power of App Center, you need to learn the pricing model Microsoft has laid out. Fortunately, the App Center has a generous free tier so you and your team can try out the features before upgrading. Table 1-1 outlines what features are free and what features have a price. As you can see, you have more than enough to get started using App Center in order to create, test, and distribute a production-ready version of your app to your users. The service only charges a price when you want to run unlimited builds, run UI tests beyond 30 days, or target more market segments.

Table 1-1. *App Center Features and Prices*

Feature	Price
Run builds up to 240 minutes per month and up to 30 minutes per build	Free
Run unlimited builds per concurrency	$40 per month
Run UI tests for 30 days	Free
Run 30 device hours of tests per concurrency	$99 per month
Unlimited distribution to unlimited users and app stores	Free
Collect analytics from your users	Free
Collect crashes from your users	Free
Target up to five audience segments with push notifications	Free
Target 100K monthly active devices for more than five audience segments	$10 per month

Let me explain some of the terminology and the rules around the premium features.

Build concurrency defines how many builds can run at the same time. For example, a build concurrency of five means five separate builds can run in the same amount of time as one build. If you are using the free tier, you will get a build concurrency of one. Therefore, if you schedule five builds, they will wait in line in a queue and compile one at a time in succession.

Device hour is a unit used by App Center to measure the amount of time consumed by a set of activities across multiple devices. In the example above of 30 hours, you can run up to 6 hours of tests on five different device configurations for a total of 30 device hours. Or you can run 10 hours of tests on three different device configurations for the same result. If you wish to run 31 device hours of tests, you'll incur an additional $99 per month.

Lastly, regarding the number of market audience segments that you want to target with push notifications, suppose you want to target six segments for 200K users. In this case, you will pay 200K/100K per $10 = $20 per month. If you want to target seven segments for 200K users, you will still pay the same amount. If you want to target six segments for 300K users, you will pay 300K/100K per $10 = $30 per month. I will go into greater detail about push notifications in a later chapter.

You can find more information about App Center pricing at `https://visualstudio.microsoft.com/app-center/pricing/`.

Market Share

I feel mobile market trends and usage are important to mention so you understand how the overall market is invested in various mobile platforms. If you follow mobile trends, it will not come as a surprise to you that Android and iOS are the two most dominant platforms in the mobile market. In fact, with the demise of Windows Phone in recent years, whatever market share was taken by Microsoft has returned back to Google and Apple. Just refer to `http://gs.statcounter.com/os-market-share/mobile/worldwide` to understand what platforms the market is using as of 2018.

Android takes up more than 70% of the market while Apple has about 25% market share. The remaining market share is split up between Windows, Samsung, and other manufacturers. In fact, at the time of this writing, Windows has less than 1% market share. Consequently, the rest of this book is dedicated toward teaching you how to use the sample Xamarin.Forms app on either Android or iOS devices only.

Account Signups

In order to get started with App Center and use the sample app later in this chapter, you will need to register for a few simple accounts first.

Visual Studio App Center

First and foremost, you need to register for a free account with Visual Studio App Center. Head over to `https://appcenter.ms/`.

Click the Get Started button at the top right. You should see the page like the one shown in Figure 1-4.

Create Account

By creating an account you accept our
Terms of use and Privacy policy.

Figure 1-4. *App Center signup*

If you already have a GitHub or Microsoft account, you can register with either of those accounts, or you can register with a social media account like Facebook or Google. The rest of the process is straightforward.

Azure DevOps (Visual Studio Team Services)

This section is optional. You can easily host your code in any source code repository like GitHub or BitBucket and integrate your builds later in the book from their repositories. But for the duration of this book, I am going to use Azure DevOps or VSTS, create a project in VSTS, and integrate the builds with the projects from VSTS. If you are a user of VSTS, then you know that Microsoft rebranded the service from VSTS to Azure DevOps in late 2018. I use the terms interchangeably in this book because VSTS is still stuck in my mind!

Head over to Azure DevOps or VSTS at `https://visualstudio.microsoft.com/team-services/`.

Follow the simple instructions either to log in with an existing Microsoft account or register with your Microsoft account. You will upload the sample code from my GitHub repository into your new Azure DevOps account later in this chapter.

Azure

Now you need to set up a free Azure account. You need an Azure account later in the book in order to export data into Azure automatically. You can always revisit this section once you reach that chapter.

If you have been following Azure on the news lately, you know Microsoft is fighting Amazon and its Amazon Web Services for customers. As a result, Microsoft has made it easy for developers to get started using Azure for free for up to 12 months. Just head over to `https://azure.microsoft.com/en-us/free/` and follow the easy sign-up instructions to set up your Azure account.

Of course, if you already have an MSDN subscription, then you know you can easily activate Azure from the MSDN Benefits section. If you have such a subscription, I trust you can navigate your way to the Benefits section to activate this feature.

Apple Developer

You will need an Apple Developer account in order to get the most out of this book. You will be creating provisioning profiles and signing certificates and testing the sample app on physical iOS devices. As a result, you will need to purchase an Apple Developer annual membership to test on real devices. If you do not already have an Apple Developer account, go to the Developer portal at `https://developer.apple.com`.

Follow the simple, easy steps to create the account. Otherwise, log in with your existing Apple account. Keep in mind the Apple Developer account is $99 per year.

Giphy

You have one last account to create. Even though I will cover the details of the sample app later, head over to the Giphy Developers site at `https://developers.giphy.com` and sign up for a free Giphy developer account. You'll see where I'm going with the sample app because I didn't want to create a boring app for this book!

After creating an account, click the Create App button, give your app a name and description, and click the Create New App option. After creating the app, you will get access to an API key that you can later embed into App Center.

Software Installations

Even though some of the upcoming chapters focus on how to use App Center and configure its settings, the other chapters will require you to integrate with App Center. Therefore, the upcoming sample app from my GitHub repository will require you to have the following knowledge and skills in order to get the most out of this book:

- Xamarin Forms

- C# and the .NET Framework

- Model-View-ViewModel design pattern

If you are coming from a different background like Unity or Cordova and if you already have a sample mobile app written in another framework, you can just as easily follow along the material in this book by ignoring the sample Xamarin Forms project in this book and using your own project. Of course, the syntax will be different in your appropriate language or technology, but you should get an idea of the concepts and logic.

Git

If you are starting from a fresh, clean machine with Git previously installed, you can skip this section. But if Git is not installed on your machine, you will need Git to clone or fork the repository from my GitHub repository.

Head over to the official Git website at `https://git-scm.com/`. The installation process is straightforward on each platform because the Git community has detailed instructions for each platform. Go to the Downloads section on the site. You will see each platform listed, such as Mac OS X, Windows, and Linux/Unix. Select the appropriate platform. Download the latest version of Git. At the time of this writing, I used Git version 2.18.0 to 2.19.0.

Since I developed the app and wrote this book on a Windows machine, the screenshots show the point of view of a Windows PC. Most of the steps during the installation wizard are kept on the default options, which is why I show you only the wizard installation steps that I have changed from the default options.

For the default editor, I personally prefer a text editor with a GUI rather than the built-in VI editor, which is why I chose TextPad 8, as shown in Figure 1-5. Feel free to choose another editor you have preinstalled or use the built-in VI editor.

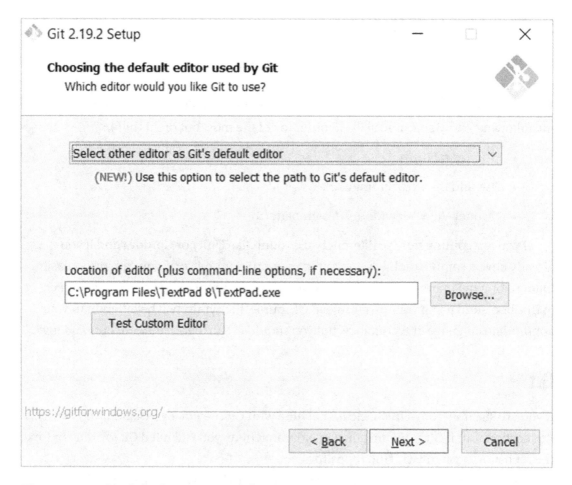

Figure 1-5. *Git default or custom editor setup*

When you have completed the wizard steps, your installation will complete, as shown in Figure 1-6.

Figure 1-6. *Git setup end*

After the installation, verify that you have Git installed using the following steps: open a command prompt window and type git --version. You should see the latest version displayed as shown in Figure 1-7.

Figure 1-7. *Git version verification*

NodeJS

NodeJS will be needed toward the end of the book because the JavaScript runtime framework is needed to install the App Center CLI locally on your machine. Navigate to https:// nodejs.org/en/, go to the Downloads section, and download and execute the latest current version of the MSI application based on your operating system and its bitness.

Visual Studio

In order to integrate App Center with the sample project, you will need Visual Studio installed on your machine. Once again, since I developed the sample app from the point of view of a Windows PC, for the rest of the book I will show you screenshots of Visual Studio on Windows when showing code from the sample project.

Head over to Microsoft's Visual Studio website at `https://visualstudio.` `microsoft.com/`. Download and install the Community Edition of Visual Studio. It has the necessary components to run a Xamarin Forms application. (All upcoming screenshots in this book are based on Visual Studio 2017 Enterprise Edition. Microsoft just released Visual Studio 2019 at the time of this writing.) I show you the screenshots of the selected features below during the installation process. I personally love how Microsoft has organized the various installation components into groups called workloads because it makes the installation easier.

Select the Mobile development with .NET workload, as shown in Figure 1-8.

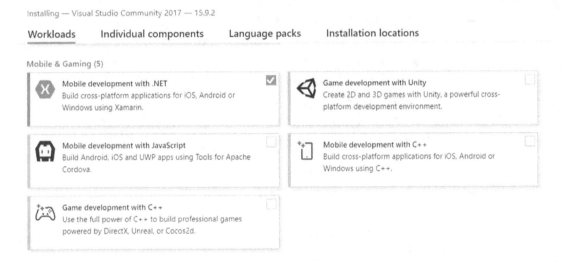

Figure 1-8. *Visual Studio setup* ➤ *Mobile development workload*

Select the .NET Framework SDK and targeting packs shown in Figure 1-9.

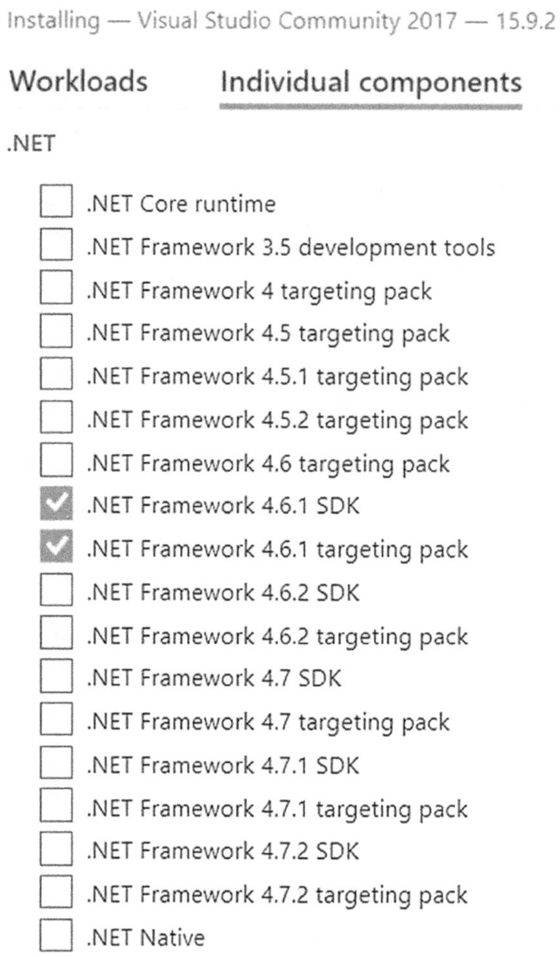

Installing — Visual Studio Community 2017 — 15.9.2

Workloads   **Individual components**

.NET

- [ ] .NET Core runtime
- [ ] .NET Framework 3.5 development tools
- [ ] .NET Framework 4 targeting pack
- [ ] .NET Framework 4.5 targeting pack
- [ ] .NET Framework 4.5.1 targeting pack
- [ ] .NET Framework 4.5.2 targeting pack
- [ ] .NET Framework 4.6 targeting pack
- [x] .NET Framework 4.6.1 SDK
- [x] .NET Framework 4.6.1 targeting pack
- [ ] .NET Framework 4.6.2 SDK
- [ ] .NET Framework 4.6.2 targeting pack
- [ ] .NET Framework 4.7 SDK
- [ ] .NET Framework 4.7 targeting pack
- [ ] .NET Framework 4.7.1 SDK
- [ ] .NET Framework 4.7.1 targeting pack
- [ ] .NET Framework 4.7.2 SDK
- [ ] .NET Framework 4.7.2 targeting pack
- [ ] .NET Native

***Figure 1-9.** Visual Studio setup ➤ Individual components*

In order to connect with GitHub directly from within Visual Studio, make sure you select the GitHub extension for Visual Studio, as shown in Figure 1-10. You can find more information about the extension at `https://visualstudio.github.com/`.

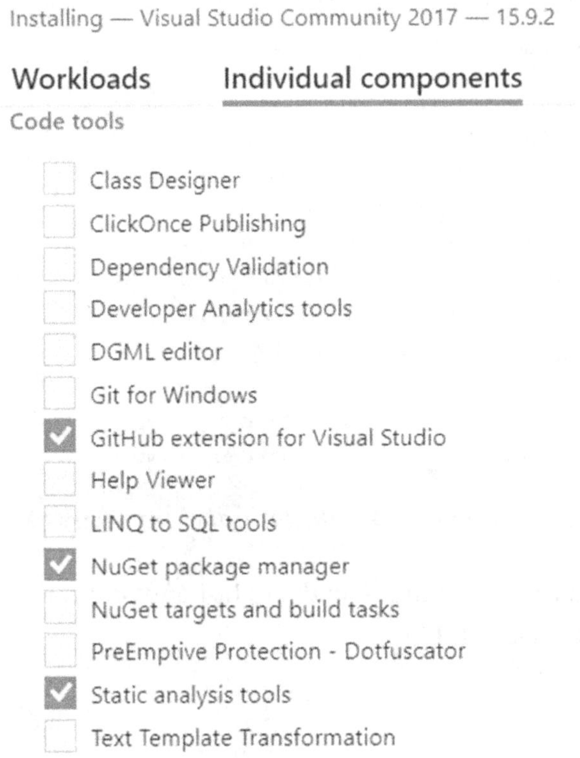

Installing — Visual Studio Community 2017 — 15.9.2

Workloads   Individual components

Code tools

- [ ] Class Designer
- [ ] ClickOnce Publishing
- [ ] Dependency Validation
- [ ] Developer Analytics tools
- [ ] DGML editor
- [ ] Git for Windows
- [x] GitHub extension for Visual Studio
- [ ] Help Viewer
- [ ] LINQ to SQL tools
- [x] NuGet package manager
- [ ] NuGet targets and build tasks
- [ ] PreEmptive Protection - Dotfuscator
- [x] Static analysis tools
- [ ] Text Template Transformation

Figure 1-10. *Visual Studio setup* ➤ *Individual components* ➤ *GitHub extension*

Now select Visual Studio Emulator for Android as shown in Figure 1-11 because you may want to use the Visual Studio emulator when running the sample app.

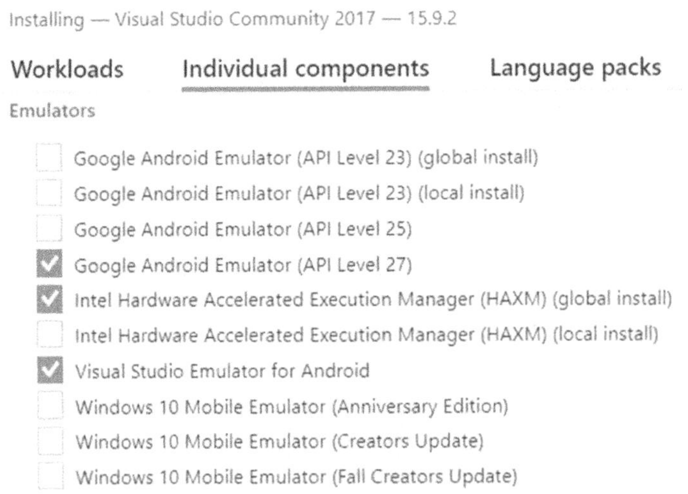

Installing — Visual Studio Community 2017 — 15.9.2

Workloads   **Individual components**   **Language packs**

Emulators

☐ Google Android Emulator (API Level 23) (global install)
☐ Google Android Emulator (API Level 23) (local install)
☐ Google Android Emulator (API Level 25)
☑ Google Android Emulator (API Level 27)
☑ Intel Hardware Accelerated Execution Manager (HAXM) (global install)
☐ Intel Hardware Accelerated Execution Manager (HAXM) (local install)
☑ Visual Studio Emulator for Android
☐ Windows 10 Mobile Emulator (Anniversary Edition)
☐ Windows 10 Mobile Emulator (Creators Update)
☐ Windows 10 Mobile Emulator (Fall Creators Update)

Figure 1-11. *Visual Studio setup* ➤ *Individual components* ➤ *Google emulator*

Verify the summary of the settings on the right-hand portion of the installation program, as shown in Figure 1-12.

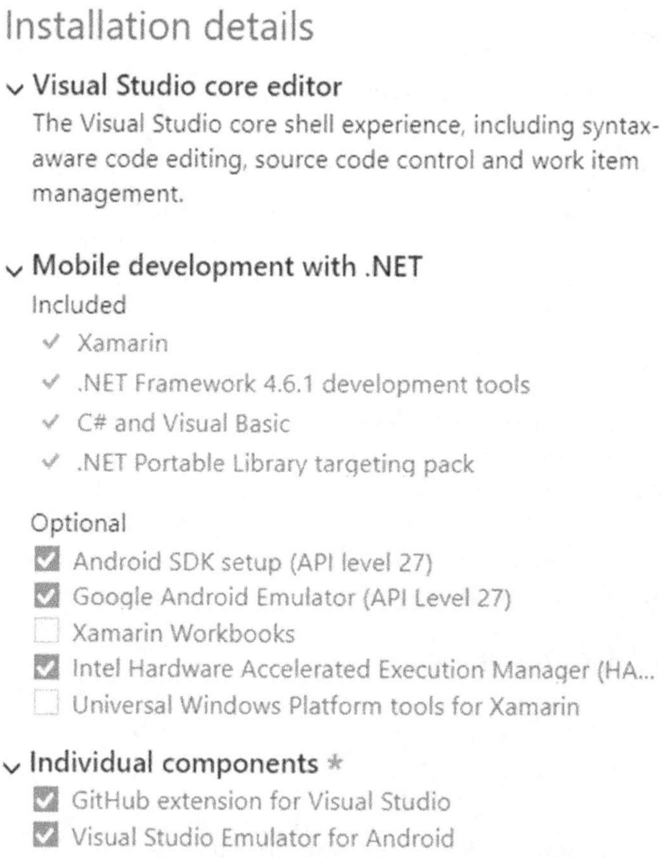

Installation details

⌄ Visual Studio core editor

The Visual Studio core shell experience, including syntax-aware code editing, source code control and work item management.

⌄ Mobile development with .NET

Included

✓ Xamarin

✓ .NET Framework 4.6.1 development tools

✓ C# and Visual Basic

✓ .NET Portable Library targeting pack

Optional

☑ Android SDK setup (API level 27)

☑ Google Android Emulator (API Level 27)

☐ Xamarin Workbooks

☑ Intel Hardware Accelerated Execution Manager (HA...

☐ Universal Windows Platform tools for Xamarin

⌄ Individual components *

☑ GitHub extension for Visual Studio

☑ Visual Studio Emulator for Android

Figure 1-12.   *Visual Studio setup review*

After the installation is complete, you have one last prerequisite to verify. You need to verify that Android 9.0 is installed because it is the Target Android Framework version in the sample Android app. Open your Visual Studio. Go to Tools menu ➤ Android ➤ Android SDK Manager. Verify you have Android 9.0 - Pie and the components shown in Figure 1-13 installed. If not, please select and install them.

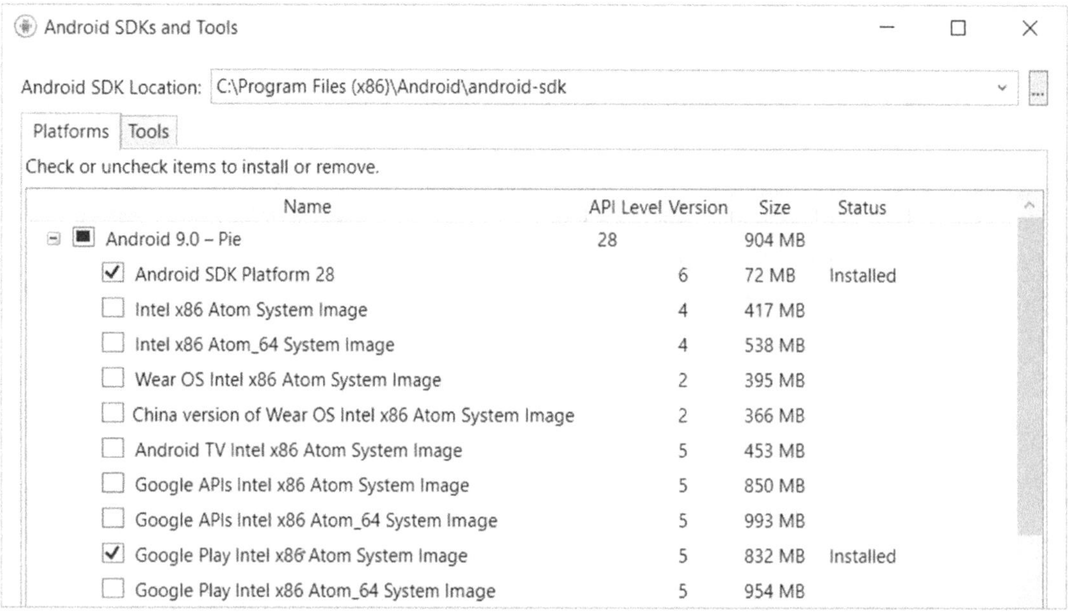

Figure 1-13. *Android 9.0 SDK setup*

Xcode

You need a Mac to develop and deploy any app to an iOS device. Just make sure you have the proper tools and the right versions installed on the Mac before moving ahead in this book. As mentioned, since you will be developing the sample Xamarin Forms app on Windows using Visual Studio, you must make sure the versions are in sync between Windows and Mac.

First, if Xcode is not already installed on your Mac, open the App Store, search for Xcode, and install it. You will not be using the Xcode IDE in the Mac, but you will need the Xcode SDK for deployment to iOS devices. As a Xamarin developer or any mobile developer who develops for Macs, you will need to ensure the Xcode versions always match between your Mac machine and your mobile development framework of choice. Once you have it installed successfully, you can go to the Xcode menu and click About Xcode to verify the version, as shown in Figure 1-14.

Figure 1-14. *Xcode version verification*

Visual Studio for Mac

Even though I am presenting all the screenshots in this book from the point of view of a Windows machine, if you have a Mac only and want to use App Center, go to https://visualstudio.com to get the free Community Edition of Visual Studio for Mac. Remember that the Community Edition is always free and it has all the Xamarin tools and SDKs packaged inside.

Since Microsoft retired Xamarin Studio and packaged all of the Xamarin tools and SDKs into Visual Studio for Mac, you only need to update Visual Studio to keep all Xamarin tools up to date. As Apple releases newer versions of Xcode, you can always update Visual Studio by clicking the Visual Studio Community menu item and selecting "Check for updates." It will download and install all the updates for you. You only need to restart Visual Studio after it finishes installing.

Android Studio

Android Studio is used in a later chapter when you need to create your Android Keystore file in order to store your signing certificates, which are necessary for your Android build on App Center to distribute your Android app to physical devices. Please install the latest version from https://developer.android.com/studio/.

GitHub Sample Project

For the purpose of this book, I built a sample project using Xamarin Forms that you will integrate with Visual Studio App Center as you progress through the chapters. I did not want to make a boring app, so I made it somewhat entertaining, which is why I asked you to create an account and app on the Giphy website.

This sample app is called GoGoGiphy. For the purpose of this book, it is a semi-functional app because you can run the app in a simulator, distribute to your test devices, and run UI tests on App Center. I made it just functional enough to give it purpose but I left out some key parts of a typical native mobile app, such as authentication, authorization, styling, and a splash screen. These design considerations should definitely be built for an app that is meant to be distributed to app stores, but for the purpose of integrating with App Center, these design features are beyond the scope of this book. Also, publication to app stores is not explained because this topic is beyond the scope, since each app store has its own set of rules, which the reader needs to read and understand from the appropriate documentation.

Why is this app somewhat entertaining? Well, this app gives the user the ability to view an endless list of gifs and search for any gif that you can find on the Giphy website. The user can create collections and save gifs to individual collections for future viewing. After all, who has ever wanted to make fun of a coworker or a boss and send gifs around the office? This app will give you ideas from which you can launch apps of your own. For example, you can share gifs via email or text. I will let your mind wander. But this app is functional enough as a sample app for integration with App Center in its current form.

Getting the Sample App

With all of that being said, now let's head over to my GitHub repository at `https://github.com/SunnyMukherjee/LearnAppCenter` to clone or fork the project. Please keep in mind that I will not be reviewing issues or looking for pull requests to merge into my project. This project is meant only as a sample app for this book. Please feel free to use the ideas from this app but not the code in your future app.

In this repository, you will find two subfolders: `Start` and `Finish`. Both are functional apps in their own right. But since some functions in the app integrate with App Center, the finished code is in the `Finish` folder of the app. The same functions are left as empty stubs in the `Start` folder.

In order to get started, you can fork the project directly from the GitHub page or you can click the Clone button and download the sample project to your local system. If you download the sample project, you will still need to upload it to a source control system like GitHub or Azure DevOps for you to integrate with App Center. After all, App Center has no visibility into your local machine! If you want to host the sample project on GitHub, I encourage you to fork the repository and I will show you in a later chapter how to connect to your GitHub repository. You can find the Fork button at the top of the repository page, as shown in Figure 1-15. GitHub will handle the rest of the process for you.

Figure 1-15. *GitHub fork project*

Importing the Sample App into Azure DevOps (VSTS)

Now I will show you how to import the sample project into your Azure DevOps (VSTS) repository. As mentioned, I assume you already have a Visual Studio Team Services (VSTS) account set up from a prior section. If not, please revisit the section to set up your Azure DevOps account.

Open your Azure DevOps account. You should see the Home page, like my page shown in Figure 1-16.

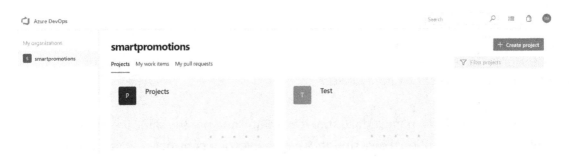

Figure 1-16. *Azure DevOps projects page*

Let's create a new project. Click the New Project button at the top right, as shown in Figure 1-17.

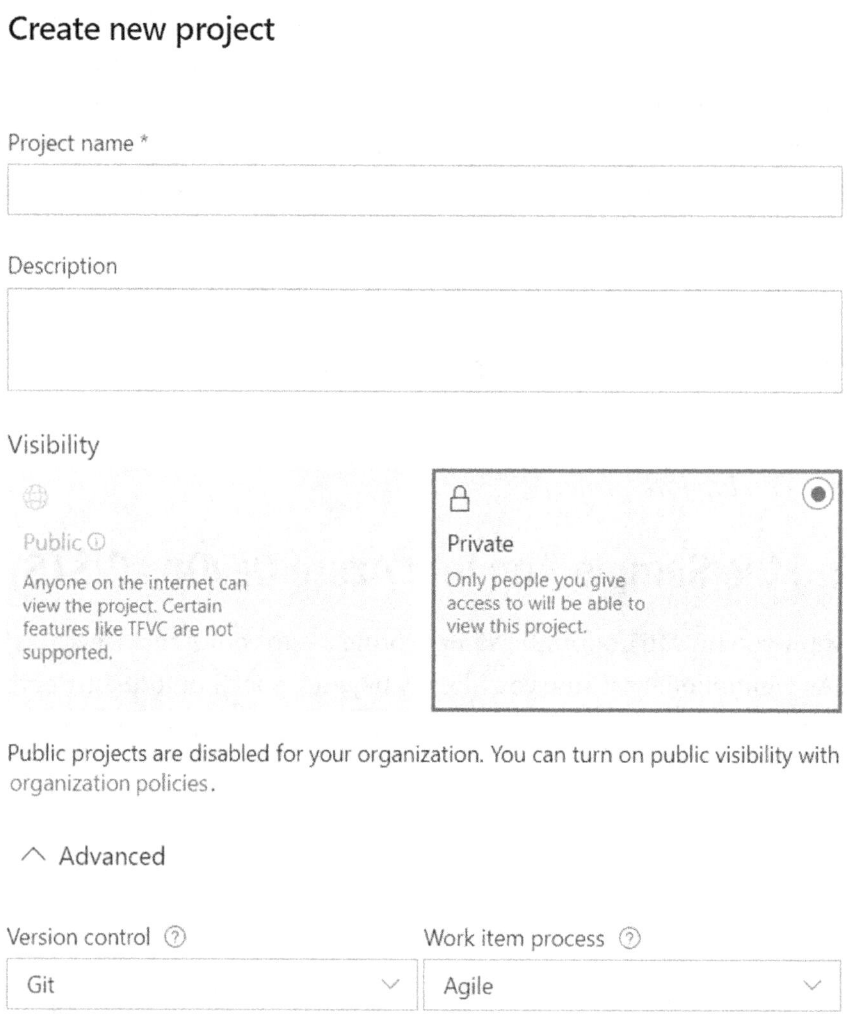

Create new project   ✕

Project name *

Description

Visibility

🌐	🔒 ⦿
Public ⓘ	Private
Anyone on the internet can view the project. Certain features like TFVC are not supported.	Only people you give access to will be able to view this project.

Public projects are disabled for your organization. You can turn on public visibility with organization policies.

⌃ Advanced

Version control ⓘ   Work item process ⓘ

| Git   ⌄ | Agile   ⌄ |

Figure 1-17. *Creating a new project*

Give your project a name. Make sure it is unique and not the same as your other projects. Give it an optional description. Keep the version control as Git and the work item process as Agile. My personal preference is keeping projects as Private.

Once your project is set up, now you can create your repository. You will take the easy route and simply import the repository from my GitHub repository. If you create a new project from scratch, you will see a screen similar to the one in Figure 1-18. You are interested in the highlighted Import button.

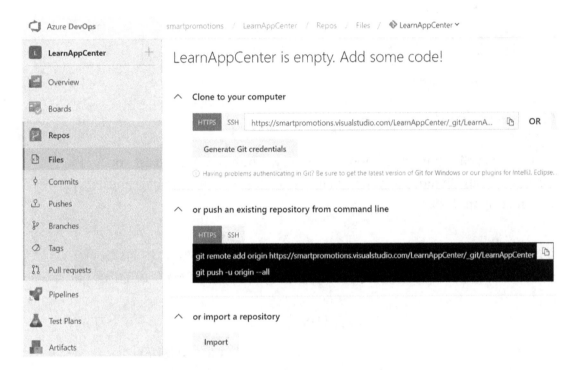

Figure 1-18. *Azure DevOps new repository*

Similarly, you can also click the breadcrumb in Figure 1-18 and select the Import repository option to go through the same actions that are coming up, as shown in Figure 1-19.

smartpromotions / LearnAppCenter / Repos / Files / ◈ LearnAppCenter ⌄

LearnAppCenter is empty. Add so

🔍 Filter repositories

◈ LearnAppCenter

+ New repository

⊼ Import repository

⚙ Manage repositories

⌃ Clone to your computer

| HTTPS | SSH | https://smartpromotions.visualstudio.co

Generate Git credentials

Figure 1-19. *Import repository*

Once you click Import or Import repository, Azure DevOps will ask you for the location of your Git repository. Return to my GitHub repository to copy the link, as shown in Figure 1-20.

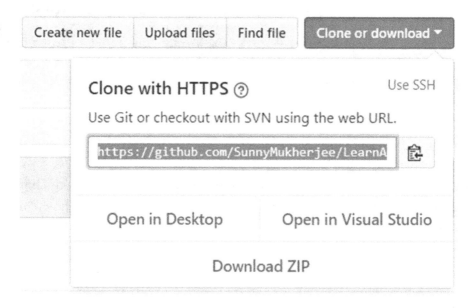

Figure 1-20. *GitHub repository URL*

Return to Azure DevOps, paste the link, and click Import, as shown in Figure 1-21.

Import a Git repository   ✕

Source type

| Git   ⌄ |

Clone URL *

| https://github.com/SunnyMukherjee/LearnAppCenter.git |

☐ Requires authorization

Import   Close

***Figure 1-21.** Importing a Git repository*

You are done importing the sample project into your Azure DevOps repository, as shown in Figure 1-22. Thankfully, the Azure DevOps team has made this process as seamless and effortless as possible.

Import successful!

Congratulations! Your https://github.com/SunnyMukherjee/LearnAppCenter.git repository has been successfully imported.

If you are not automatically redirected to your repository page Click here to navigate to code view.

***Figure 1-22.** Successful GitHub repository import*

Getting the App Ready

After either forking the project into your own GitHub repository or importing the project into your DevOps repository, now it's time to get your app ready for prime time! It needs to be ready for you to integrate with App Center starting in Chapter 2.

1. Update your Visual Studio 2017 to the latest version. This step should already be complete from the prior "Software Installation" section about Visual Studio if you installed VS for the first time. But if you already had Visual Studio installed from before, you need to update to the latest version to use the latest Xamarin features.

    a.   Go to Tools ➤ Get Tools and Features.

    b.   If the installer asks you to update, start the update.

    c.   Close Visual Studio.

    d.   If Visual Studio is not the latest version, run the update.

2. Update the NuGet packages.

    a.   Right-click the solution and click "Manage NuGet Packages for Solution."

    b.   Update every package except the NUnit package. This version needs to be on 2.6.4 because the UI tests that you will run in a future chapter will fail if this package is updated to a later version.

3. Rebuild the solution.

    a.   If you get any Xamarin errors, based on my experience developing mobile apps, Xamarin tends to throw false errors and leaves you scratching your head trying to figure out the reason. After updating Visual Studio and/or Xamarin.Forms NuGet package, I always recommend closing and restarting Visual Studio. And I recommend deleting the Bin and Obj folders of each project from Windows Explorer. After restarting VS, try rebuilding because these steps will take care of most of Xamarin's false errors.

4. If the build was successful, do not try running the app just yet. If
    you do run it, it will crash and for good reason. You need to go into
    the Settings class in the GoGoGiphy.Core project and replace the
    values for AppCenterSecretiOS and AppCenterSecretAndroid.
    The app uses these variables. You will not do this step just yet
    because you will set up your builds in Chapter 2.

The Technologies Used in the Sample App

I do make use of some important frameworks and toolkits in this sample app. Even
though this book is not about teaching these individual concepts or Xamarin Forms and
its concepts, it is important for you to understand these technologies because otherwise,
the syntax in this app will seem alien and unintelligible. Our jobs are hard enough as it is
now, so I will point you in the right direction for you to read the documentation of each
technology from the original authors.

FreshMvvm

First and foremost, this app is designed using the FreshMvvm framework. If you
understand the Model-View-ViewModel design pattern, then you understand the eventual
need of page navigation, use of the BindingContext from XAML pages, dependency
injection, and inversion-of-control practices. I will not go into great detail about each of
these concepts, but I made use of the FreshMvvm framework because the author, Michael
Ridland, has done a wonderful job of creating an MVVM framework specifically for
Xamarin Forms and made it easy to integrate in a Xamarin Forms app. You can find more
information at his GitHub page at https://github.com/rid00z/FreshMvvm.

You can find more useful information on his Quick Start guide from his blog at
https://michaelridland.com/xamarin/freshmvvm-quick-start-guide/.

Xamarin Essentials

The next big toolkit I used in the app is Xamarin Essentials. This toolkit gives a developer
the power to use a single cross-platform API to tap into cross-platform–specific features
like Connectivity, Battery, Clipboard, etc. instead of having to learn each API separately
for Android, iOS, and Windows. You can find the GitHub page for Xamarin Essentials
at https://github.com/xamarin/Essentials. In this sample app, I do make use of the

Connectivity, MainThread, and File System Helper APIs. If you decide to use my sample app as a base for your own app and if you come up with more ideas, you can leverage the cross-platform APIs from Xamarin Essentials. I encourage you to read through the documentation at `https://docs.microsoft.com/en-us/xamarin/essentials/`.

James Montemagno, who has been a major voice on the Xamarin Forms scene for a long time, is a major contributor among a team of other open-source contributors to Xamarin Essentials. If you do not know much about him, you can always follow his blog at `https://montemagno.com/` because he publishes a lot of relevant how-to articles relating to Xamarin Forms and other technologies. He regularly publishes sample code from which you can learn.

FFImageLoading

Another crucial library used in this sample app is the FFImageLoading library. This library is crucial because it gives the app the ability to display gifs. This library is available in a number of different frameworks like Xamarin.iOS, Xamarin.Android, and of course, Xamarin.Forms. I personally love this library because you can simply plug and play the controls, modify a few settings, and never worry about it. I encourage you to read more about this library as you browse through the code in the sample app.

```
https://github.com/luberda-molinet/FFImageLoading
https://github.com/luberda-molinet/FFImageLoading/wiki
```

SQLite

Of course, these gifs need to be stored somewhere locally so the user can save the images in collections for later viewing. That is why I implemented SQLite into the Core project of the solution because it was easy to implement and easy to learn even for a beginner. The NuGet package integrated into the Core project is the .NET wrapper package around the SQLite client. You can find more information at the links below:

```
https://github.com/praeclarum/sqlite-net
www.nuget.org/packages/sqlite-net-pcl
www.sqlite.org/index.html
```

Lastly, the final important framework to learn about is Json.NET. If you have ever developed a website, web API project, or a mobile app, JavaScript Object Notation (JSON) has become our payload of choice because it is easy to use, easy to read, and easy to serialize or deserialize into a .NET object. If you are new to Json.NET, I encourage you to read through the documentation at `www.newtonsoft.com/json` and `www.newtonsoft.com/json/help/`.

That's it! If you study the above documentation, you should gain a basic understanding of how all the different frameworks and libraries work within this sample app.

Tips, Tricks, and Links

Before leaving this chapter, I do want to highlight a couple of important tips, tricks, and links because you will need them when the time is right. It is better for you to have these links bookmarked on your browser now.

First and foremost, the App Center support team is very helpful and courteous to users of their service. You can reach out to them anytime for help from the icon at the bottom right of the site. You can ask a question and a support person will be in touch usually within 24 hours. The support icon is shown in Figure 1-23.

Figure 1-23. *App Center support icon*

Second, you may get stuck when using App Center. Most errors that people run into are common and you can rest assured that many others have run into the same error before. As a result, Microsoft has done a splendid job of making the articles to the most common errors available online at `https://intercom.help/appcenter`. You can simply search for your error or question and it will return a list of all matching articles.

Third, on rare occasions, the App Center services may experience downtimes or may be down due to scheduled maintenance. You can see what services are operational or not from `https://status.appcenter.ms/`. Of course, you can also subscribe to updates so you are alerted to them when they happen.

Fourth, the App Center teams advertise what features are coming and how to use new features on the blog at `https://devblogs.microsoft.com/appcenter/`. The blog will show you how to use both easy and advanced features beyond this book after you have mastered the basics.

Finally, App Center does provide an API for you to query or execute important actions directly from the API endpoints without having to use the website. I will cover the details of how to use the API, how to get an authorization token, and how to use the token with the API in later chapters. Moreover, the API is the only way for you to run UI tests that I will explain in a later chapter. But you can bookmark this site now and browse through the list of available endpoints that App Center offers: `https://openapi.appcenter.ms/`.

Summary

If you followed all the steps above, you should now be ready to use the sample app and App Center at the same time. You have also accomplished the following:

- Understand the history of HockeyApp and various Xamarin tools and how they are now incorporated into App Center

- Understand what DevOps is about and how App Center is the DevOps solution for mobile applications

- Signed up for the following accounts:

  - Visual Studio App Center

  - Azure DevOps

  - Azure

  - Apple Developer

  - Giphy

- Downloaded and installed the following applications:

  - Git for Windows

  - Visual Studio 2017

  - Visual Studio 2017 components for Git

  - Xcode on Mac

  - Android Studio

- Either forked the sample project to your GitHub repository or imported the sample project to your Azure DevOps repository

Roadmap

Before starting any journey, an informed traveler always has an itinerary. As a result, it is only natural to want to know what is coming ahead in this book before flipping one more page.

- **Chapter 2**: In this chapter, you will begin creating your first iOS and Android builds. I will walk you through the process of authorizing App Center to connect to your GitHub, connecting either to your GitHub or Azure DevOps project (depending on your source code location), setting up your iOS and Android builds, setting up teams and adding collaborators to your teams, and setting up notifications to an external communication service like Slack so you stay informed of build successes and failures as they happen.

- **Chapter 3**: If we followed the typical DevOps workflow where the Test step came immediately after Build, then this chapter would be about setting up your tests. But I am saving UI tests until the end of the book for two reasons. First, UI tests are by far the most difficult topic for you to learn. Therefore, I do not want to overwhelm you with an advanced topic this early in the book. Second, some teams and some organizations may find this topic optional because they may not elect to use the App Center Testing feature for all their apps since a certain price is incurred monthly and based on usage. As a result, Chapter 3 covers setting up your distribution to test devices. You will learn about registering your Apple device, creating your certificate signing request, creating your developer certificate, creating your provisioning profile, creating your Android keystore file, registering your devices on App Center, and configuring your builds for distribution. This chapter is packed with a ton of critical information.

- **Chapter 4**: This chapter is all about the Continuous Feedback portion of DevOps where the reader learns how to report analytics and crashes from their mobile app as the users of the app use it in the wild. You will learn how to set up custom events, simulate test crashes, handle crashes from within your code, and export data to Azure for persistent storage.

- **Chapter 5**: This chapter will teach you how to interact with users of your app through push notifications. You will learn how to configure Apple Push Notification Service, configure Firebase Cloud Messaging, send push notifications from App Center, handle push notifications from within your code, send silent notifications when the app is minimized to the background, send custom data in your notification, and automate notifications using the App Center API.

- **Chapter 6**: I will conclude this book with UI tests. As mentioned, this chapter is the most advanced topic in this book simply because it requires a lot of customization and trial and error. You will understand as you begin setting up your own tests. But do not worry. I went through most of the trials and errors and documented my experiences for you. This chapter will teach you how to set up Post-Build scripts, App Center variables, the iOS UITest command in the build script, and the Android UITest command in the build script. You'll also learn how to use REPL, a tool created to help you test UI test commands on your app through the simulator.

I recommend following me on this journey sequentially from chapter to chapter. But if you are comfortable with the beginner topics, feel free to jump around from topic to topic or to jump ahead to an advanced topic.

CHAPTER 2

Creating Builds

It's time to begin your journey of a thousand miles with the first step!

In the last chapter, you set up your Visual Studio App Center account, you set up your Apple Developer account, and you downloaded the sample project to use through the rest of this book.

In this chapter, you will tiptoe into the waters of App Center and begin setting up your builds. But just like anything else in the software world, before you can begin using it, you must set up a couple of things. This chapter has a lot of material. For me, the best way to learn is by attacking one topic at a time when I need to use it. If you are like me, please feel free to revisit this chapter from time to time. Or you can try to set up everything up all at once.

Here is all the material we will cover from start to finish:

- How to set up an organization

  - How to add collaborators

  - How to create your teams

- How to set up more branches on Azure DevOps (VSTS)

- How to set up the sample app to run locally

- How to connect your GitHub project to App Center

- How to connect your VSTS project to App Center

- How to set up your Xamarin Forms iOS build

- How to set up your Xamarin Forms Android build

- How to set up your build notifications

- How to set up notifications to your Slack account

© Sunny Mukherjee 2019
S. Mukherjee, *Learn Microsoft Visual Studio App Center*, https://doi.org/10.1007/978-1-4842-4382-4_2

As you can see, you have a lot to do before you can realize the full potential of App Center. And do remember I performed every action before writing it in this book, so every topic is a first-hand account of a developer using App Center.

Setting Up Your Organization

Before you create any builds, you need to set up an organization. An organization allows you to manage the collaborators of an app and their permissions. Since you created your App Center account, you are an admin automatically. And you will have the ability to add more collaborators to an app later.

Go to the Home Screen of App Center. You will see an Add New button at the top right, as shown in Figure 2-1. Click the Add new organization option.

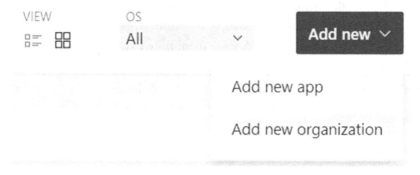

Figure 2-1. *Adding a new organization*

Give your organization a name like the one in Figure 2-2.

Figure 2-2. *Organization name*

You will now see three sections under your organization, shown in Figure 2-3.

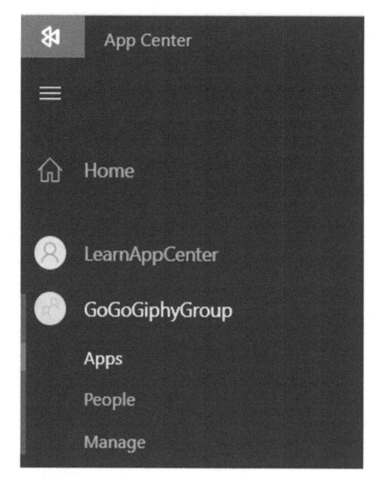

Figure 2-3. *Organization menu*

Adding Collaborators

Go to the People section. You will see only one user (you) in there as the admin. You can add a collaborator to your organization in the textbox, as in Figure 2-4. (I have redacted my personal email in the image.)

Figure 2-4. *Collaborators*

You will see the invitation for your new collaborator listed as in Figure 2-5. The Invited message will disappear once your collaborator has accepted the invitation.

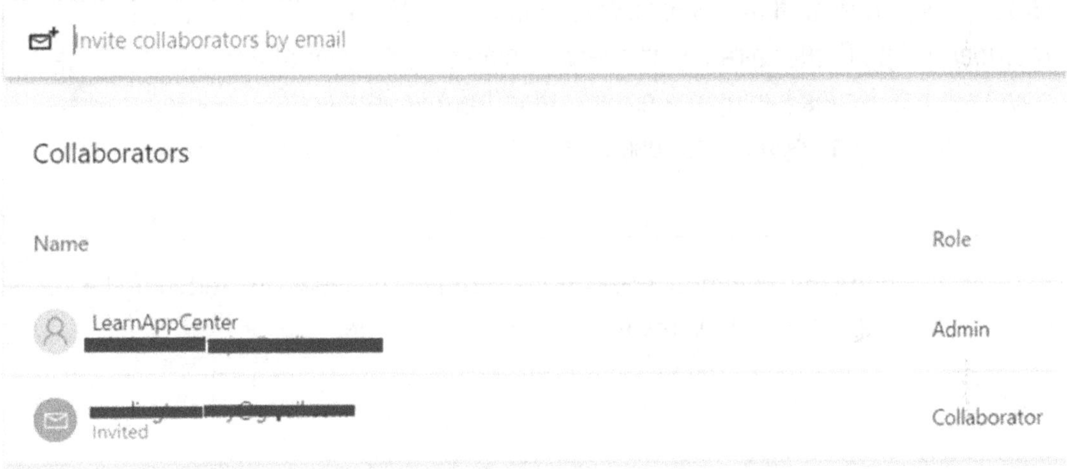

Figure 2-5. *A collaborator and the Invited message*

Your new collaborator will see an email similar to Figure 2-6. Once your collaborator accepts the invitation, they will be brought to a webpage in the next figure where they can click the Join organization option.

Figure 2-6. *Email invitation (top) and webpage after clicking Accept (bottom)*

Note   Keep in mind that the user who gets the invitation either needs to be a member of App Center already or needs to sign up as a user of App Center. If the new user has issues joining the organization from your invitation, ask the user to verify if they are an App Center user. If not, they can follow the registration steps in Chapter 1.

Upon accepting the invitation, you will see your new collaborator added to the list, as shown in Figure 2-7. Notice how the Invited message is gone.

Collaborators

Name	Role
LearnAppCenter	Admin
Sunny Mukherjee	Collaborator

Figure 2-7. *Collaborators list showing accepted members*

Creating Your Teams

App Center offers the feature of setting up multiple teams in your organization. Why would you need this? If you are using App Center for an enterprise, your organization conceivably can manage multiple apps across multiple teams. In this scenario, each team has its own team members and manages its own apps. For example, if a team member has access to App 1 but not to App 2, they will not be able to manage App 2. Team members who are not admins cannot access other teams and access other apps. Now let's go through a few easy steps on how to set up your first team.

Go to the People section on the left-hand side. Click the Teams option. You will the page shown in Figure 2-8.

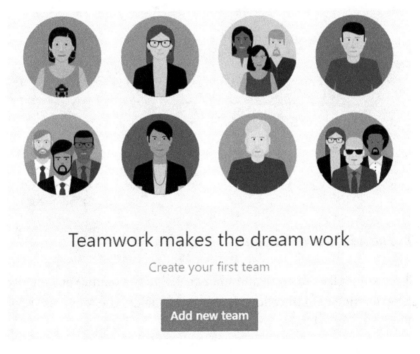

Teamwork makes the dream work

Create your first team

Add new team

Figure 2-8. *Add new team page*

Give your team a name as in Figure 2-9.

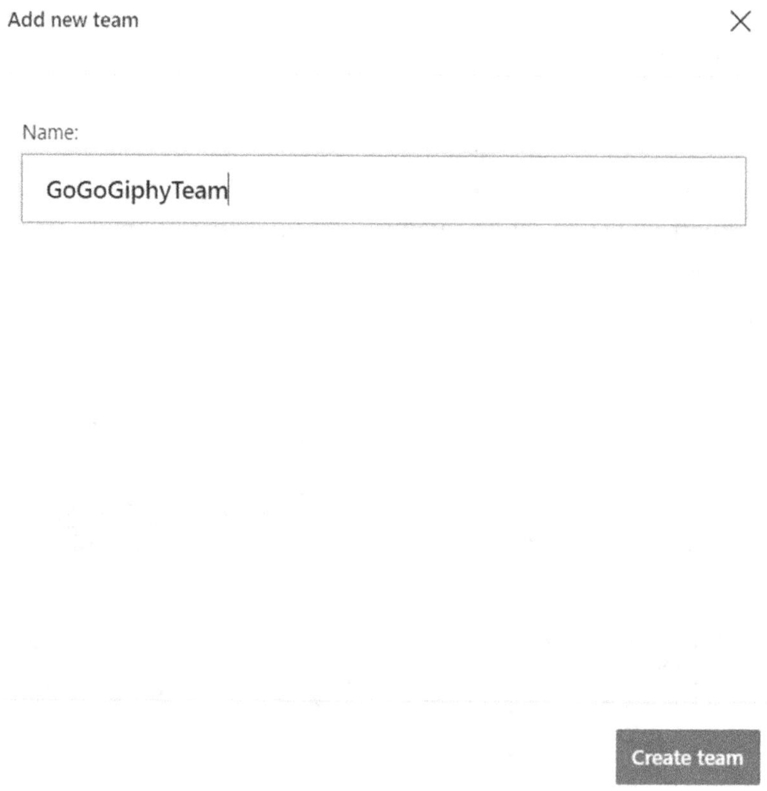

Add new team   ✕

Name:

> GoGoGiphyTeam|

Create team

Figure 2-9. *The Add new team panel*

You will see yourself as the only member added to the team. You can always click the highlighted wrench icon in yellow to rename or delete the team, as shown in Figure 2-10.

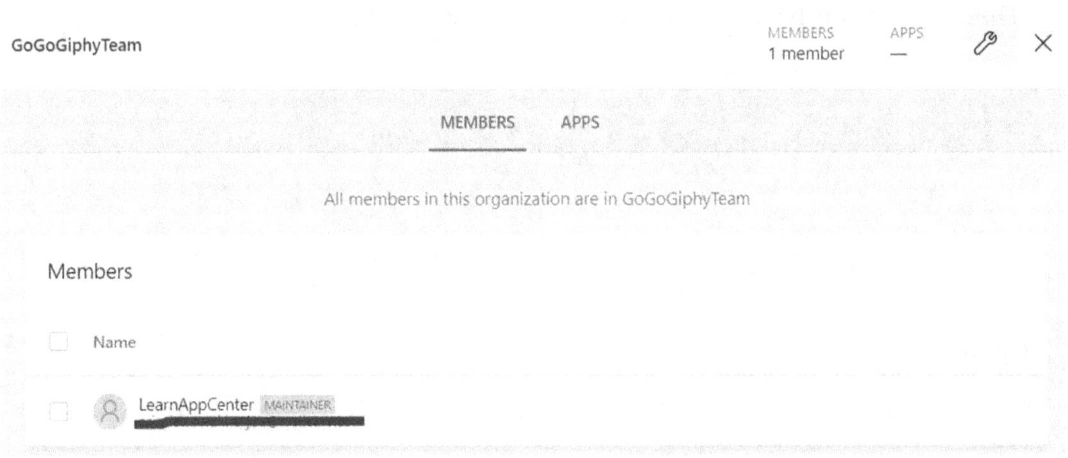

GoGoGiphyTeam

MEMBERS
1 member

APPS
—

MEMBERS   APPS

All members in this organization are in GoGoGiphyTeam

Members

Name

LearnAppCenter MAINTAINER

Figure 2-10. *The Team page*

Go ahead and add your new collaborator from the previous section to your team (Figure 2-11).

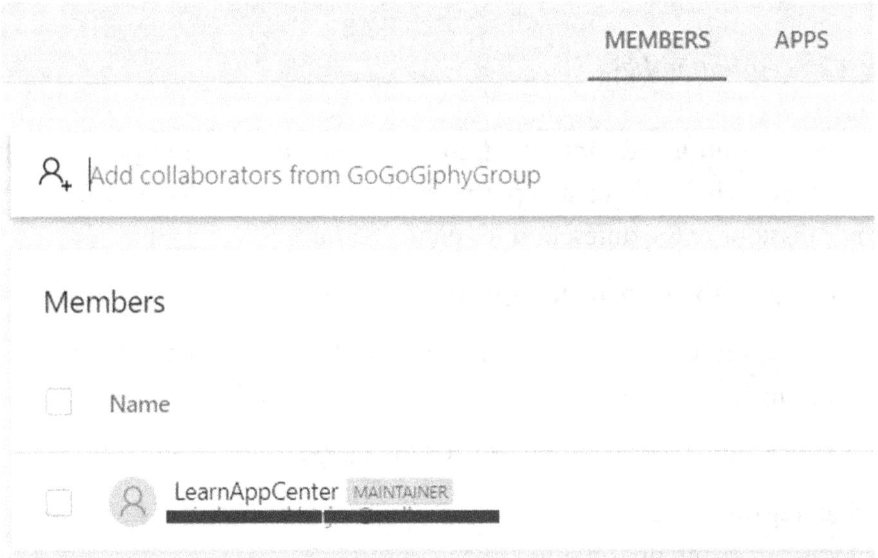

MEMBERS   APPS

Add collaborators from GoGoGiphyGroup

Members

Name

LearnAppCenter MAINTAINER

Figure 2-11. *Adding collaborators*

That's it. You now have two members on your new team (Figure 2-12).

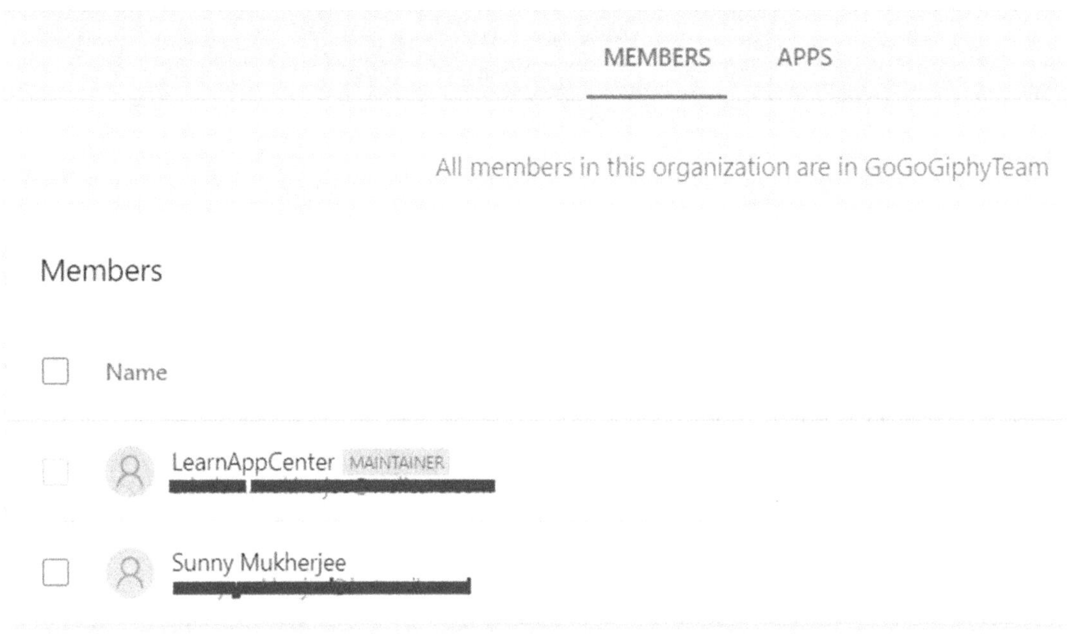

MEMBERS   APPS

All members in this organization are in GoGoGiphyTeam

Members

☐   Name

☐   ⃝ LearnAppCenter MAINTAINER

☐   ⃝ Sunny Mukherjee

Figure 2-12. *Team members*

As mentioned, only an admin has the ability to jump across multiple teams. But even team members have segregated permissions within a team. Let's briefly cover the different permissions of the different roles on the team.

- **Manager**: Ability to invite new members and access settings

- **Developer**: Ability to manage services, such as creating builds or running UI tests

- **Viewer**: Ability only to view or download app data

Note that, regardless of the permission, team members can only view and manage apps within the team and not on other teams.

Please have some patience now because there are many steps to set up both on App Center and locally before you can set up your first builds. You only need to do this once and never again. You set it and forget it.

Setting Up Your Solution Configuration Mappings

In this section, you will set your configuration mappings from the sample project. Open the sample project. If this is the first time you are opening the project, please remember that Visual Studio will take some time to restore the NuGet packages. Be patient. Once it is finished, right-click the solution and go to Configuration Manager.

Verify that your active solution configuration and active solution platforms match Figures 2-13 and 2-14.

Notice how the Build and Deploy checkboxes are not selected for the Android and UWP projects when the Active solution configuration is Debug or Release and the Active solution platform is either iPhone or iPhoneSimulator. You do not want to build or deploy Android or UWP projects when the active solution platform is for iPhone.

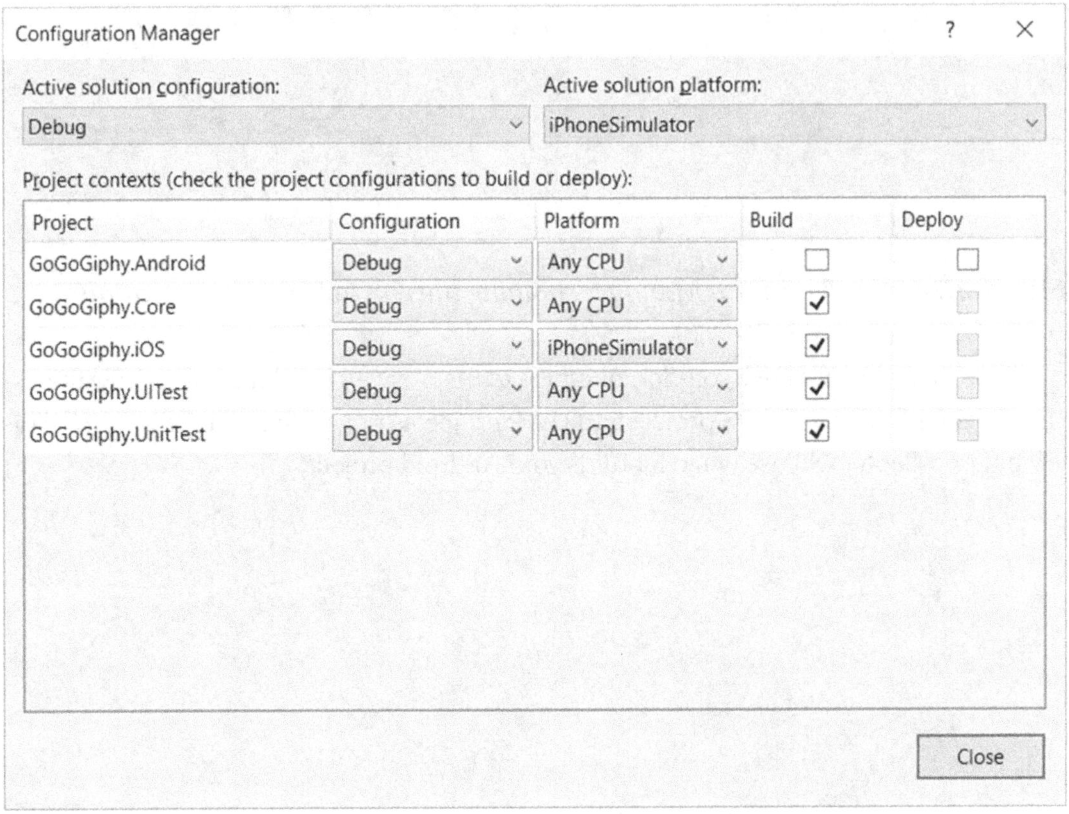

Figure 2-13. *Configuration Manager showing the iOS Debug configuration*

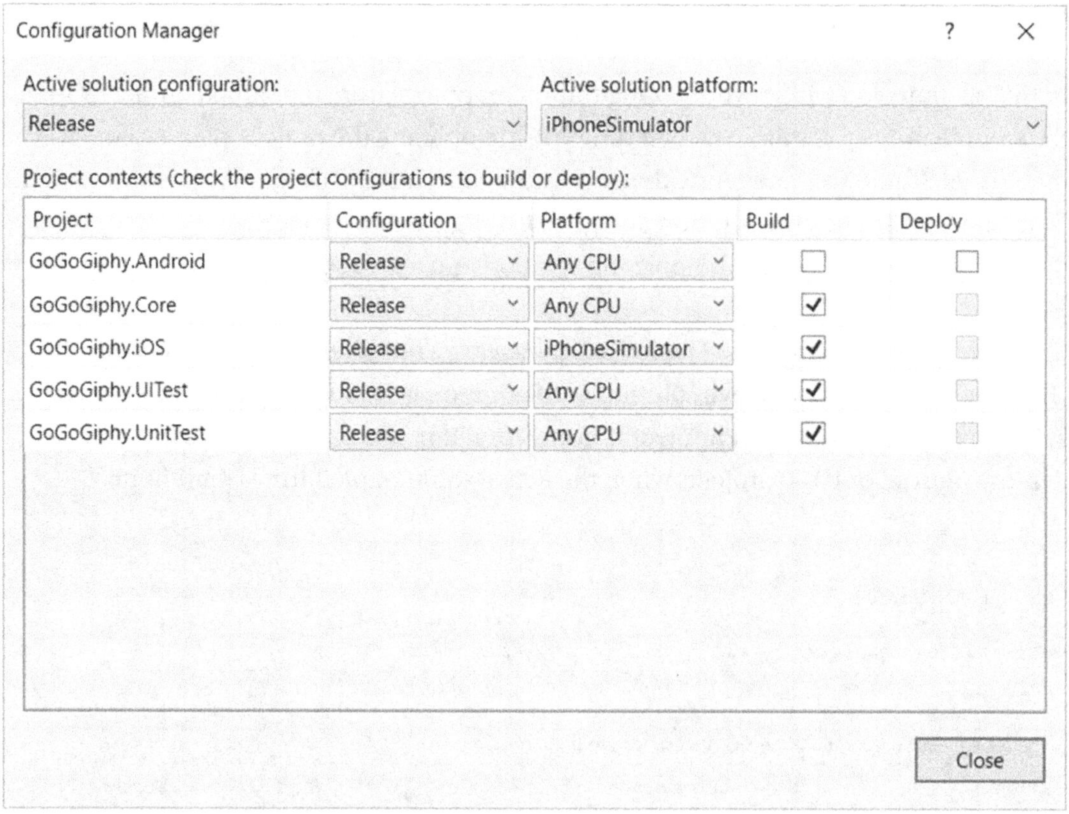

Figure 2-14. *Configuration Manager showing the iOS Release configuration*

Now change your active solution platform to the Any CPU option. Notice how the checkbox for Build in the iOS project and UWP project is not selected in Figure 2-15. This is what App Center will use when it builds your Android project.

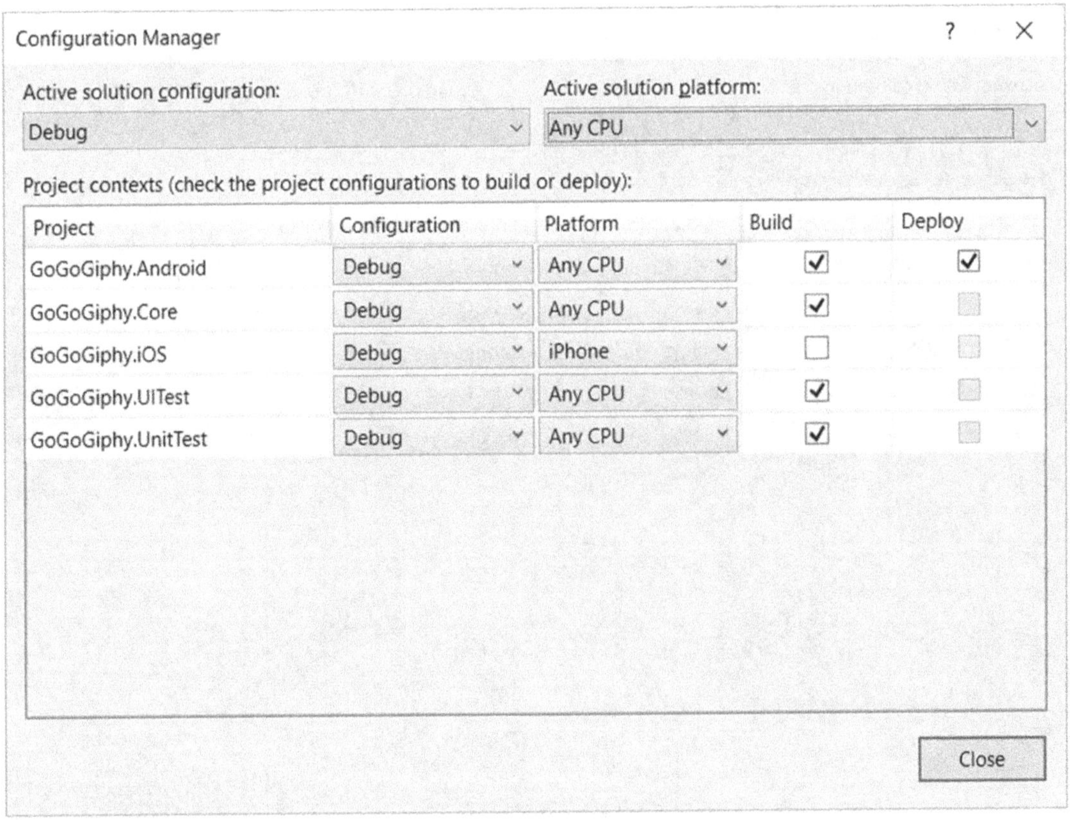

Configuration Manager				? ✕

Active solution configuration:

Debug	⌄

Active solution platform:

Any CPU	⌄

Project contexts (check the project configurations to build or deploy):

Project	Configuration	Platform	Build	Deploy
GoGoGiphy.Android	Debug ⌄	Any CPU ⌄	✓	✓
GoGoGiphy.Core	Debug ⌄	Any CPU ⌄	✓	☐
GoGoGiphy.iOS	Debug ⌄	iPhone ⌄	☐	☐
GoGoGiphy.UITest	Debug ⌄	Any CPU ⌄	✓	☐
GoGoGiphy.UnitTest	Debug ⌄	Any CPU ⌄	✓	☐

Close

Figure 2-15. *Configuration Manager showing the Android Debug configuration*

Change the active solution configuration to Release and active solution platform to Any CPU, like before, and verify that the same settings are selected as the Debug configuration. Refer to Figure 2-16.

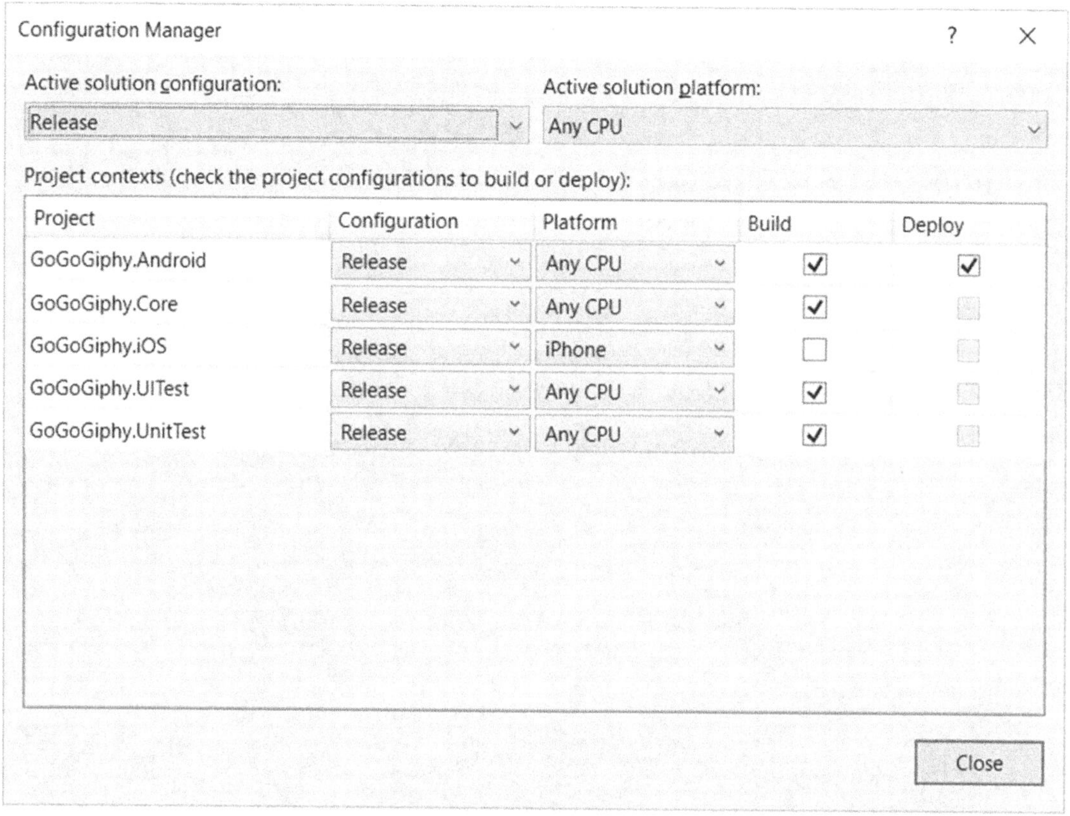

Figure 2-16. *Configuration Manager showing the Android Release configuration*

Note   You can disregard the UnitTest project entirely for this book. I included a sample UnitTest project using the NUNit Framework in order to test specific endpoint functionality with the Giphy API. It will not be needed within the App Center builds.

Next, you need to set up your app to connect to the various services and run locally in your simulator.

Setting Up More Branches on Azure DevOps

In this section, I will show you how easy it is to create and configure multiple branches on Azure DevOps (VSTS) so you can maintain a different build for each branch in your repository. You only have a single branch in your code repository called master now, so the master branch serves as your development branch because it is where the developers are committing code and pulling code from other developers in the remote master branch into their local master branch.

In a real-life scenario, you should separate the source code where you have new branches for QA teams and even business teams to sign off your changes. Ideally, you even want to have another branch called Staging or Pre-Prod where you can run your UI tests just before the code is published to the App Stores. For the purpose of this chapter, I will show you how to create a QA branch on Azure DevOps and set up a new build on App Center against the QA branch so you understand the entire process and you can create your own branch structure based on your organization's needs.

Let's get started.

- Sign into your Azure DevOps account.

- Switch to your source code repository.

- Expand the Repos section on the left-hand panel, as shown in Figure 2-17.

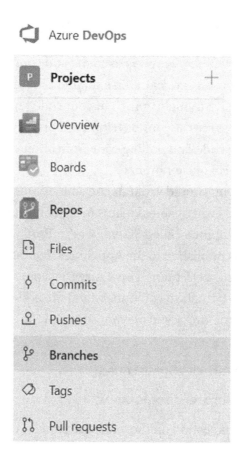

Figure 2-17. *Azure DevOps Repos*

- Click the Branches option. You should now see only the master branch on the right-hand part of the screen.

- Click the New Branch button located at the top-right corner of the webpage.

- In the pop-up box, give your new branch a name, such as QA. Since master is the only branch available at this time, the code will be based on master automatically. Your page should look like Figure 2-18.

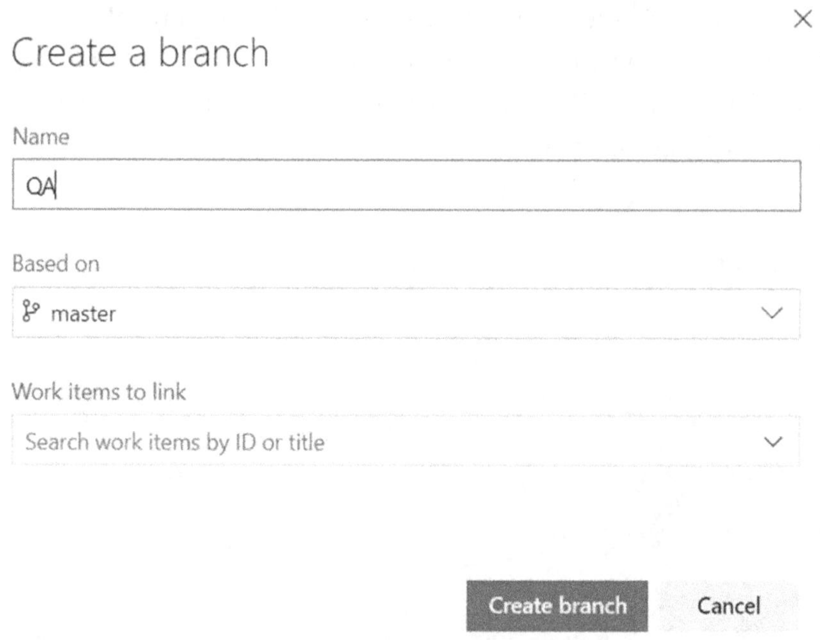

Create a branch

×

Name

QA|

Based on

⅄ master   ⌄

Work items to link

Search work items by ID or title   ⌄

Create branch   Cancel

Figure 2-18. *Creating a new branch on Azure DevOps*

- Click the Create branch button. Your branches should look like those in Figure 2-19. I created an additional Staging branch for demonstration purposes.

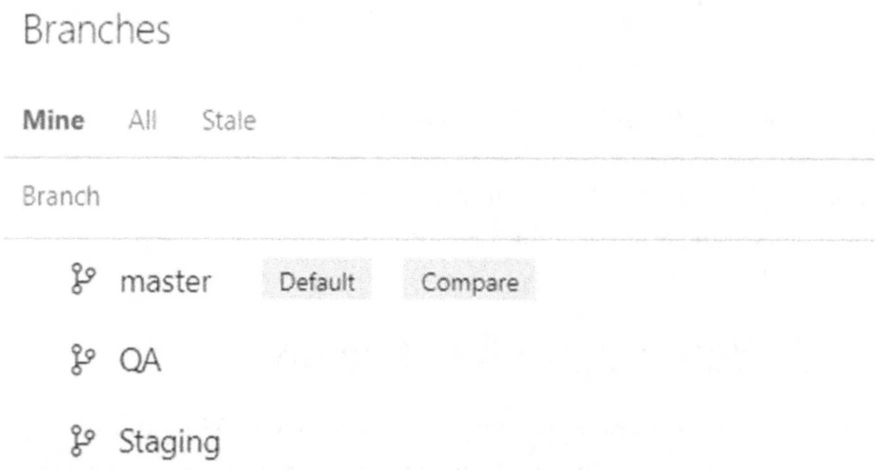

Branches

Mine   All   Stale

Branch

⅄ master   Default   Compare

⅄ QA

⅄ Staging

Figure 2-19. *Viewing branches on Azure DevOps*

- Return to App Center. The service will detect the new branches automatically for you. Click in the Build section. You should see the branches shown in Figure 2-20. Notice how the master branch has been configured thus far.

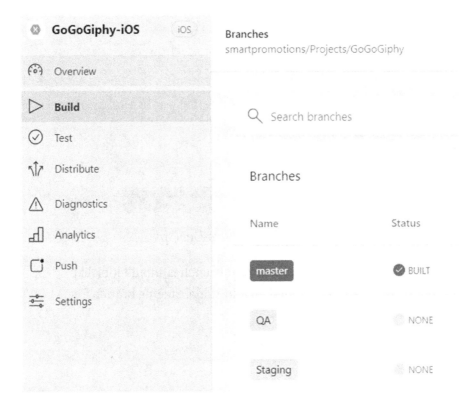

Figure 2-20.   *Viewing branches in App Center*

By this point, the source code in your master and QA branches will be identical. I will show you why this segregation of code is important in Chapter 3.

Setting Up Your App to Run Locally

Before performing any setup on App Center with either your iOS or Android build, you must verify that your app runs fine locally in your simulator. You need to perform a few steps first to get your app to connect to the various services, such as App Center and Giphy.

- Verify that your Xcode versions match between your Visual Studio on Windows and the Xcode version on your Mac. If you forgot the steps, please revisit the section from Chapter 1.

- Switch to the master branch in Visual Studio. If you don't know how to perform this action, here is how to switch between branches easily within Visual Studio itself:

  - Open Team Explorer. If it is not already open, you can find it at View ➤ Team Explorer.

  - Select Branches. The master branch should be checked out locally to you.

  - Expand remotes/origin to explore the remote branches on your Azure DevOps repository. You should see the QA branch that you created earlier.

  - Double-click the branch to check out the branch locally on your machine. Your Team Explorer should look like Figure 2-21. You can peruse through the source code and see that the files are identical to the master branch when you first created your repository.

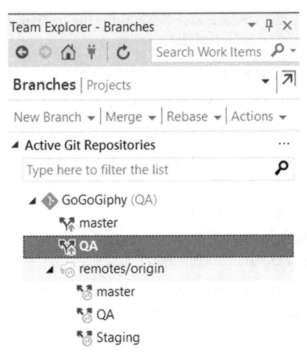

Figure 2-21. *Local QA branch checked out*

- Open the GoGoGiphy solution file.

- Remember from Chapter 1 I asked you to ignore the variables in the `Settings.cs` file at the time. Return and open `Settings.cs` from the GoGoGiphy.Core project. In this class, you will find several static strings that are used throughout the code. Two of the variables pertinent to this topic are `AppCenterSecretiOS` and `AppCenterSecretAndroid`. You will need to replace the `iOSSecret` string with the actual App Secret value from App Center because this is how App Center identifies your app from the millions of other apps out there.

Follow these simple steps to get the App Secret value for iOS:

- Go to the GoGoGiphy-iOS app in App Center.

- Go to the left-hand panel and click Settings at the bottom.

- At the top right corner of the page, you will see a vertical dot icon button. Click the button.

- Click the Copy App Secret.

- Paste and replace the value for `iOSSecret` in the `AppCenterSecretiOS` variable.

Follow these simple steps to get the App Secret value for Android:

- Go to the GoGoGiphy-Android app in App Center.

- Go to the left-hand panel and click Settings at the bottom.

- At the top right corner of the page, you will see a vertical dot icon button. Click the button.

- Click the Copy App Secret option.

- Paste and replace the value for `AndroidSecret` in the `AppCenterSecretAndroid` variable.

Now return to your Giphy account that you set up from Chapter 1. Go to `https://developers.giphy.com` to access your dashboard.

If you did not set up your Giphy account, return to Chapter 1 to follow the instructions. If you did set up your account, you will find your app listed under Your Apps and your API key is given inside. Copy the value and replace the `GiphyApiKey` string value in the `ApiKey` variable.

Now your app is set up locally for you to run in either the iOS or Android simulators. Follow these steps to test your iOS app in the simulator:

- Open Visual Studio and the GoGoGiphy solution. Verify that you are in the master branch.

- Right-click the GoGoGiphy.iOS project and click on the Set as Startup Project option.

- Connect to your Mac machine. Verify that the connection is successful.

- Select an iOS device from the Debug Target combo-box in Visual Studio, such as iPhone 8 or iPhone X.

- Rebuild the iOS project. Verify that the build is successful. If you get any errors, please visit the "Troubleshooting" section at the end of the chapter.

- Run the project.

Follow these steps to test your Android app in the simulator:

- Open Visual Studio and the GoGoGiphy solution. Verify that you are in the master branch.

- Right-click the GoGoGiphy.Android project and click the Set as Startup Project option.

- Go to Tools menu ➤ Android Device Manager.

- Start one of your preconfigured Android devices.

- Right-click the Android project and click Deploy. If the build is successful, Visual Studio will deploy the app to the Android emulator. If the build failed, please visit the "Troubleshooting" section at the end of the chapter.

- After the deployment has succeeded, click the Play button to run in the Android emulator.

After verifying the sample app runs locally, you can commit your changes now into the Master branch. However, you must keep one safety precaution in mind. It is unsafe to commit your App Secret and your Api Key values into source control by simply committing the changes in the Settings class as they currently exist. For now, for the purpose of getting your first build to work in App Center, go ahead and commit your changes into your source code repository of choice. I will show you in the next chapter how to avoid committing these secret values into source control by using the magic of App Center environment variables and a sprinkle of Bash scripting to replace these secret values dynamically on the cloud before the build. This is the reason why you have a separate QA branch.

Creating Your iOS Build

You need to create two separate build definitions, one for iOS and one for Android. Two separate build definitions need to be set up because this is how App Center uses the appropriate configuration settings to build the corresponding projects for iOS or Android.

Let's create your initial iOS build definition. You are only going to create it for now and set it up for a debug. You need to create an empty build definition in order to connect to external source code repositories, like GitHub or VSTS services, from where you can retrieve your code. You will return to the build definition multiple times through the book as you configure the settings for later chapters.

Go into the organization you created in the previous section. On the first page, click the button named Add new app.

You will see a sliding panel similar to Figure 2-22. Fill out the information as shown and click the Add new app button.

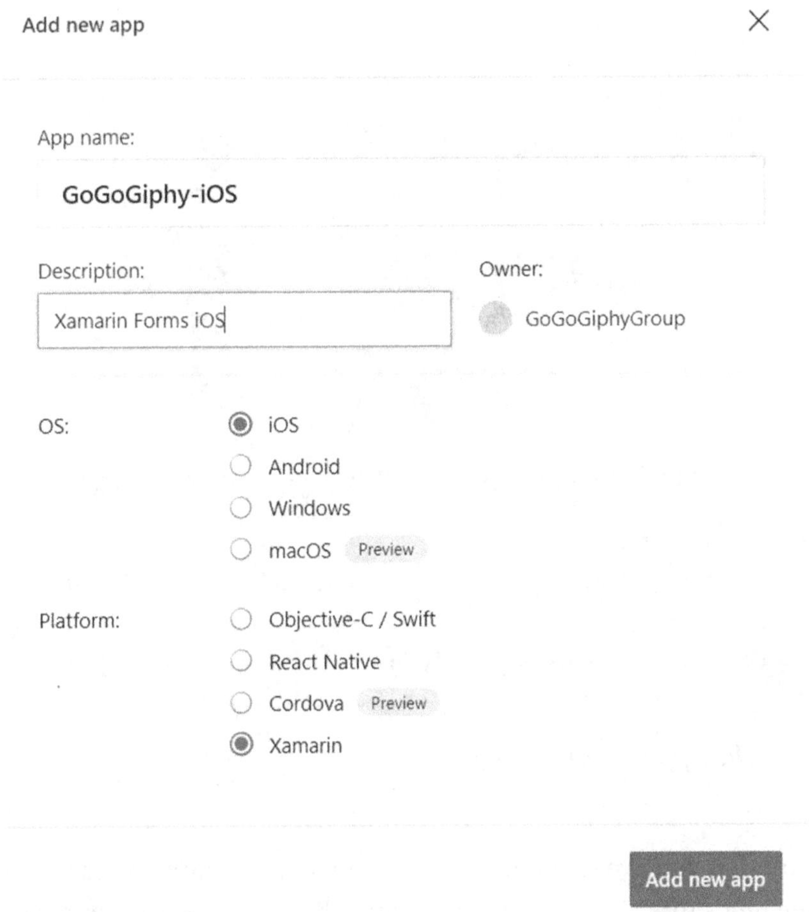

Add new app   ✕

App name:

GoGoGiphy-iOS

Description: Owner:

Xamarin Forms iOS   GoGoGiphyGroup

OS: ◉ iOS
                 ○ Android
                 ○ Windows
                 ○ macOS Preview

Platform: ○ Objective-C / Swift
                 ○ React Native
                 ○ Cordova Preview
                 ◉ Xamarin

Add new app

Figure 2-22. *The Add new app panel*

You will now see the welcome page of the app with a lot of useful instructions on how to integrate the App Center SDK into your Xamarin or Xamarin Forms app. Figure 2-23 shows a snippet of the front page. Disregard these instructions for now. You will revisit them later as you go through this book.

Add App Center's SDK to your app.

For detailed instructions on SDK integration go to:
Getting Started with the Xamarin SDK

XAMARIN   XAMARIN.FORMS

Figure 2-23. *The app welcome page*

Now I will show you two different ways to connect your empty build definition to a source code repository. The first way is GitHub. The second way is Azure DevOps or Visual Studio Team Services. Let's start with GitHub.

Connecting Your GitHub Project

First, verify that you are in the app you created. Click the Build option on the left-hand panel, as shown in Figure 2-24. Notice the name of the app, GoGoGiphy-iOS, at the top of the panel.

Figure 2-24. *App Center left pane*

The page will show the services shown in Figure 2-25. Select GitHub.

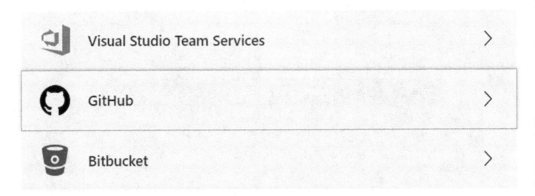

Figure 2-25. *The Select a service page*

App Center will ask for your authorization to connect to your repositories. Just click the Authorize button, shown in Figure 2-26, and you are on your way toward setting up your first build with source code from GitHub!

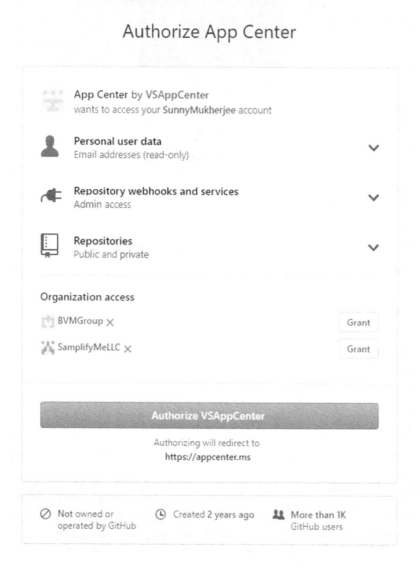

Figure 2-26. *GitHub authorization for App Center*

Connecting Your VSTS Project

Now I will show you the second way to connect to your project on Azure DevOps (VSTS). If you followed the steps in Chapter 1 to upload the sample project into your Azure DevOps repository, this section will be the next step. For the remainder of this book, this book will assume that you have connected your builds to your Azure DevOps repositories. You are welcome to follow along this book and use your GitHub project fork as the source code going forward.

Click the Visual Studio Team Services option, as shown in Figure 2-27.

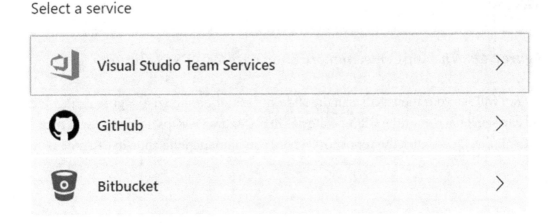

Figure 2-27. *The Select a service page*

If you are signing into Azure DevOps for the first time, you will see a page like Figure 2-28. Click the Accept button to give App Center the right to access your VSTS account.

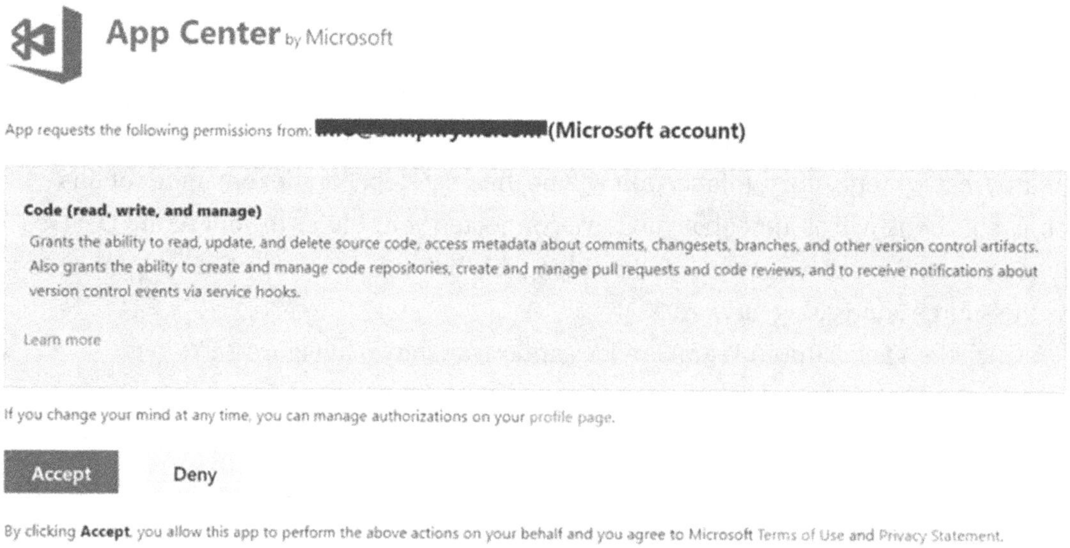

App requests the following permissions from: ▓▓▓▓▓▓▓▓▓▓▓▓▓▓(Microsoft account)

Code (read, write, and manage)

Grants the ability to read, update, and delete source code, access metadata about commits, changesets, branches, and other version control artifacts. Also grants the ability to create and manage code repositories, create and manage pull requests and code reviews, and to receive notifications about version control events via service hooks.

Learn more

If you change your mind at any time, you can manage authorizations on your profile page.

Accept   **Deny**

By clicking **Accept**, you allow this app to perform the above actions on your behalf and you agree to Microsoft Terms of Use and Privacy Statement.

Figure 2-28. *The App Center authorization page for a VSTS account*

You will see your repositories in the slide-out panel, as shown in Figure 2-29. As you can see, I have multiple Git repositories in my Azure DevOps account. I will click GoGoGiphy. Please click the repository where you uploaded the code in Chapter 1.

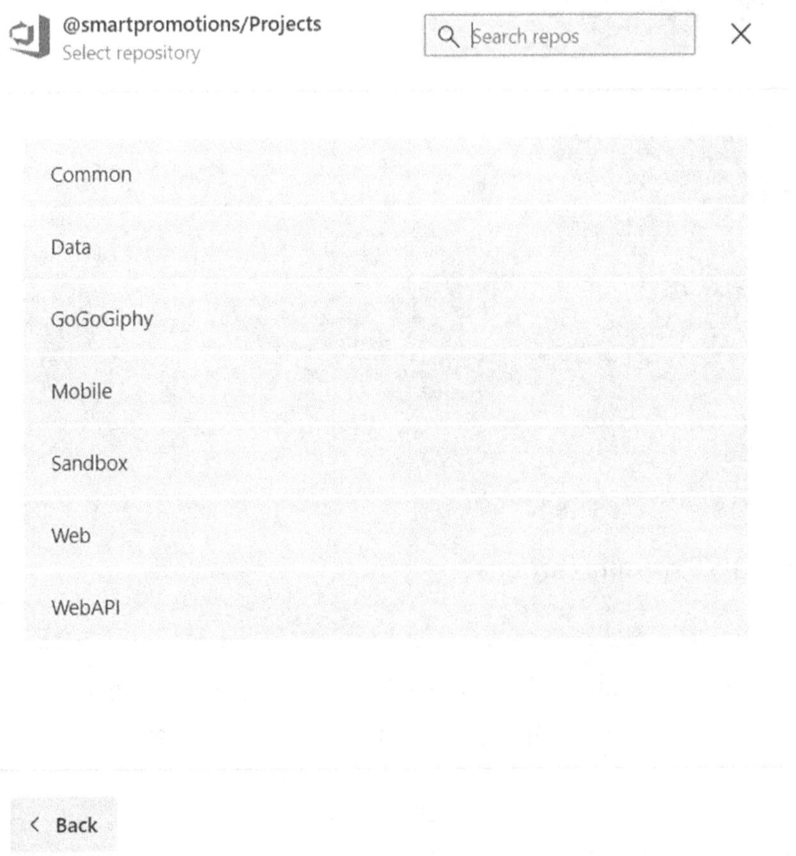

@smartpromotions/Projects
Select repository

Q Search repos   ✕

Common

Data

GoGoGiphy

Mobile

Sandbox

Web

WebAPI

‹ Back

Figure 2-29. *Azure DevOps Git repositories*

Revoking App Center Privileges from VSTS

But what if you ever need to revoke privileges for App Center for the specified Azure DevOps account and add a different Azure DevOps account? How do you do it? When you sign into Azure DevOps for the first time, you will see your name and account information on the left side of the page, as shown in Figure 2-30. Click the Manage authorizations option highlighted. In the pop-up panel, you can revoke your App Center tokens.

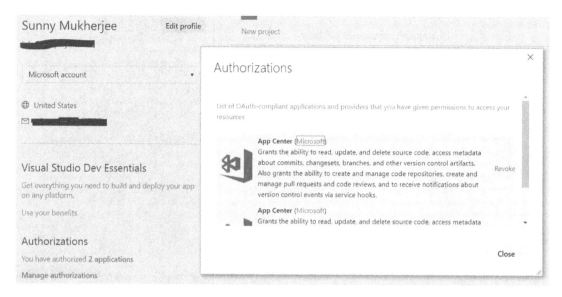

Figure 2-30. *VSTS authorizations*

Note   Once you remove the App Center token, go for a long walk because it can take up to an hour for Azure DevOps to remove the authorization.

Setting Up Your iOS Build

Now you will finish setting up your iOS build. Once you have connected to your source code repository, you will see a page similar to Figure 2-31. App Center will ask you to configure the build for the master branch since you only have a single branch. Click the Configure build button.

This branch has not been configured to build yet.

It sure looks intriguing, though!

LAST COMMIT

- Modifying solution file configurations
Sunny Mukherjee

14 hours ago   Configure build

Figure 2-31. *The Configure build page*

The slide-out panel will show you all the different configuration parameters. Configure your iOS build and match the parameters according to Figure 2-32.

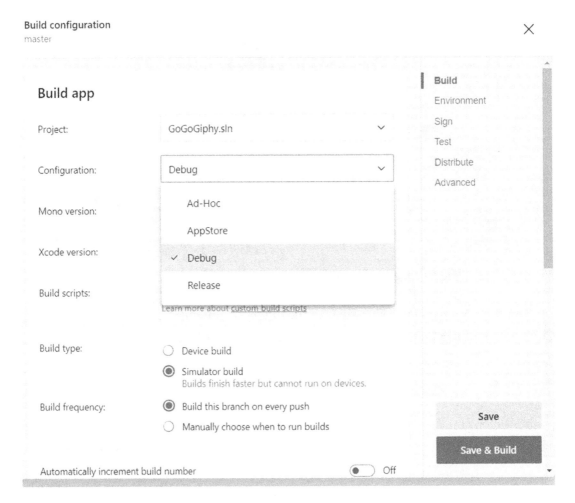

Figure 2-32. *iOS build configuration*

The following is an explanation of the parameters shown in Figure 2-32:

- **Project**: App Center will show all the solution files and project files in this combo-box. Select the GoGoGiphy solution file that you configured before (Figure 2-33).

Figure 2-33. *Project selection*

- **Configuration**: App Center automatically detects the configuration mappings from your solution file. Select Debug, as shown in Figure 2-34.

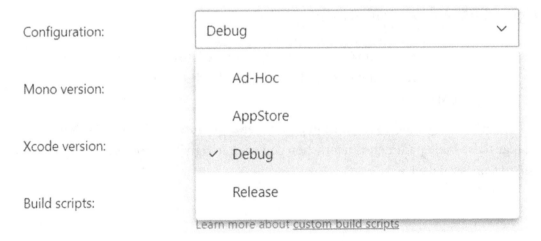

Figure 2-34. *Configuration selection*

- **Mono version**: App Center will default always to the latest stable version of Mono. If needed, you can always build using an older version of Mono for older versions of frameworks or libraries. At the time of this writing, Xamarin.iOS 11.12 is the most stable version (Figure 2-35).

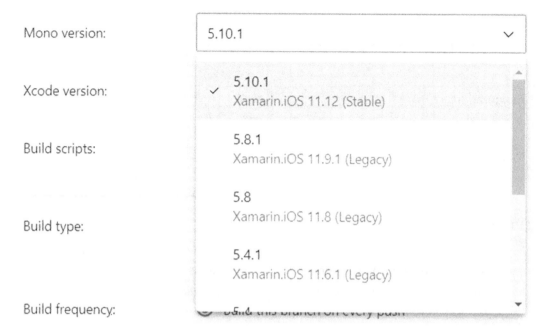

Figure 2-35. *Mono version selection*

- **XCode version**: App Center will default to the latest stable version
  of XCode. Verify that this version matches the XCode version on
  your Mac.

The remaining build configuration parameters are shown in Figure 2-36. You will
change these build parameters later when you want to sign your builds and deploy your
app to a physical device.

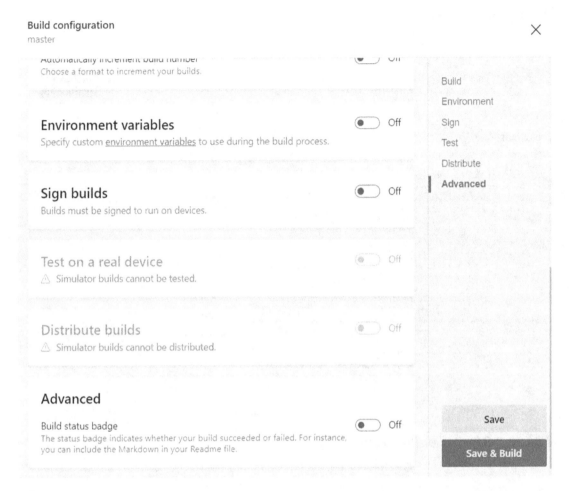

Figure 2-36. *iOS build configuration*

Now click the Save & Build button. This action will save your changes and initiate a new build. If everything goes well, once the build finishes, you will see the build output (Figure 2-37).

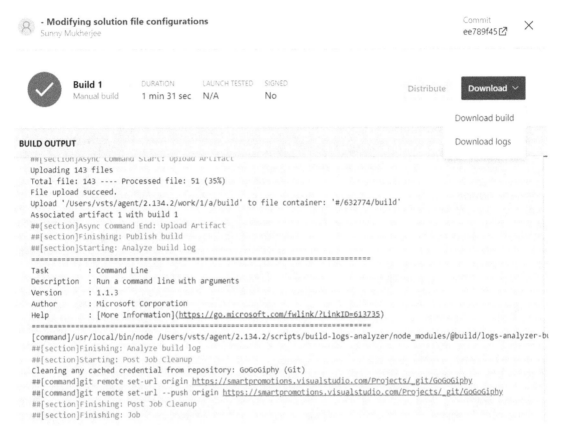

Figure 2-37. *iOS build output*

A couple of important pieces of information stand out in Figure 2-37.

- Notice the latest Git commit message of "Modifying solution file configurations" at the top, which is the comment you added when you committed your code into the repository.

- Notice the commit ID at the top right. This commit ID corresponds to your Git commit ID in your Git repository. You can click the arrow and navigate to VSTS showing the changes for this commit.

- Notice the build number, duration, etc. at the top.

- Notice the expanded Download button at the top right. You have the option of downloading the build and logs for troubleshooting purposes. You will need to know this feature when you run into trouble with your builds.

- Notice the build output. You can scroll up and down through the output to view success, errors, and warnings in each step of the build.

You have done it! You have created your first Xamarin Forms iOS build definition. Now it is time to complete the Android build definition.

Setting Up Your Android Build

In this section, you will follow a similar set of steps as for the iOS build. Let's begin.

Go to the front page of your organization again. Click the Add new app button shown at the top right of Figure 2-38.

Figure 2-38. *The Apps page*

Configure the parameters on the slide panel to match Figure 2-39.

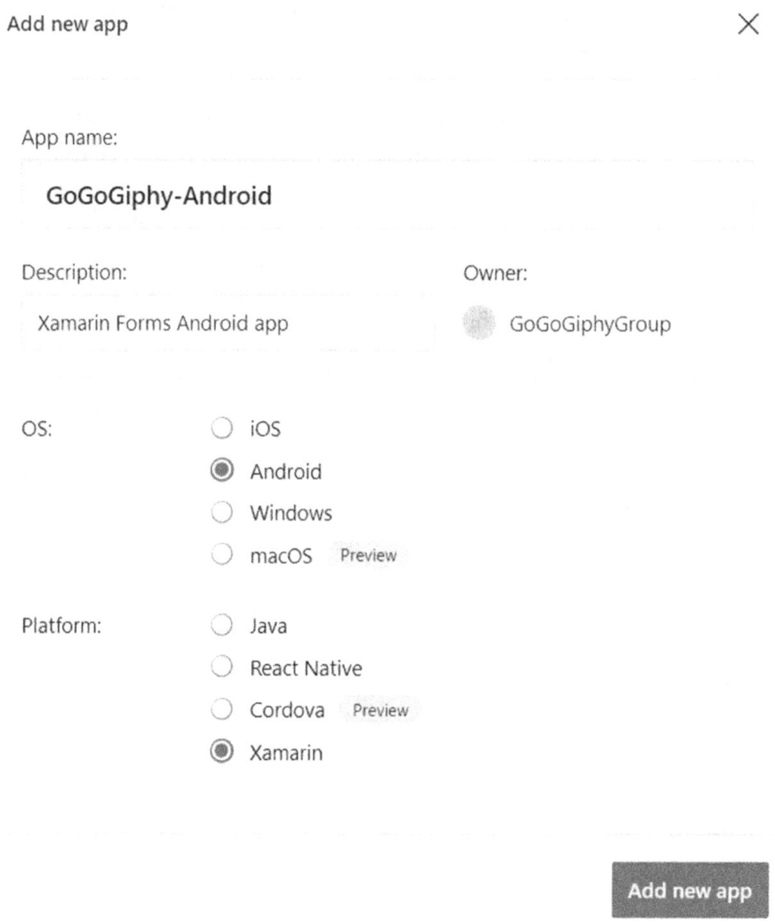

Add new app   ✕

App name:

GoGoGiphy-Android

Description: Owner:

Xamarin Forms Android app   GoGoGiphyGroup

OS: ◯ iOS
                         ◉ Android
                         ◯ Windows
                         ◯ macOS   Preview

Platform: ◯ Java
                         ◯ React Native
                         ◯ Cordova   Preview
                         ◉ Xamarin

Add new app

Figure 2-39. *The Add new app panel*

Go to the Build option in the left-hand panel. Click Visual Studio Team Services to select your repository. Select the GoGoGiphy repository again (Figure 2-40).

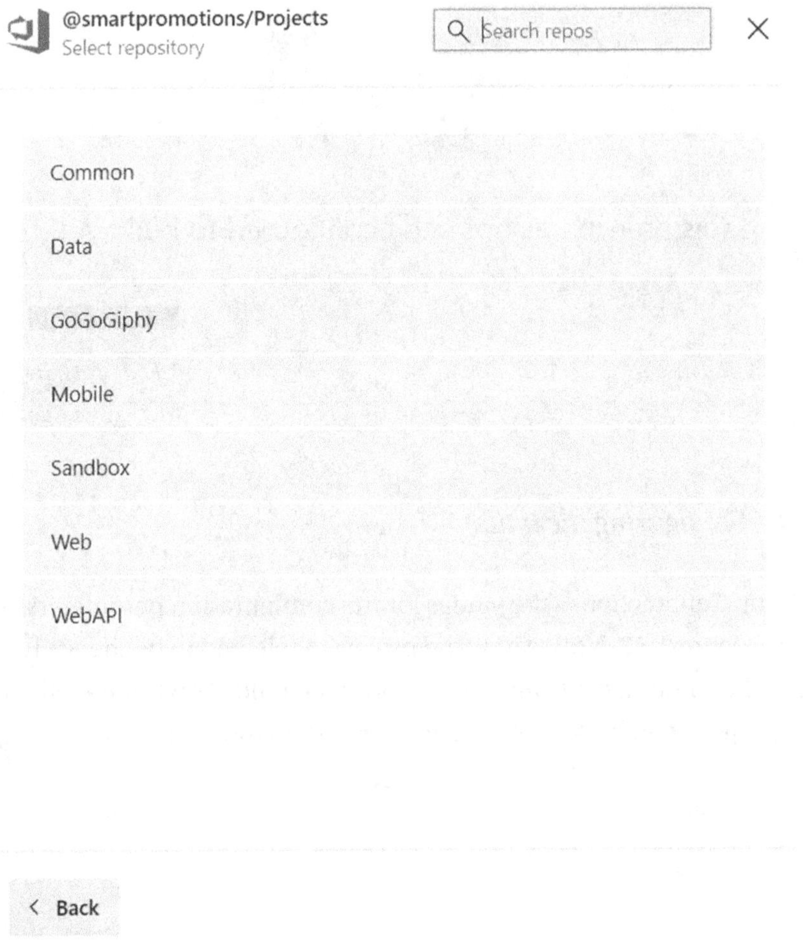

@smartpromotions/Projects
Select repository

🔍 Search repos   ✕

Common

Data

GoGoGiphy

Mobile

Sandbox

Web

WebAPI

‹ Back

Figure 2-40. *VSTS Git repositories*

Click the master branch. Click the Configure build button shown in Figure 2-41.

This branch has not been configured to build yet.

It sure looks intriguing, though!

LAST COMMIT

- Modifying solution file configurations   15 hours ago   **Configure build**
Sunny Mukherjee

Figure 2-41. *Configuring the build*

Now let App Center choose the values for the configuration parameters. Match the
parameters to Figure 2-42. Notice how the project is selected to be the Android project
file instead of the solution file from the previous iOS build. App Center will match up the
appropriate projects and build dependencies based on the project and configuration
parameters.

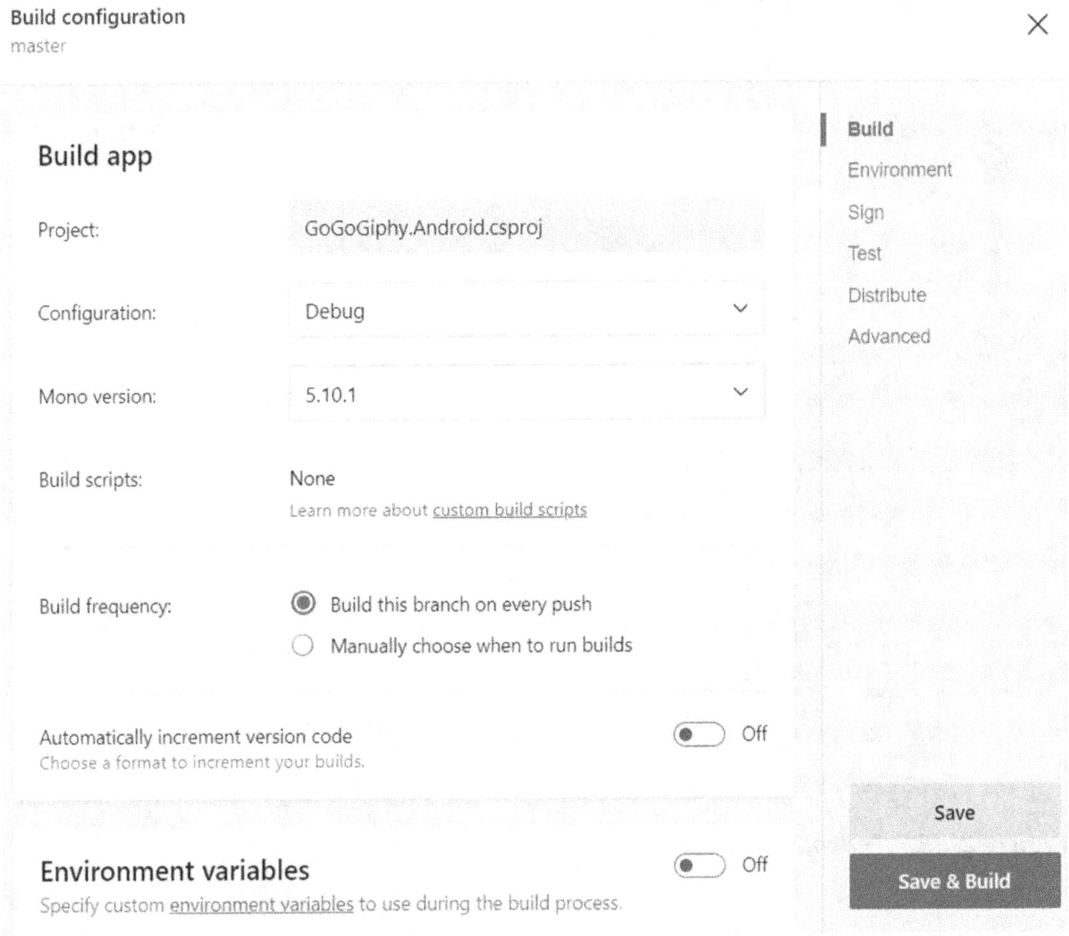

Build configuration   ×
master

Build app

| | Build |
| Environment |
| Sign |
| Test |
| Distribute |
| Advanced |

Project: GoGoGiphy.Android.csproj

Configuration: Debug   ∨

Mono version: 5.10.1   ∨

Build scripts: None
                            Learn more about custom build scripts

Build frequency: ◉ Build this branch on every push
                            ○ Manually choose when to run builds

Automatically increment version code   (●) Off
Choose a format to increment your builds.

Save

Environment variables   (●) Off
Specify custom environment variables to use during the build process.

Save & Build

Figure 2-42. *Android build configuration*

Once the build finishes, you will see a page similar to Figure 2-43. Notice that the layout of the page is the same as before. You still have access to the same build artifacts and logs.

Figure 2-43. *Android build output*

Integrating App Center from GitHub

Even though I already showed you how to connect your GitHub project from App Center, I do want to show how the same integration can be done from GitHub itself. I show this different method because the pages you will see in this approach will show you different information that you may find useful. Keep in mind the screenshots you see in this section and GitHub may be different between the time this book was written and the current status of the website after Microsoft's acquisition and integration with other services.

Sign into GitHub. Go to the link called Marketplace in the header at the top of the page. You should see a search bar on this page. Type in App Center, as shown in Figure 2-44.

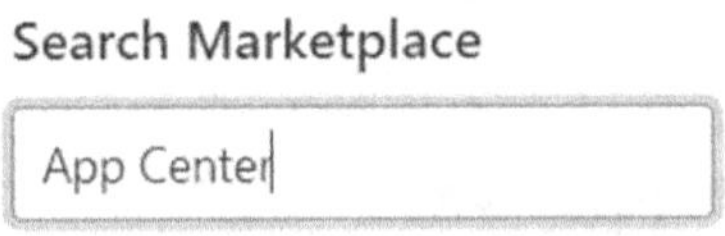

Search Marketplace

App Center

Figure 2-44. *GitHub Search Marketplace*

Click the App Center app. You will be brought to the page shown in Figure 2-45.

App Center

ⓘ You have already purchased this app on GitHub Marketplace.
To complete this installation, you must grant this app access to your GitHub account.

Set up a new plan   Edit your plan ▾

Categories

Continuous Integration

Mobile CI

Ship Your Mobile Projects Faster

Automate the Build-Test-Distribute process for your mobile projects. Continuous Integration and Continuous Delivery (CI/CD) are at your fingertips.

Figure 2-45. *The App Center app*

As you can see, I already set up App Center with my repository and removed it, which is why it says that I have already purchased this app. Your screen may look slightly different if you are a first-time user.

Click the Set up a new plan button. You will see the different pricing tiers explained in the first chapter. Click the Free option since you are learning; you always have the option of returning and applying the other pricing tiers. Click the Install it for free button, as shown in Figure 2-46.

Pricing and setup

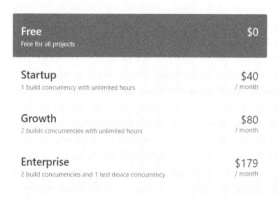

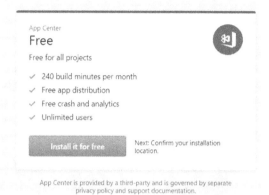

Figure 2-46. *App Center pricing tiers*

Figure 2-47 shows the next page. Click the button titled Complete order and begin installation.

Review your order

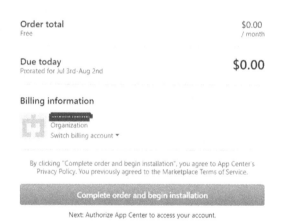

Figure 2-47. *Reviewing your order*

Figure 2-48 shows the screen where you can choose the repositories where App Center will be installed. I chose the All Repositories option for simplicity. Click Install.

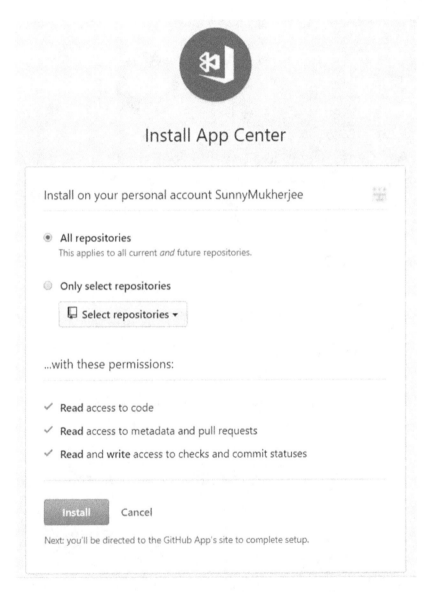

Figure 2-48. Installing App Center

You have one last screen left where you need to authorize App Center (Figure 2-49). After installing, you will be redirected back to App Center where you can log in and create your app. These are the same steps you followed when you set up your builds.

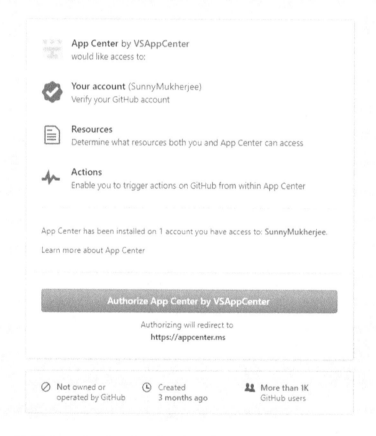

Figure 2-49. *GitHub authorization for App Center*

Revoking App Center Privileges from GitHub

If you ever need to revoke App Center privileges on GitHub itself, go to the Settings page and click Applications on the left-hand pane highlighted in Figure 2-50. Click the Authorized GitHub Apps tab.

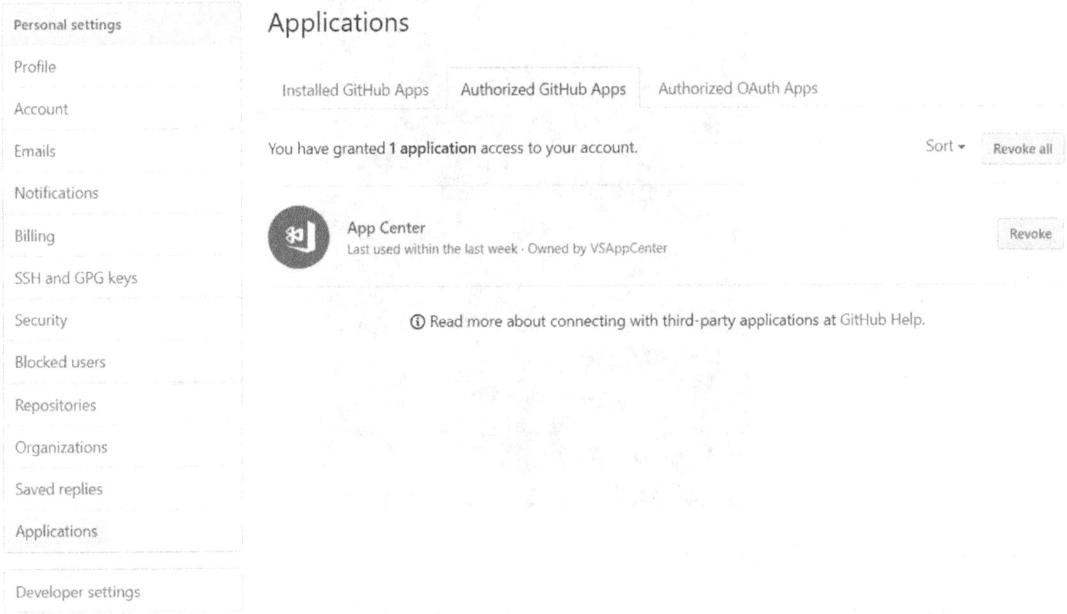

Figure 2-50. *The GitHub Applications page*

Setting Up Your Notifications to Slack

In this section, I will show how easy it is to set up notifications from App Center to your Slack account. I like to know if my build has succeeded or failed. In order for App Center to know about your Slack account, you will need to configure a few settings on Slack first, copy the URL, and paste it into your App Center account. I am assuming you already have a Slack account and the Slack mobile app downloaded to your phone. I will show you all the steps. Let's get started.

Go to the Settings section for the GoGoGiphy-iOS app, as shown in Figure 2-51.

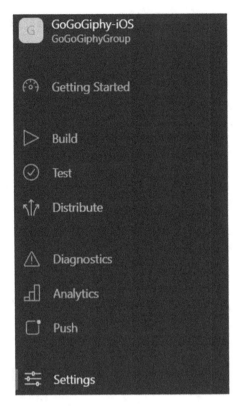

Figure 2-51. *The Settings link*

Click Webhooks on the left-side panel and click the Slack link, as highlighted in Figure 2-52. You can click the New Webhook button to see your options. But the Slack link will show you how to configure and get the URL so App Center knows where to publish the notifications.

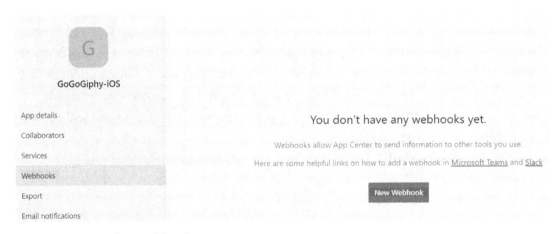

Figure 2-52. *The Webhooks page*

Upon clicking the Slack link, the navigation will bring you to a page like Figure 2-53. Click Add Configuration to get started.

Figure 2-53. *The Add Configuration page*

Now you should see a page like Figure 2-54. As you can see, I already have a channel set up called #builds selected in the combo-box. You can create a new channel in the link highlighted below the combo-box. Click the button named Add incoming Webhooks integration.

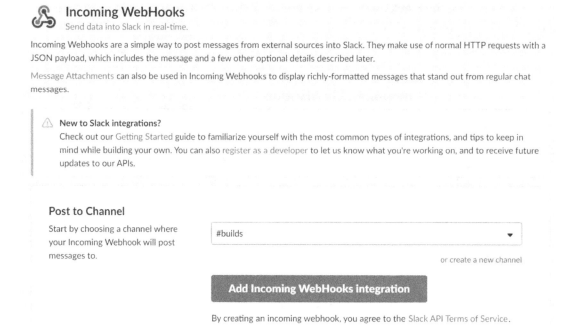

Figure 2-54. *The Incoming WebHooks page*

The following page will have a lot of options about customizing your username, icon, and message that you post to your Slack channel from App Center. Please feel free to browse the options and play with the different options.

Keep your configuration simple for the moment and only customize the description, name, and icon. Mimic the settings shown in Figure 2-55. I included a custom iOS icon so I know it is a build notification for my iOS app on the build channel. You will notice also that the preview message changes as you type in the different settings so you can see how it will look on your build channel.

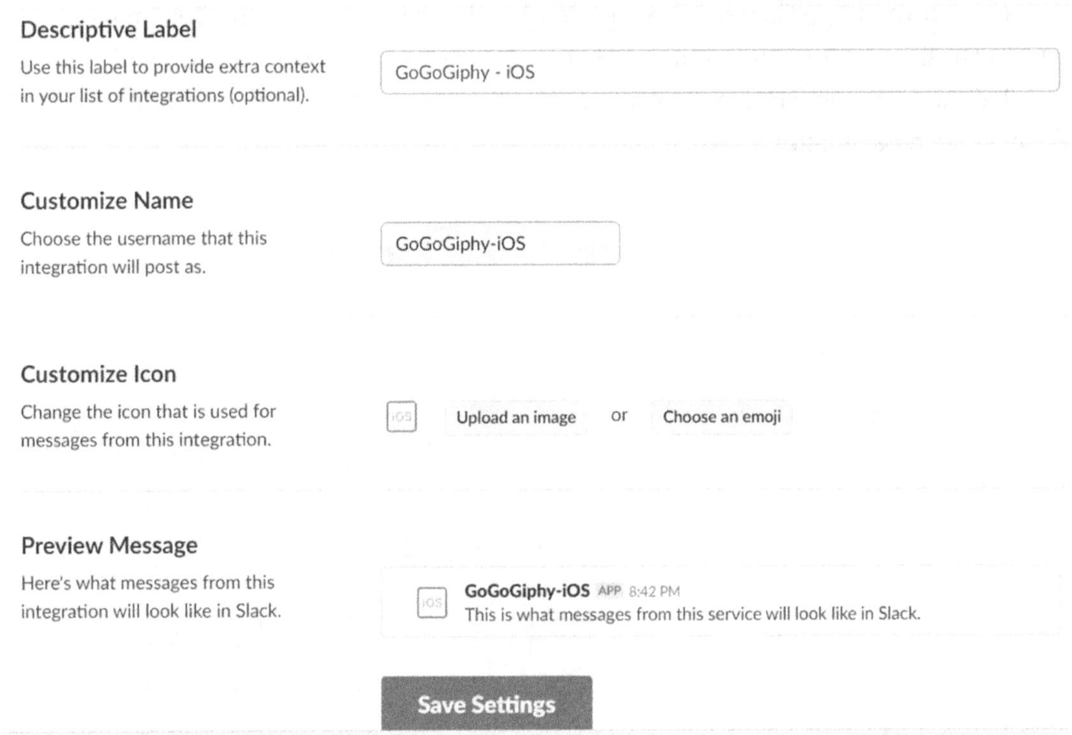

Descriptive Label

Use this label to provide extra context in your list of integrations (optional).

GoGoGiphy - iOS

Customize Name

Choose the username that this integration will post as.

GoGoGiphy-iOS

Customize Icon

Change the icon that is used for messages from this integration.

iOS   Upload an image   or   Choose an emoji

Preview Message

Here's what messages from this integration will look like in Slack.

iOS   **GoGoGiphy-iOS** APP 8:42 PM
This is what messages from this service will look like in Slack.

Save Settings

Figure 2-55. *The Incoming WebHooks page*

Upon clicking the Save Settings button above, you will return to the same page. Copy the Webhook URL, as shown in Figure 2-56.

Integration Settings

Post to Channel

Messages that are sent to the incoming webhook will be posted here.

#builds ▾

or create a new channel

Webhook URL

Send your JSON payloads to this URL.
Show setup instructions

https://hooks.slack.com/services/T1F99JVFV/BBLAN0ZEV/iHFDYvWEZvVxcrDI

Copy URL • Regenerate

Figure 2-56. *The Integration Settings page*

Now return to App Center. Click the New Webhook button from the first image. A panel will slide out from the right. Mimic the settings shown in Figure 2-57. Notice how I copied the URL from Slack and how I configured the webhook to notify me "always" during a success or failure.

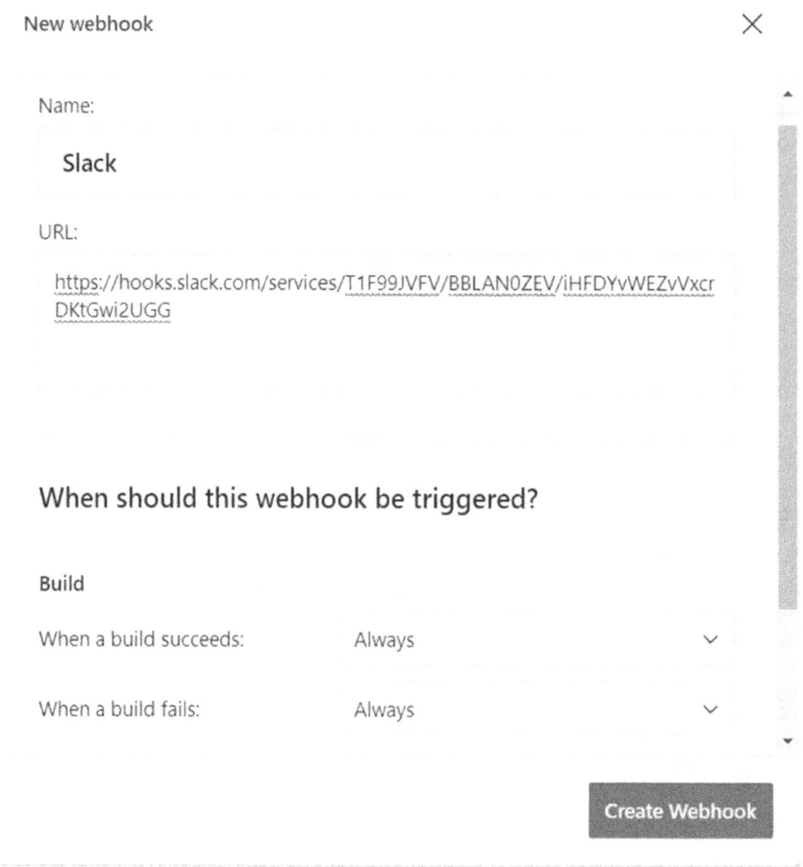

New webhook   ✕

Name:

Slack

URL:

https://hooks.slack.com/services/T1F99JVFV/BBLAN0ZEV/iHFDYvWEZvVxcr
DKtGwi2UGG

When should this webhook be triggered?

Build

When a build succeeds: Always   ⌄

When a build fails: Always   ⌄

Create Webhook

Figure 2-57. *The App Center New Webhook panel*

Figure 2-58 shows the webhook added to App Center. Click the icon on the right. Click Test. This will send a test message to your Slack channel.

Figure 2-58. *The App Center Webhooks page*

Now let's trigger a manual build so you know the notification is working. Go to your app and the Build link on the left panel. Click the Build now button on the right, as shown in Figure 2-59.

Figure 2-59. *The iOS App Build Page*

When the build completes, return to your iOS device. As mentioned, I assume you already have the Slack app downloaded and installed. Open your Slack app. You should see something similar to Figure 2-60 in your Slack app and channel. Notice all the messages published from Slack to App Center in order from the webhook integration, the test message, and the build notification. You can click the View Details button on the build message to see the details of the build. It will navigate you back to App Center and ask you to sign in.

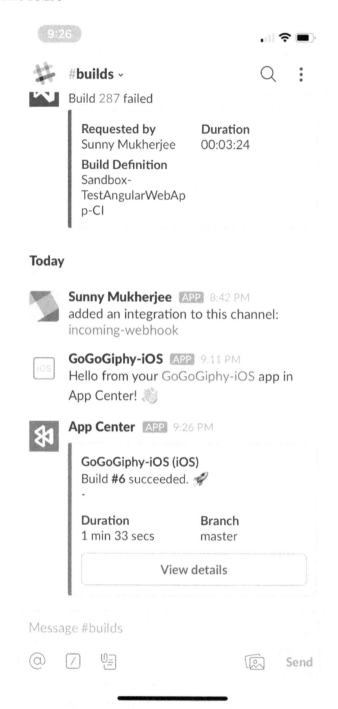

Figure 2-60. *The Slack mobile app showing an App Center build message*

Just for your knowledge, if you ever want to remove your webhook integration on Slack, you can click the Manage link at the top of your Slack page and go to Custom Integrations, as shown in Figure 2-61.

Figure 2-61. *The Custom Integrations page*

Now your exercise is to repeat the same steps for the Android app that you set up before. Keep in mind that you can add another configuration to your existing webhook on Slack without creating a new configuration.

If you complete the above steps, you will have your builds and notifications set up to alert you whenever a build succeeds or fails.

Troubleshooting

I wrote this section because I ran into a few of these errors as I downloaded a fresh copy of my own app onto a different repository! That's Xamarin Forms for you. Microsoft is still working through a few bugs.

Keep in mind that most Xamarin Forms errors are not true errors. For whatever reason, Visual Studio does not perform a thorough job even when asking to rebuild the solution. By definition, a rebuild action is a clean build. But apparently the clean actions do not always work as intended.

Follow the steps below to resolve most Xamarin Forms errors:

- If the solution is open in Visual Studio, exit Visual Studio.

- Open the folder where the project is located in Windows Explorer.

- Locate the `Bin` and `Obj` folders for each of the projects, including the Core, iOS, and Android projects.

- Delete the `Bin` and `Obj` folders.

- Restart Visual Studio.

- Reopen the solution.

- Rebuild the solution.

- Redeploy the app to the simulator.

The follow are some of the errors I encountered during my journey of creating this sample app. You may encounter these errors too and you may find this section useful.

Visual Studio iPhone Simulators Are Not Showing in Debug Target Combo-box

You may encounter this error if versions are out of sync between Visual Studio and Mac. Follow the steps below to resolve this error:

- Update XCode on Mac.

- Verify that the Xamarin.ios versions are the same on VS and Mac.

- Verify that the Xamarin.Forms NuGet package is the correct version.

- Launch XCode and verify that the components are installed.

Visual Studio Android Emulator Does Not Start

You may encounter this error if Hypervisor is not running on your machine. Follow the steps below:

- Verify that Hypervisor is running.

- Open the command prompt in Admin mode.

- Enter the following command:

  `bcdedit /set hypervisorlaunchtype on`

- Restart your Windows machine.

- Restart the Android emulator.

Deployment failed: Mono.AndroidTools. InstallFailedException: Failure [INSTALL_FAILED_NO_ MATCHING_ABIS

You may encounter this error when trying to deploy the Android project to the Android emulator. Follow the steps below to resolve the error:

- Right-click the Android project.

- Go to Properties.

- Go to Android Options ➤ Advanced.

- Enable all options in Supported Architectures.

Xamarin.Forms Tasks Do Not Match Targets

If you see this error when building the Xamarin Forms project, try the following steps to solve the error:

- Go to Windows Explorer.

- Go to your project folder.

- Open the targets file located at the relative path below:

  `\GoGoGiphy\GoGoGiphy.iOS\obj`

- Locate the Import tag.

- Verify that the Xamarin Forms path is the same version as the Xamarin Forms NuGet package.

- If they do not match, delete the `obj` and `bin` folders from each project.

- Close Visual Studio.

- Reopen Visual Studio and the solution.

- Rebuild the solution.

The above steps of deleting the `obj` and `bin` folders, closing VS, and reopening VS usually resolves most Xamarin errors.

Error Java.Lang.OutOfMemoryError: Failed to Allocate a 132710412 Byte Allocation with 1048576

This error occurs because an Android project does not use a large heap by default. The error message itself explains that it is trying to allocate a larger byte allocation for a smaller size. Follow the steps below:

- Open `AndroidManifest.xml` in Properties.

- Change the appropriate line in your XML file:

  ```
  <application
  android:label="GoGoGiphy.Android" android:largeHeap="true">
  </application>
  ```

Ibtool Exited with Code 1

You may encounter this error when building the iOS project. Follow the steps below to resolve the error:

- Open `Info.plist`.

- Change the Deployment Target to a value later than 6.0.

Foundation.MonoTouchException: Objective-C Exception Thrown. Name: NSInternalInconsistencyException Reason: -[UISearchBar sizeThatFits:] Does Not Support Passing Non-Finite Values ({inf, 56})

Note that iOS 11 has an issue with setting an infinite value to a SearchBar control. Set the WidthRequest on the SearchBar control. You can find more information on the Xamarin bug at `https://bugzilla.xamarin.com/show_bug.cgi?id=59595`.

The "DebugType" Parameter Is Not Supported by the "XamlCTask" Task

Newer versions of Xamarin Forms may reintroduce this bug. Follow the steps below to resolve the error:

- Go to the following folder: Project ➤ Packages ➤ Latest Xamarin. Forms ➤ Build ➤ Portable.

- Find the `Xamarin.Forms.targets` file.

- Remove following code from the file:

  `DebugType = "$(DebugType)`

You can find more information about this error at `https://forums.xamarin.com/discussion/95724/xamarin-forms-2-3-4-247-update-project-wont-build`.

Summary

Congratulations! You have accomplished a lot in this chapter. If you followed all the steps above, you should have completed the following:

- Set up your organization, collaborators, and team

- Set up more branches on Azure DevOps

- Set up the app to run locally

- Configured your solution configuration mappings

- Connected to either your GitHub or VSTS code repository

- Set up your iOS build

- Set up your Android build

- Set up your build notifications

- Set up notifications to your Slack account

In the next chapter, you will learn how to set up test distributions for your app.

CHAPTER 3

Setting Up Distribution

In the last chapter, you set up your builds, collaborators, and teams. In this chapter, you will cover a lot of ground as well. You need to be able to set up your distribution as your first step in your journey through App Center because you will set up analytics, crash reporting, and push notifications in later chapters. You will send data to App Center, and App Center will send data back to you. In order to get the most out of these chapters, you need to be able to use the app on a physical device. And it is a lot more fun when you have a real app working on real device instead of a simulator! Let's get started.

This chapter is about distributing your app within your team, including your developers and testers, but not to public app stores. The sample app with this book is good enough for internal distribution because it was designed to show the capabilities of App Center with Xamarin Forms, but it does not meet the requirements of a public app, such as an app icon or a splash screen.

In this chapter, you will learn about the following topics. Please feel free to go through this chapter in a single sprint or in repeated visits because you will cover a lot of material.

- How to create your iOS App ID

- How to register your Apple device

- How to create a certificate signing request

- How to create a developer certificate

- How to create an iOS provisioning profile

- How to register devices in App Center

- How to create distribution groups

- How to configure builds for developer distribution

© Sunny Mukherjee 2019
S. Mukherjee, *Learn Microsoft Visual Studio App Center*, https://doi.org/10.1007/978-1-4842-4382-4_3

- How to set up the QA branch for build scripts

- How to set up your post-clone build script

You will spend the better part of this chapter in the Apple Developer portal. Please make sure you have already signed up for a Developer account (explained in the first chapter) and you can access the page shown in Figure 3-1.

Figure 3-1. *Apple Developer Portal*

Creating Distribution Groups

Before you do anything with distribution to iOS or Android, you need to set up your distribution groups in App Center. Why should you create distribution groups? For example, distribution groups are needed when you want to distribute iOS builds only for iOS developers or testers and when you want to distribute Android builds for Android developers or testers. Distribution groups give you the ability to assign members to each group. Distribution groups also allow you to segregate certain builds to certain groups. For example, let's suppose you have a Developer branch and a QA branch. Logically, you can set up your distribution to deliver your app to your developers only when the build for the code from the Development branch completes. Likewise, you can set up your distribution for QA only when the build from the QA branch completes. Let's create the distribution groups you need through the rest of this book.

Locate the Distribute link on the left pane. Click Groups. Click the Add Group button on the right, as shown in Figure 3-2.

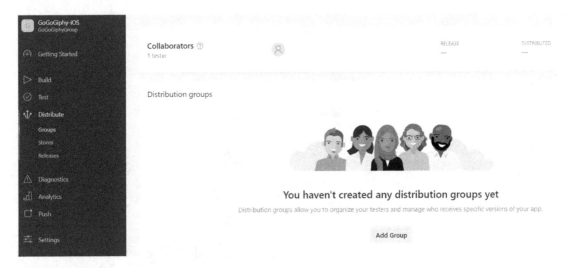

Figure 3-2. *Adding groups*

Next you will see a panel from the right that prompts you to enter details for the group. Create a distribution group for iOS Testers, as shown in Figure 3-3. Go ahead and give it a name, disable the Allow public access option, and enter the email addresses of your testers. Upon saving the Distribution group, your iOS testers will get an email invitation, at which point they can either sign into or sign up for an App Center account and register their device with App Center. I will explain how to register your physical device in App Center later in the chapter.

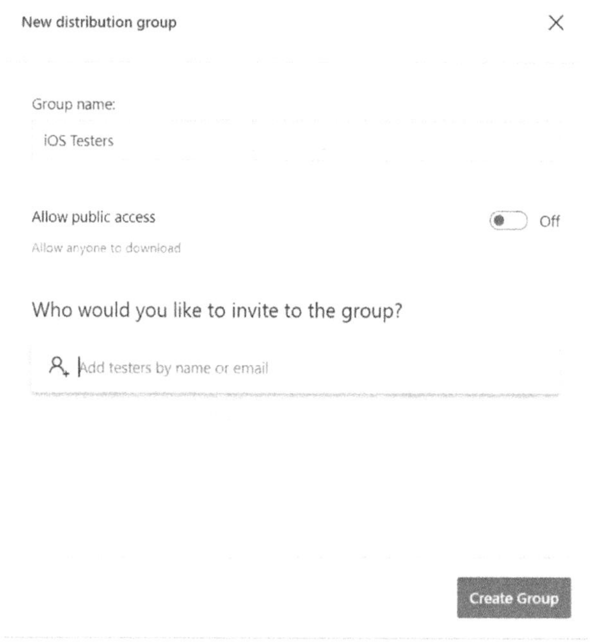

New distribution group   ✕

Group name:

iOS Testers

Allow public access   ⬤◯ Off
Allow anyone to download

Who would you like to invite to the group?

👤₊ Add testers by name or email

Create Group

Figure 3-3. *New distribution group*

After saving your new distribution group, you will see your new group. Click Devices
and you will see the registered device of the person who received the email invitation, as
shown in Figure 3-4.

Figure 3-4. *iOS Tester distribution group*

Now repeat these steps to create a new Distribution group called Developers.
Remember to add your developers to your new group. Ask your developers to register
their devices. Upon device registration, you will see the developer devices in a list similar
to Figure 3-4. And your new list of groups should look like Figure 3-5.

			RELEASE	DISTRIBUTED	
Collaborators ⑦ 3 testers	👤 👤 👤		1.0 (1.0)	Jul 10, 2018	
Distribution groups					+
Developers 1 tester	👤		RELEASE 9 (9)	DISTRIBUTED Jul 10, 2018	⋮
iOS Testers 1 tester	👤		RELEASE —	DISTRIBUTED —	

Figure 3-5. *iOS distribution groups*

Remember to set up your Android distribution group as well. Follow the same set of steps, except within the GoGoGiphy-Android app in App Center. Figure 3-6 shows one Android device set up to use as a Developer device with a separate email address. After you are finished, your group should look similar to my group shown in Figure 3-6.

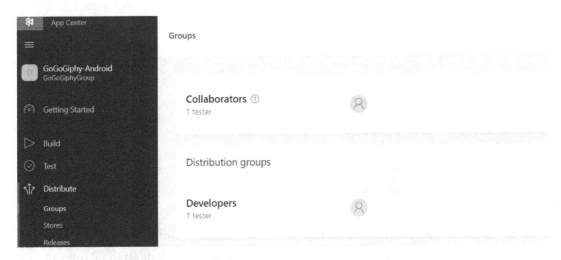

Figure 3-6. *Android distribution groups*

Creating Your iOS App ID

The first step in this chapter is to enable your Apple Developer Account to identify your app. The App ID will be needed later when creating your provisioning profile.

Go to the Certificates, Identifiers & Profiles section shown in Figure 3-7. Go to the Developer Portal, click App IDs under Identifiers in the left pane, and click the + button highlighted.

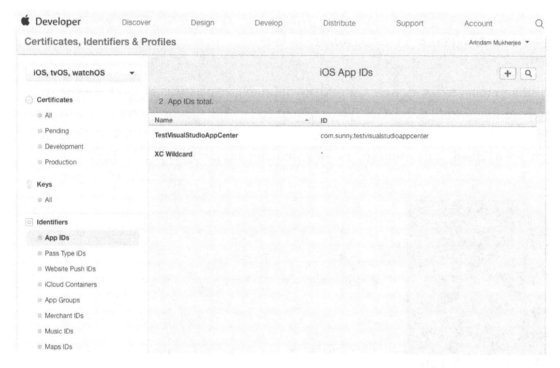

Figure 3-7. *Adding an iOS App ID*

After clicking the + button, the Developer Portal will ask you for the name of the new App ID. It will assign an App prefix for you automatically. You will need to fill out the Bundle ID in reverse domain name style. You can use the same reverse domain name as mine, but I suggest replacing my name, sunny, with yours (Figure 3-8).

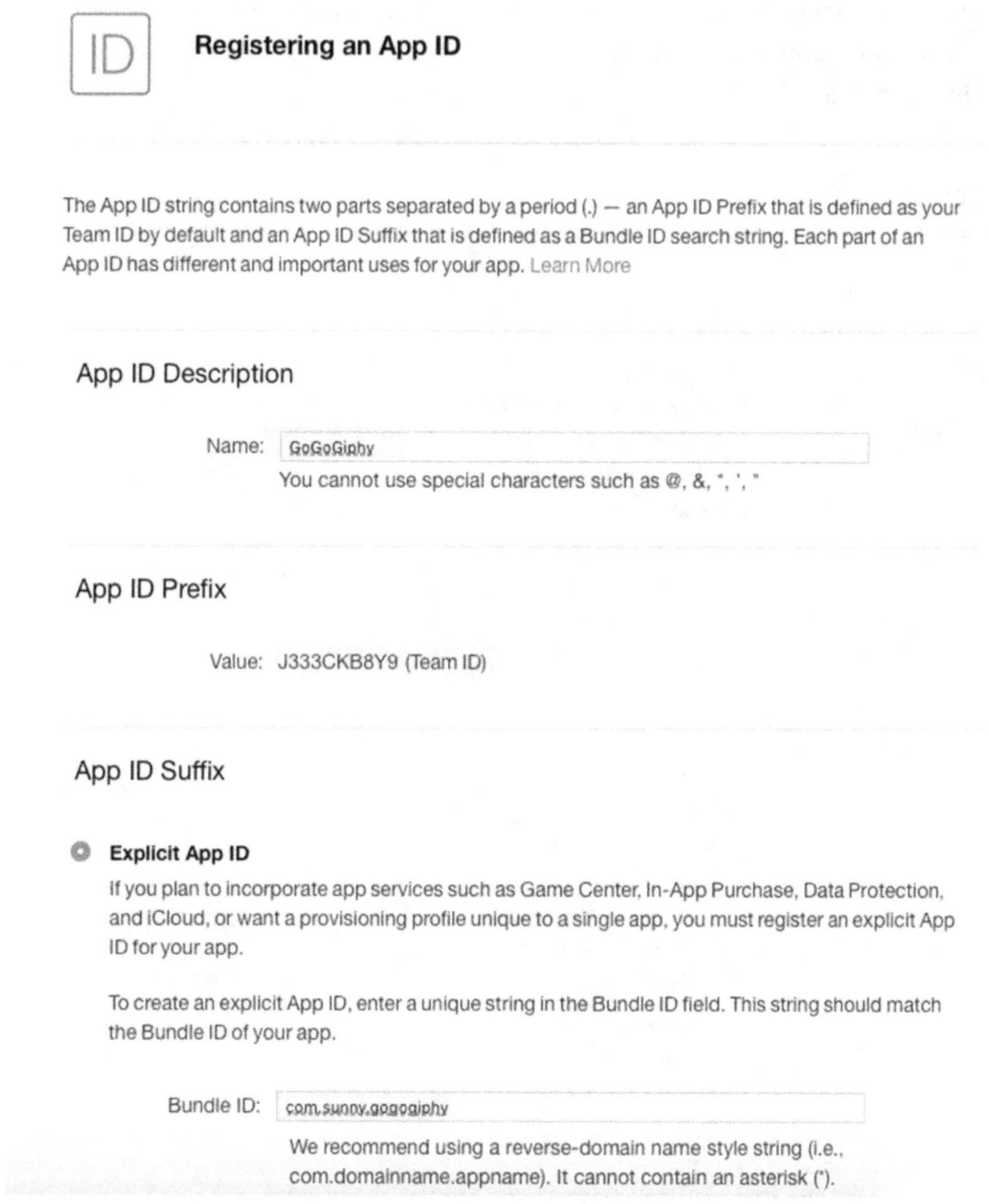

| ID | **Registering an App ID** |

The App ID string contains two parts separated by a period (.) — an App ID Prefix that is defined as your Team ID by default and an App ID Suffix that is defined as a Bundle ID search string. Each part of an App ID has different and important uses for your app. Learn More

App ID Description

Name: GoGoGiphy

You cannot use special characters such as @, &, *, ', "

App ID Prefix

Value: J333CKB8Y9 (Team ID)

App ID Suffix

● **Explicit App ID**

If you plan to incorporate app services such as Game Center, In-App Purchase, Data Protection, and iCloud, or want a provisioning profile unique to a single app, you must register an explicit App ID for your app.

To create an explicit App ID, enter a unique string in the Bundle ID field. This string should match the Bundle ID of your app.

Bundle ID: com.sunny.gogogiphy

We recommend using a reverse-domain name style string (i.e., com.domainname.appname). It cannot contain an asterisk (*).

Figure 3-8. *Registering an App ID*

On the next screen, Apple will ask you to supply what services you would like to enable in your new app. For the purpose of a future chapter, enable push notifications, as shown in Figure 3-9.

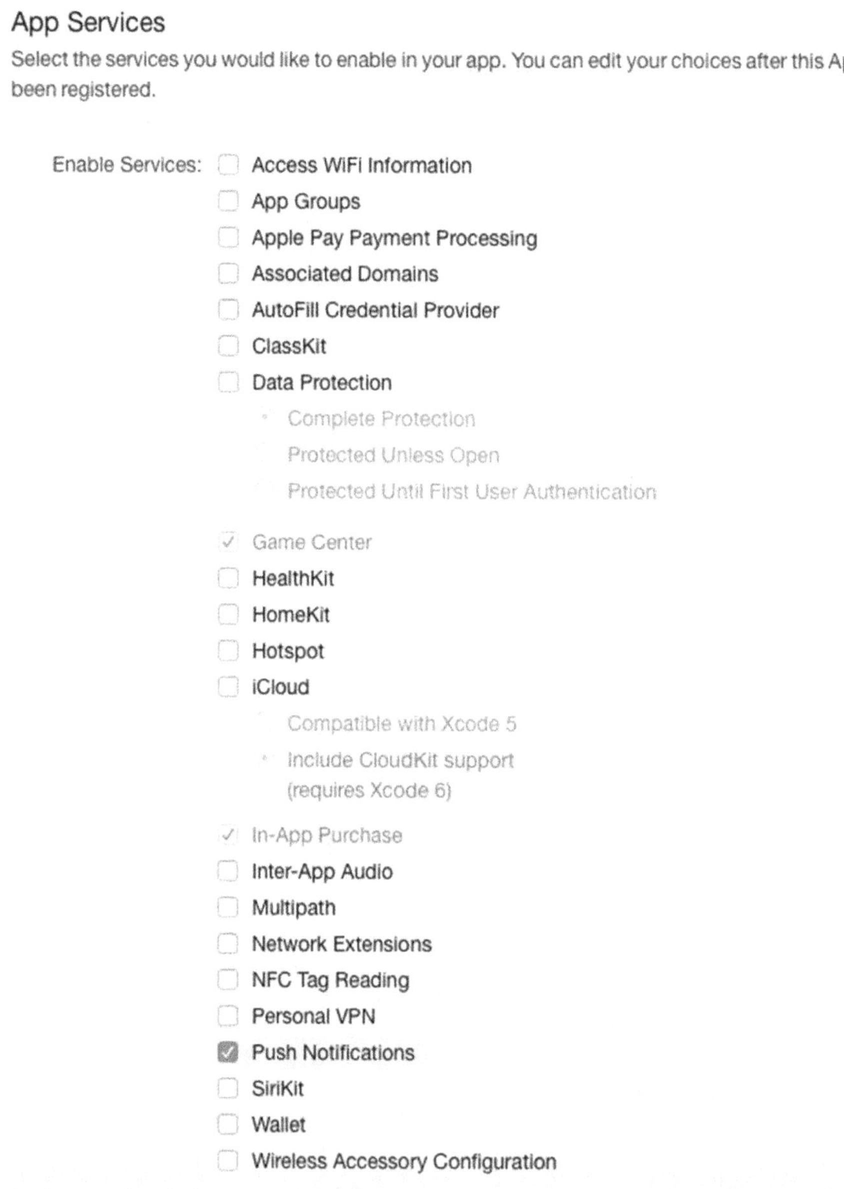

App Services

Select the services you would like to enable in your app. You can edit your choices after this App ID has been registered.

Enable Services:
- ☐ Access WiFi Information
- ☐ App Groups
- ☐ Apple Pay Payment Processing
- ☐ Associated Domains
- ☐ AutoFill Credential Provider
- ☐ ClassKit
- ☐ Data Protection
  - Complete Protection
  - Protected Unless Open
  - Protected Until First User Authentication
- ☑ Game Center
- ☐ HealthKit
- ☐ HomeKit
- ☐ Hotspot
- ☐ iCloud
  - Compatible with Xcode 5
  - Include CloudKit support (requires Xcode 6)
- ☑ In-App Purchase
- ☐ Inter-App Audio
- ☐ Multipath
- ☐ Network Extensions
- ☐ NFC Tag Reading
- ☐ Personal VPN
- ☑ Push Notifications
- ☐ SiriKit
- ☐ Wallet
- ☐ Wireless Accessory Configuration

Figure 3-9. Enabling app services

In the summary page, verify all the app settings one last time, as in Figure 3-10. Click
Register.

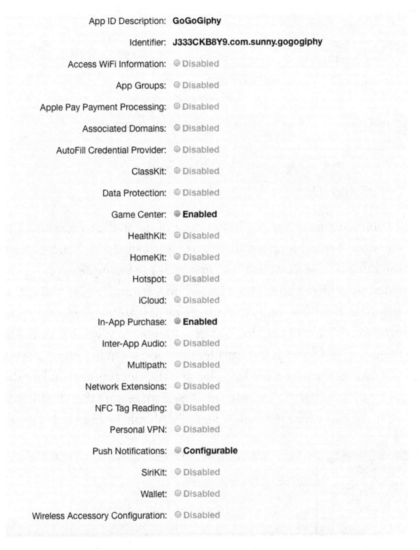

App ID Description:	**GoGoGiphy**
Identifier:	**J333CKB8Y9.com.sunny.gogogiphy**
Access WiFi Information:	Disabled
App Groups:	Disabled
Apple Pay Payment Processing:	Disabled
Associated Domains:	Disabled
AutoFill Credential Provider:	Disabled
ClassKit:	Disabled
Data Protection:	Disabled
Game Center:	**Enabled**
HealthKit:	Disabled
HomeKit:	Disabled
Hotspot:	Disabled
iCloud:	Disabled
In-App Purchase:	**Enabled**
Inter-App Audio:	Disabled
Multipath:	Disabled
Network Extensions:	Disabled
NFC Tag Reading:	Disabled
Personal VPN:	Disabled
Push Notifications:	**Configurable**
SiriKit:	Disabled
Wallet:	Disabled
Wireless Accessory Configuration:	Disabled

Figure 3-10. *The App Summary page*

You will now see your new App ID listed, as shown in Figure 3-11.

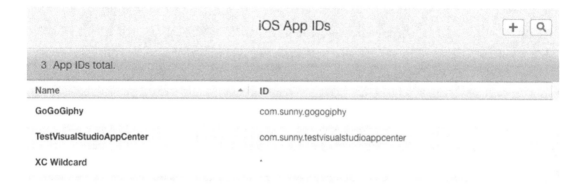

iOS App IDs

3 App IDs total.

Name	ID
GoGoGiphy	com.sunny.gogogiphy
TestVisualStudioAppCenter	com.sunny.testvisualstudioappcenter
XC Wildcard	

Figure 3-11. *iOS App IDs*

You must complete one more step before continuing to the next section. The sample project that you downloaded from my GitHub repo already has a bundle identifier specified in the Info.plist file that I used when creating the sample app.

Open the sample project and solution file. Open the Info.plist file in the iOS project. You will see a Bundle Identifier textbox. If you changed your bundle identifier in the Developer Portal to be different than the one in the images above, change the bundle identifier in the Info.plist to match the app identifier you set in the Apple Developer Portal. If Apple sees a mismatch between the Info.plist and the Developer Portal for the bundle identifier, your distribution of the app will fail. Please make sure that they always match!

Figure 3-12 highlights where the bundle identifier should be changed in the Info.plist file.

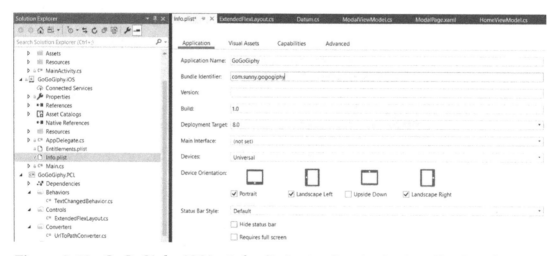

Figure 3-12. *GoGoGiphy.iOS* ➤ *Info.plist* ➤ *Application* ➤ *Bundle Identifier*

Registering Your Apple Device

The second step is registering your Apple device. When I created the sample app, I tested with two iOS devices, an iPhone X and an iPhone 6 Plus. The first is a developer device and the second is a tester device.

Go to the Devices section on the left pane and click All, as shown in Figure 3-13.

Figure 3-13. *All Apple devices*

Click the + icon on the top right to add your device (Figure 3-14).

Figure 3-14. *Adding a device*

Give your device a unique name. You now need to find the UDID of your iOS device. There are a couple of ways to do so.

If you have not already registered your iOS device with App Center, go to http://whatsmyudid.com/. This webpage gives you simple set of screenshots on where and how to find your UDID. The steps are as follows:

- Connect your iPhone to your PC.

- Open iTunes.

- Open the Summary page and locate the UDID.

- Copy it.

If you have already registered your iOS device with App Center, App Center already has this information and you can get it from the site easily. Just go to the distribution group you created earlier where your device is one of the devices as part of the group. Go to Devices and click the vertical dot icon. You will see the Copy UDID button shown in Figure 3-15.

Figure 3-15.   *Finding the UDID of a registered iOS device in the distribution group*

Now return to the Apple Developer Portal and paste the UDID of your device into the UDID textbox, as shown in Figure 3-16. (I redacted a part of my UDID on purpose.)

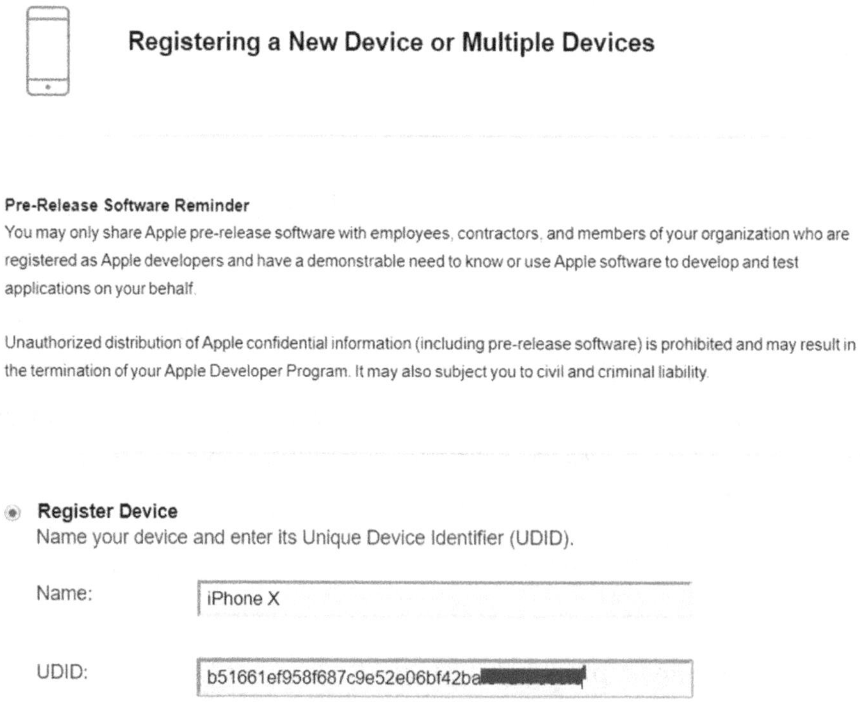

Registering a New Device or Multiple Devices

Pre-Release Software Reminder
You may only share Apple pre-release software with employees, contractors, and members of your organization who are registered as Apple developers and have a demonstrable need to know or use Apple software to develop and test applications on your behalf.

Unauthorized distribution of Apple confidential information (including pre-release software) is prohibited and may result in the termination of your Apple Developer Program. It may also subject you to civil and criminal liability.

⦿ **Register Device**
Name your device and enter its Unique Device Identifier (UDID).

Name: iPhone X

UDID: b51661ef958f687c9e52e06bf42ba

Figure 3-16.   *Apple Developer Portal ➤ Registering a Device*

After registering your device, you will see your device listed under All Devices, as in Figure 3-17. (I show both my developer and tester iPhones here with their UDIDs redacted again.)

Name	Identifier
Sunny's iPhone 6 Plus	413ea956908739a16b7c04fb▓▓▓▓▓▓
iPhone X	b51661ef958f687c9e52e06bf4▓▓▓▓▓

Figure 3-17. All iOS devices

Creating a Certificate Signing Request

The next step is to create your certificate signing request. What is a signing certificate exactly? It is used for signing your apps. A certificate is a public-private key pair issued by Apple. The public part of the certificate is stored on the Apple Developer portal and the private part of the certificate is stored locally on your Mac in your keychain. You can learn more information about app signing at `https://help.apple.com/xcode/mac/current/#/dev3a05256b8`.

About the private part of the key, remember that if this key is lost, you will not be able to use the signing certificate again to sign your app. Therefore, secure the key as you would secure a password. You can learn more about backing up your developer account and your signing certificates at `https://help.apple.com/xcode/mac/current/#/dev8a2822e0b`.

In the next section, you will generate a developer certificate based on this signing certificate you create in this section. So open your Mac machine now.

On your Mac, go to Applications ➤ Utilities. Open the Keychain Access, as shown in Figure 3-18.

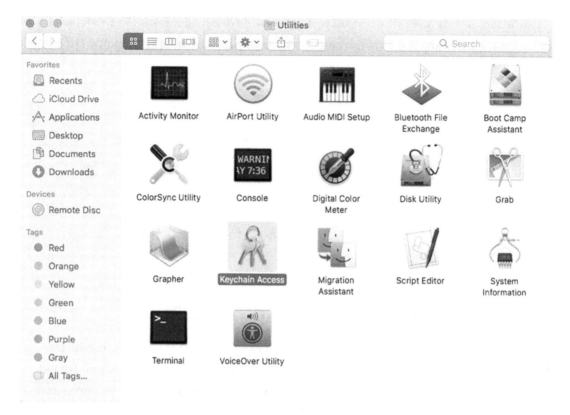

Figure 3-18. *Mac Utilities* ➤ *Keychain Access*

Go to the menu, click Keychain Access ➤ Certificate Assistant ➤ Request a Certificate from a Certificate Authority. In this method, you are asking Apple to generate a signing request file containing a public key (Figure 3-19).

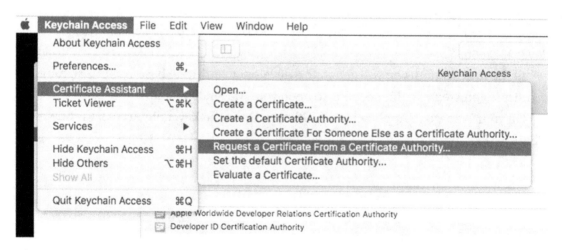

Figure 3-19. *Requesting a certificate from a certificate authority*

Enter your values for email and name. Make the common name memorable so you can identify it later. Verify that the Save to disk option is selected because you will save this signing request file to your desktop (Figure 3-20).

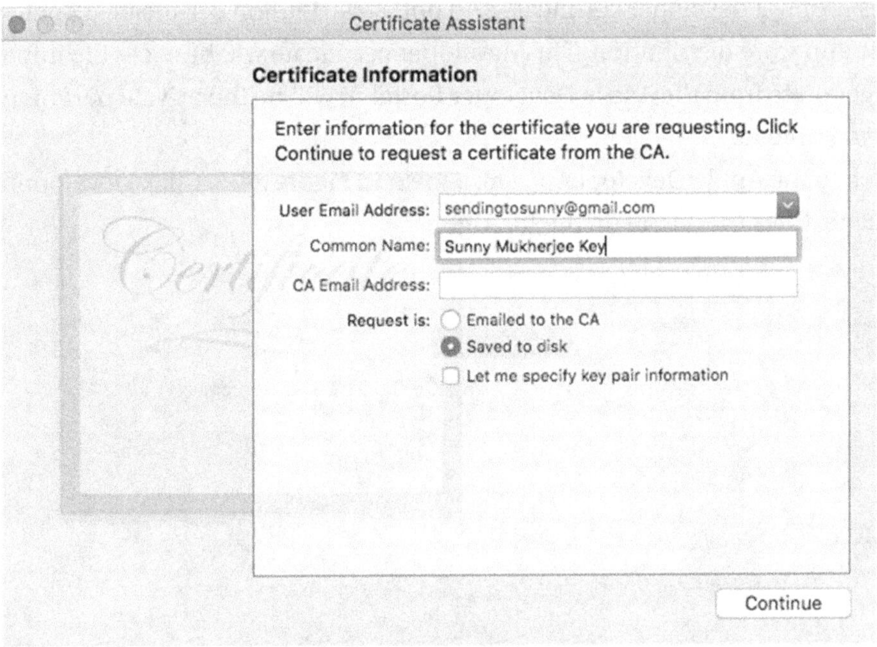

Figure 3-20. *Requesting certificate information*

In the next dialog, save your certificate file to an easily searchable location, such as your desktop, because you will need the certificate file in a later section (Figure 3-21).

Figure 3-21. *Saving the certificate file*

Creating a Developer Certificate

Next, you will create your first developer certificate. This developer certificate will be an iOS development certificate so you can run your app on iOS, tvOS, and watchOS. Keep in mind this is only a developer certificate and not a distribution certificate, which is used for public app store distribution. This developer certificate will be a .cer file initially that you will generate from the Apple Developer Portal. It will be the private part of the public key that you upload.

Return to the Apple Developer portal, shown in Figure 3-22. Click Development in the left pane. Click the + icon on the top right.

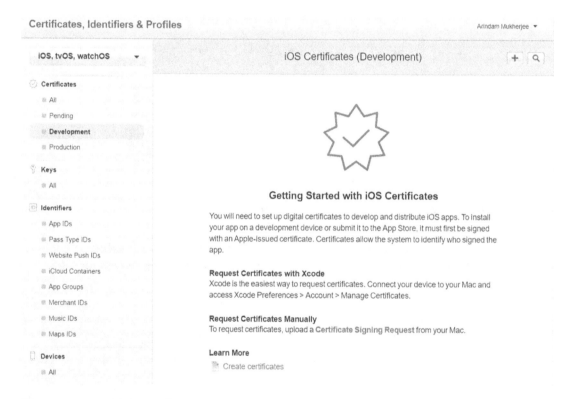

Figure 3-22. *iOS certificates*

As shown in Figure 3-23, select the iOS App Development radio button because you are creating a developer certificate.

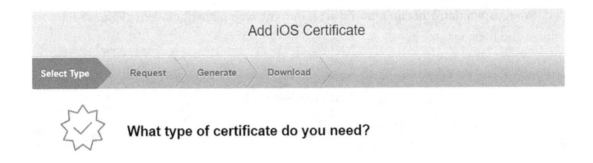

Figure 3-23. *Choosing an iOS certificate type*

Add the certificate signing request file you created in the previous section to sign your developer certificate, as shown in Figure 3-24. Remember it is the public part of the key pair. Apple will generate the private part of the key pair for you shortly. Apple will tell you how to upload it. You can either drag it into the web page or click the Choose File button and locate your file.

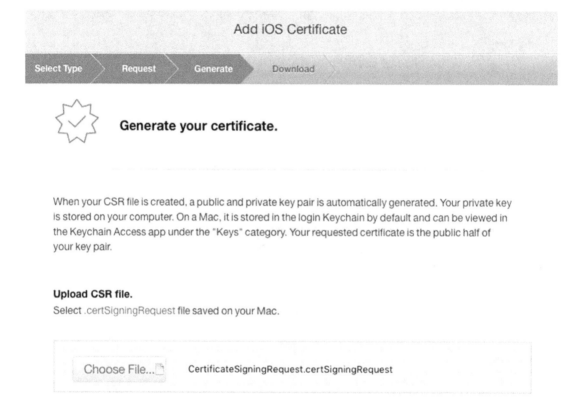

Figure 3-24. *Generating an iOS developer certificate*

Click the Download button and save the iOS Development certificate to your desktop, as shown in Figure 3-25. It is a file with a .cer extension type. Remember to keep it in a safe place.

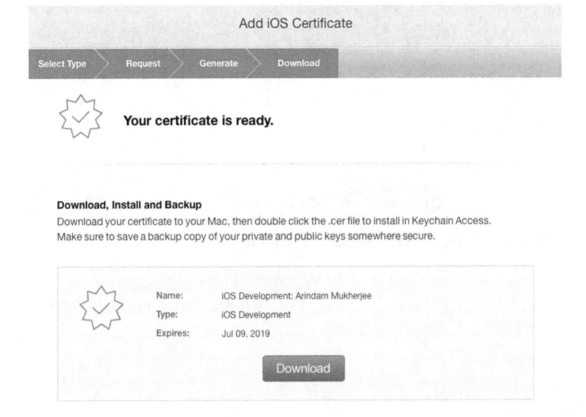

Figure 3-25. *Downloading an iOS developer certificate*

Now you need to install the certificate locally. Double-click the downloaded certificate to install it to your Keychain Access. Open Keychain Access to see that your developer certificate was installed, as shown in Figure 3-26.

Figure 3-26. *Verifying an iOS developer certificate*

Next, you will create your certificate file. Right-click iPhone Developer and the private key and select Export. Your Mac will ask you where to save the P12 certificate file. Choose your desktop, as shown in Figure 3-27.

Figure 3-27. *Exporting a developer certificate*

Enter a password for the certificate file. Remember this password because App Center will ask you for this password when signing your build (Figure 3-28).

Figure 3-28. *Securing the developer certificate*

Your Mac will now ask for your Mac password when exporting a key from Keychain Access. Enter your Mac password to export the key and click Always Allow so you do not have to keep repeating this step (Figure 3-29).

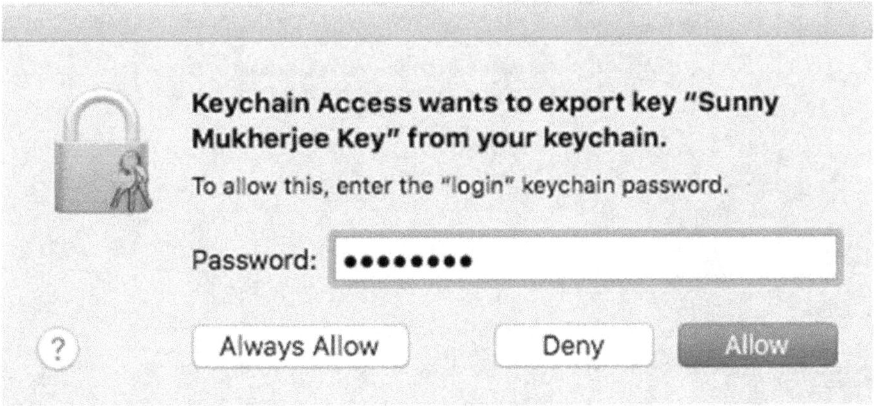

Figure 3-29. *Exporting the developer certificate*

Creating an iOS Provisioning Profile

In this section, you will create your first iOS provisioning profile. A provisioning profile allows you to install and run apps on a physical device. A development provisioning profile is used for testing purposes on test devices. It is not used for distribution to the App Store. An ad-hoc or App Store distribution certificate is used for distributing to testers and for distributing to the general public from the App Store. The developer signing certificate you created earlier will be included within the developer provisioning profile.

Go to the Provisioning Profiles section on the left pane. Click Development. You will see the webpage shown in Figure 3-30.

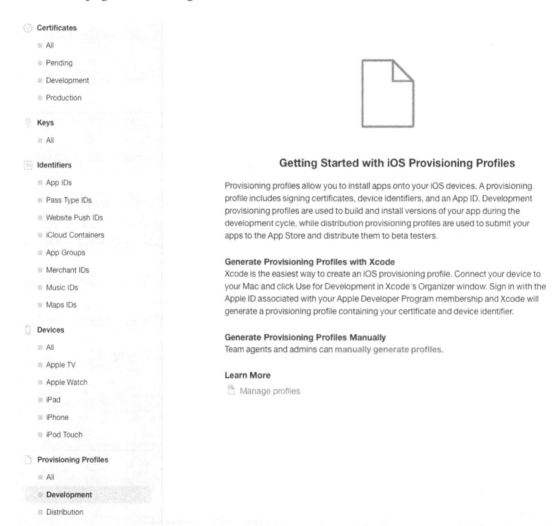

Figure 3-30. *Provisioning profiles*

Like you did when creating your signing certificate, click the iOS App Development radio button because you are creating a developer provisioning profile (Figure 3-31).

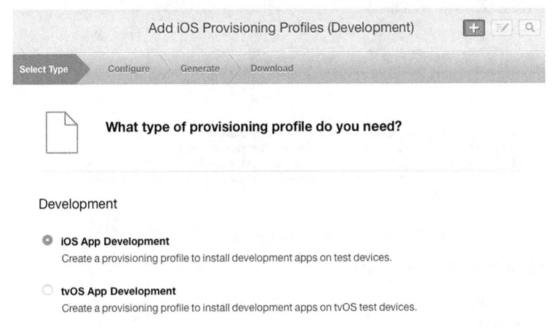

Figure 3-31. *Adding an iOS provisioning profile*

Select the App ID you entered in the previous section so Apple can associate the developer provisioning profile to the right app (Figure 3-32).

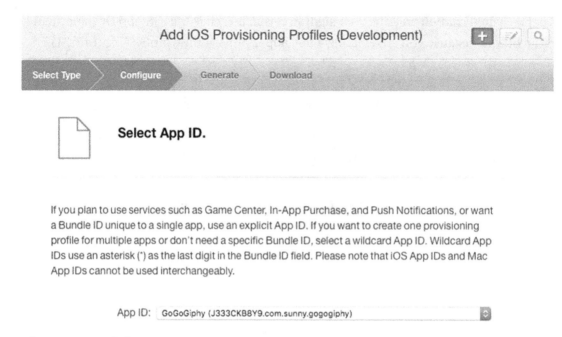

Figure 3-32. Selecting an App ID

Select the developer certificate you created in the previous section, as shown in Figure 3-33.

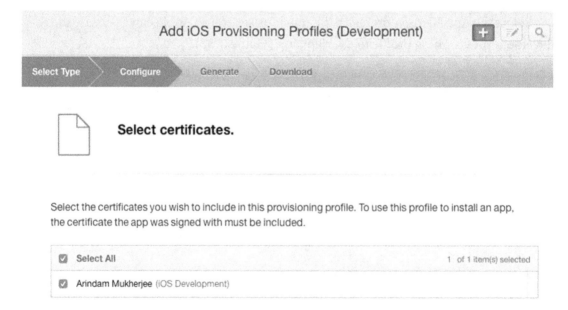

Figure 3-33. Selecting the iOS certificate

In the next page of the wizard, select the list of devices that you want to test on. As you can see in Figure 3-34, I have two devices registered; my iPhone X is the developer device and the iPhone 6 Plus is the testing device, so I select my iPhone X for this developer provisioning profile.

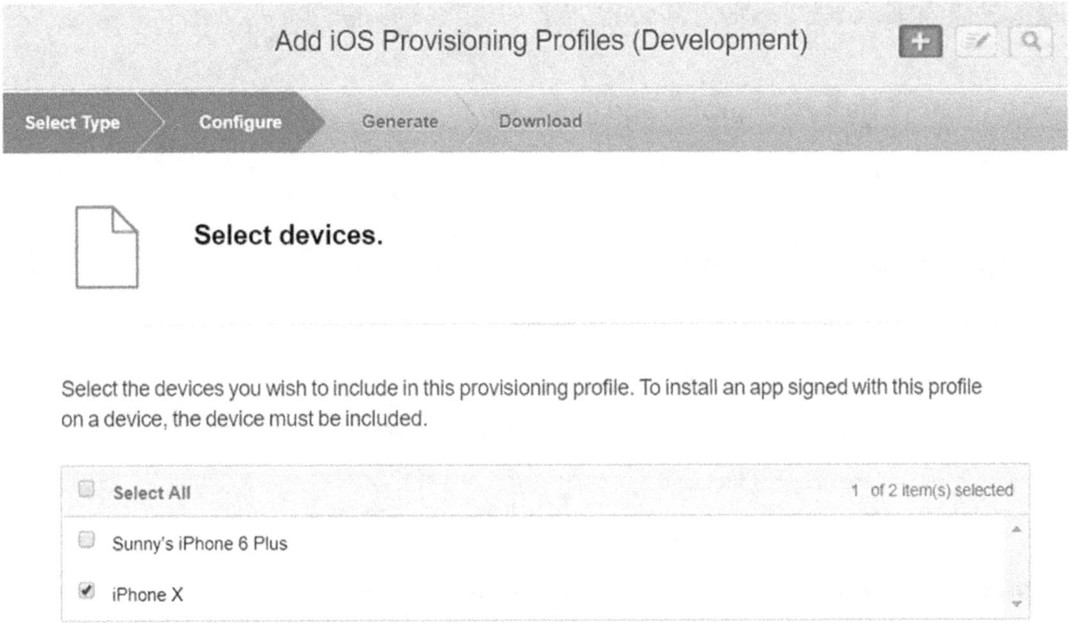

Figure 3-34. *Selecting the devices to include in the provisioning profile*

Give your developer provisioning profile a memorable name, as shown in Figure 3-35.

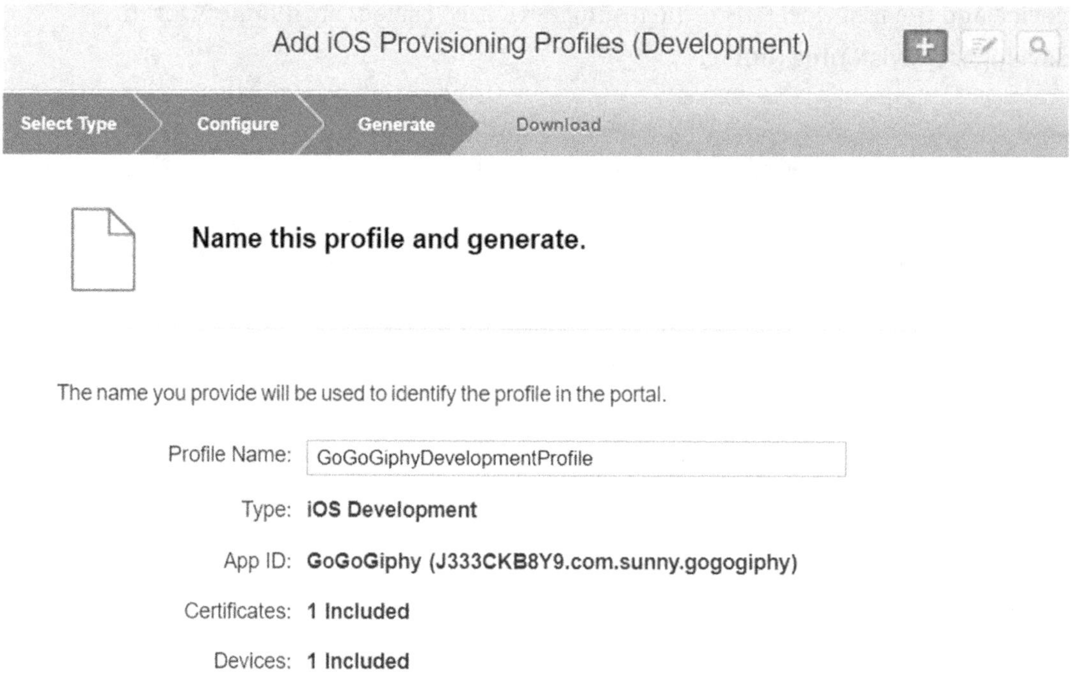

Figure 3-35. *Naming the developer provisioning profile*

Finally, download the provisioning profile to your desktop because it will be uploaded into your App Center build later for distribution (Figure 3-36).

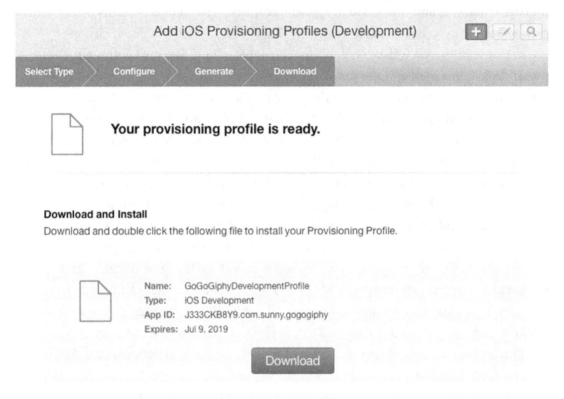

Figure 3-36. *Downloading the provisioning profile*

Creating an Android Keystore

In this section, you will follow a similar set of steps for your Android build to set up distribution to Android devices. However, you will find this section will take less than half the time and less than half as many steps to set up as you performed with Apple. Why? It is because Apple is crazy secure and wants to make sure you are creating certificates from an actual Mac! You have no idea how many hours I've spent figuring out the past few sections.

Before you dive into the stressful part, let's briefly talk about Android Keystore so you understand what it is about. Android Keystore is a system-level secure storage container where you can store both public and private parts of a key pair. Similar to Apple, the public part of the key pair is used to encrypt an application secret and the private part is used to decrypt the application secret. As a result, Android Keystore can be used for more than just app signing for distribution. It can be used for storing signing certificates and encrypted data. But unlike Apple, you do not need to create a public certificate first, upload it to Apple, and download the private certificate. It handles both the public and private parts for you in a single keystore file. This section will be so much easier!

In this section, you will explore the specific topic of app signing. Let me explain the Android concept of app signing. Android requires a digital or identity certificate identifying the author of an app. It is the same public key certificate that I explained before. The act of signing an APK file attaches the public part of the key to the APK. It associates the APK file to the author, which is you. It is important also to note that the app uses the same identity signing certificate throughout the lifetime of an app in order to install new versions or updates of the app. Because you will use Android Studio shortly to create a keystore file storing your key, Android Studio by default signs an app with a debug certificate. It is important to understand that this debug certificate is used to sign apps for internal distribution for developers and testers, but Google will not allow you to publish apps to the Google Play Store signed with a debug certificate. Finally, similar to Apple, treat your keystore file as you would treat a password. Store it in a safe place because if it is compromised, Google will not be able to recover the lost or stolen keystore and you will need to generate a new keystore and sign your app again. You can find information about app signing at `https://developer.android.com/studio/publish/app-signing`.

Now that you understand the concept, let's dive into it. The first action you must perform is to open Android Studio. If you do not have Android Studio installed, please revisit Chapter 1 about installing Android Studio. Once Android Studio is open, click Build in the menu bar and select Generate Signed Bundle/APK, as shown in Figure 3-37.

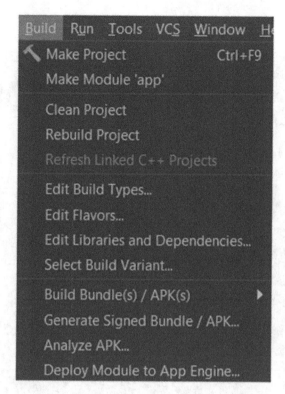

Figure 3-37. *Build menu* ➤ *Generate Signed Bundle/APK*

Android Studio will ask you either to sign an app bundle or an APK. For your needs, you want to sign an APK file, as shown in Figure 3-38.

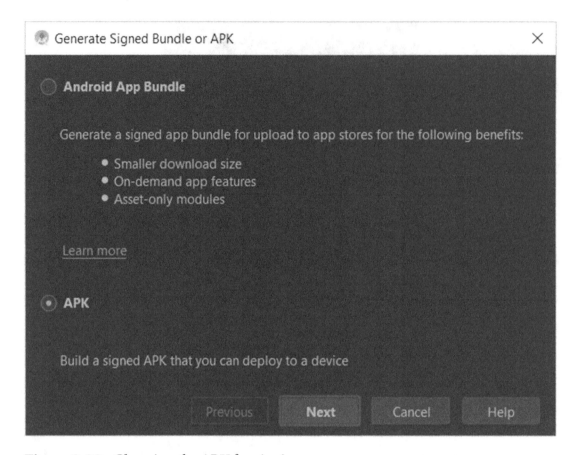

Figure 3-38. *Choosing the APK for signing*

Android Studio will open a dialog prompt for you to create your new keystore. If you already have a keystore file created, you can choose the existing keystore file to store your key. Since you do not have a keystore file, you need to create one first. Click Create new, as shown in Figure 3-39.

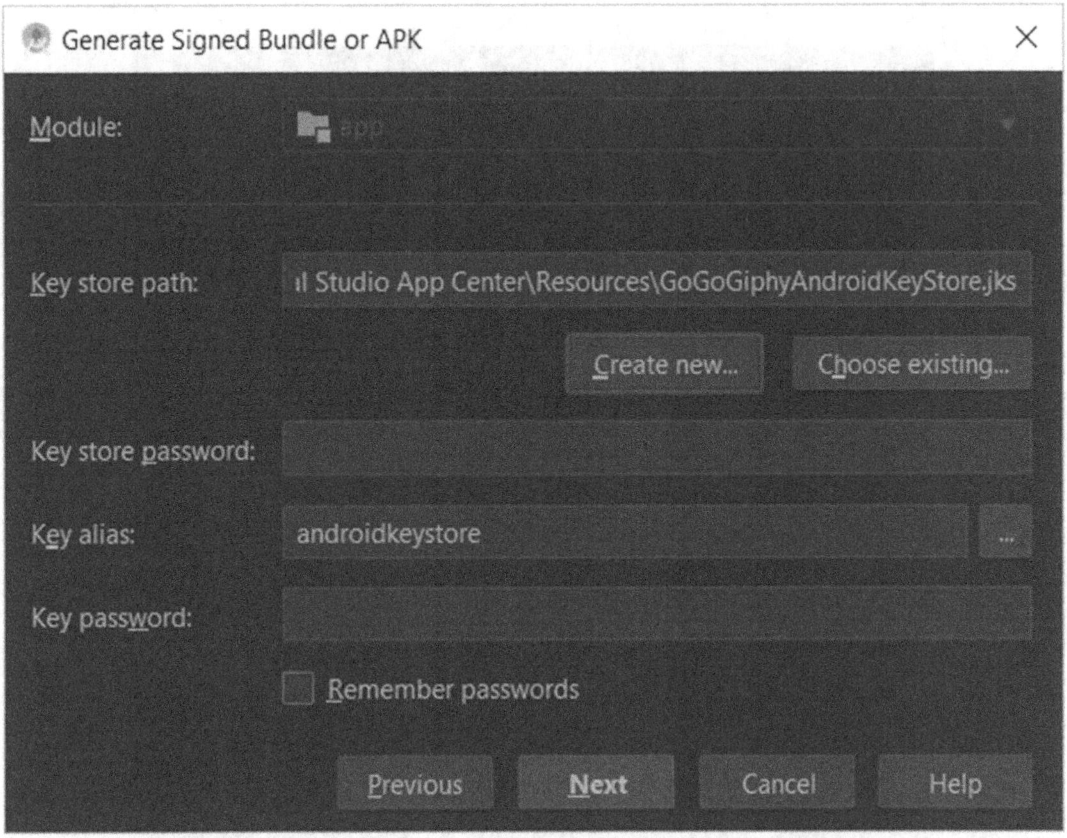

Figure 3-39. *Creating new or using existing keystore file*

You will see a new dialog asking you for details about the keystore file. Choose where the file will be saved in the keystore path. Enter a password and confirm the password for the keystore file. App Center will ask you for this password to unlock the keystore and retrieve your debug certificate to sign your APK file for distribution. In the same dialog, Android Studio gives you the ability to create the first key. Enter a name for the alias and the password of the key stored in the keystore. An alias is a name for your key. App Center will ask you for this key password too when you configure your Android build.

It's best to make the password of the key different than the password of the keystore. (For the purpose of this chapter, I kept the password the same for simplicity.) Finally, enter your first name, last name, organizational unit, and organization, as shown in Figure 3-40. Click Ok.

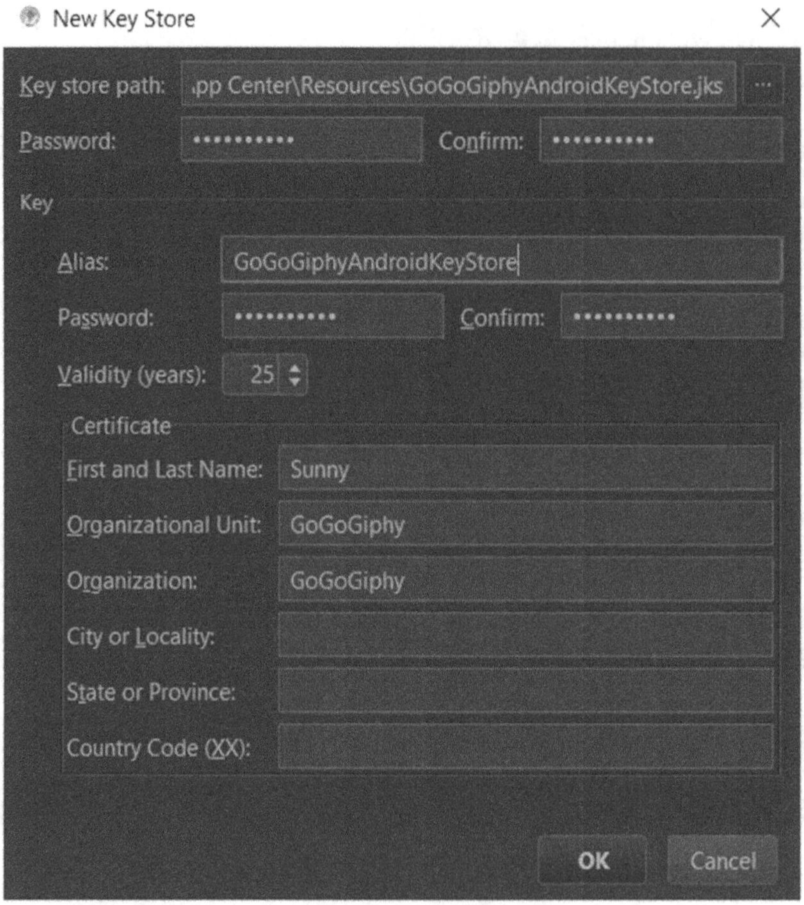

Figure 3-40. *Creating new keystore file and new key*

Fill out the keystore password and confirm the password again. Click Next (Figure 3-41).

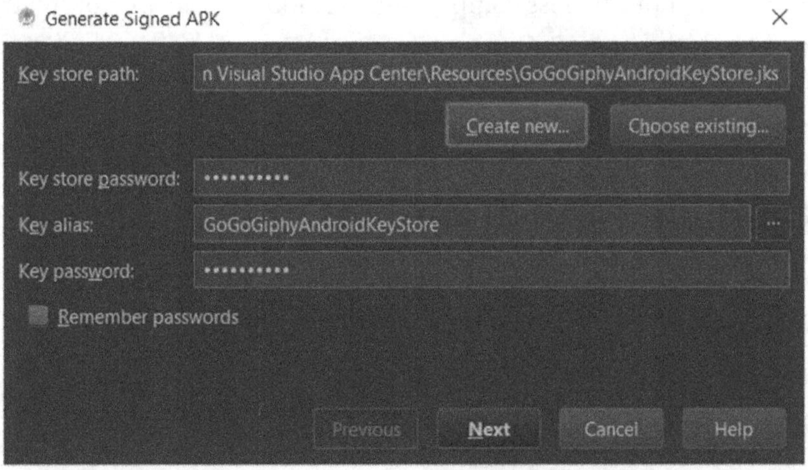

Figure 3-41. *Confirming keystore password, key alias, and key password*

Choose a destination folder where it will be saved. Make sure the build type is Debug since it is a Debug build. And choose V2 as the APK signature. Click Finish. You should see a pop-up message and an event log entry in Android Studio showing that it has finished generating the signed APK at the specified location. Make sure you navigate to the folder you specified and see if the keystore file was created there (Figure 3-42).

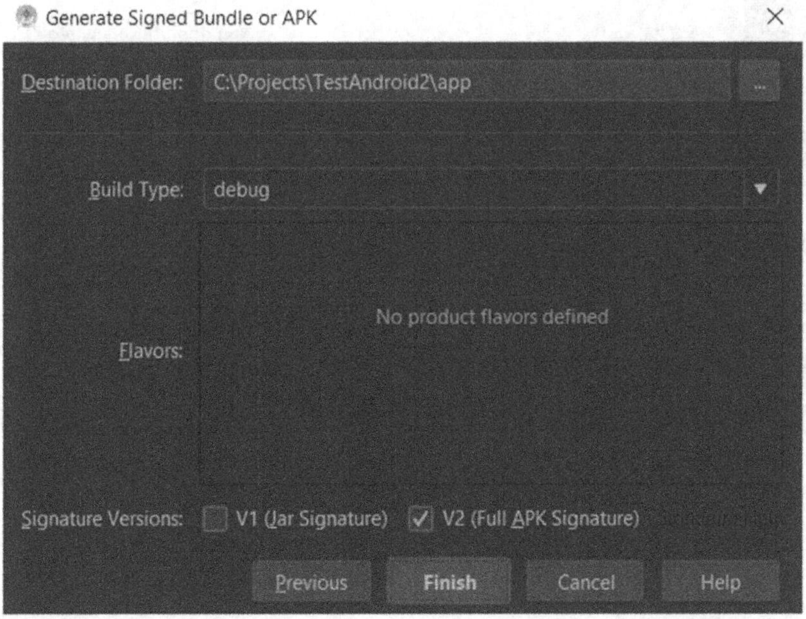

Figure 3-42. *Saving a keystore file*

That's it! Was that not a lot less complicated in Android? You are now ready with your iOS developer provisioning profile and your Android Keystore when you sign your App Center builds later.

Registering Devices in App Center

Now you must go through the device registration steps in App Center. This is necessary for App Center to authorize your devices. I will show you how I registered both my developer and tester iOS devices in App Center.

Go to Account Settings and then My Devices, as highlighted in Figure 3-43. Your page will be empty because you have no registered devices.

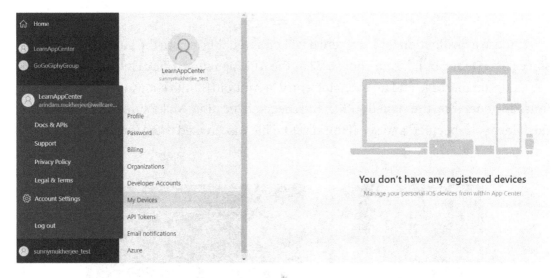

Figure 3-43. *Account Settings* ➤ *My Devices*

You need to register the devices individually on each device. Remember you will log in to App Center using the different accounts for the Developer and the Tester. Navigate to the following URL on each device: `https://install.appcenter.ms/`.

You will see the webpage shown in Figure 3-44 on each device. Sign into your App Center account using either the Developer or Tester account. Remember you added these accounts as collaborators in the previous chapter. App Center will associate these accounts with their new devices.

Figure 3-44. *Signing into App Center*

Once signed in, you will see your My apps page, as shown in Figure 3-45. No apps are shown because you have not distributed any apps yet to either the developer or the tester. Click the Profile icon highlighted at the top right of the image.

Figure 3-45. *Signed into App Center*

You are now on the device registration page. Click the + Add New Device button (Figure 3-46). The webpage will now ask for your permission to install a new configuration profile in your settings. Click Allow (Figure 3-47).

Figure 3-46. *My devices*

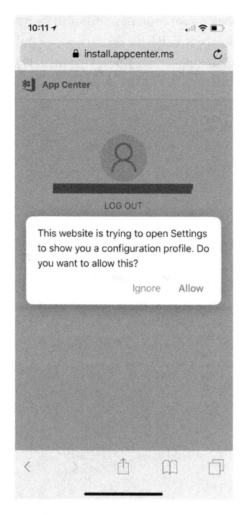

Figure 3-47. *Adding a new device*

Install the profile on your device, as shown in Figures 3-48 and 3-49.

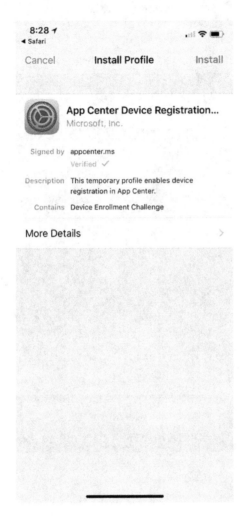

Figure 3-48. *App Center profile*

Figure 3-49. *Installing a profile*

Navigate back to the same URL on your iOS device for App Center given before. You will see your registered device, as shown in Figure 3-50.

Figure 3-50. *New device*

Now return to App Center, sign in with your admin account, and navigate to the My Devices page again. You will see all the registered devices associated with all the collaborator emails, as shown in Figure 3-51.

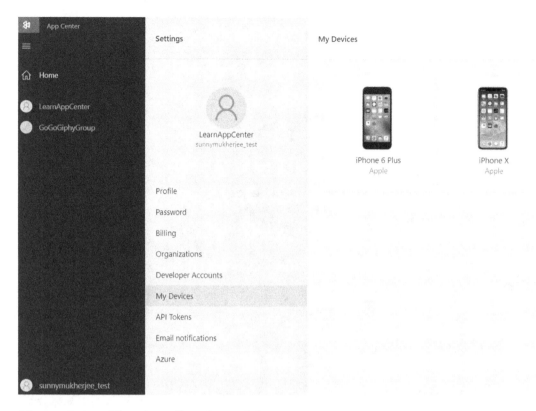

Figure 3-51. *Showing all registered devices*

Configuring iOS Build for Distribution

In this section, you finally arrive at the whole point of this chapter. You are now going to configure the build that you created in the prior chapter to get it ready for distribution. This section is one of the pillars of mobile DevOps. You are automating the Continuous Delivery part of the DevOps cycle. Keep in mind this is only limited distribution to internal developers and testers only and not public store distribution.

Click the Builds link on the left pane. Open the master branch. Click the configure icon at the top right of the page. You will see the Build configuration panel again, as shown in Figure 3-52. First, change the build type from Simulator build to Device build.

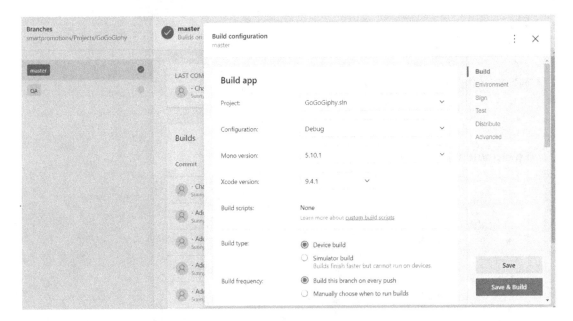

Figure 3-52. *Selecting Device build for iOS Build*

Scroll down the panel. Copy the development provisioning profile and the developer certificate from your Mac desktop that you created in the prior section. Enter the password that you entered when creating the P12 file. Also, change the build number format to Build ID so it auto-increments upon building. Please see Figure 3-53 and the highlighted provisioning profile and certificate files.

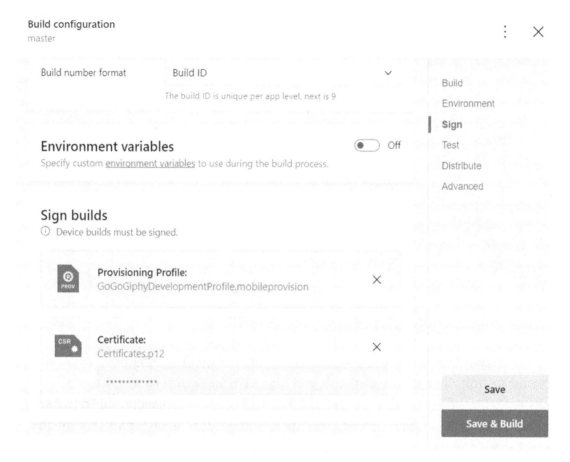

Figure 3-53. *Uploading a provisioning profile and signing certificate*

Scroll down the panel. Select the new distribution group that you created in the previous section called Developers. Remember this build will be sending an iOS distribution only to your developers (Figure 3-54).

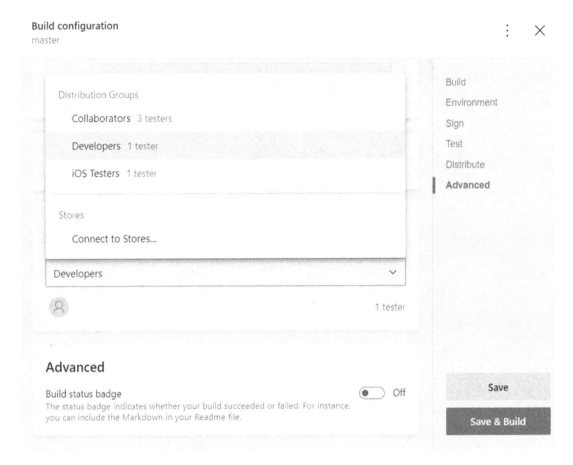

Figure 3-54. *Selecting the Developers group from the distribution groups*

Verify all of the new settings above. Click the Save & Build button. Once the build completes, you should see an email invitation like Figure 3-55. Click the Install button and you will navigate to a webpage like in Figure 3-56 where you can install the app. Your app will now download and install to your desktop on your phone.

Figure 3-55. *App Center email*

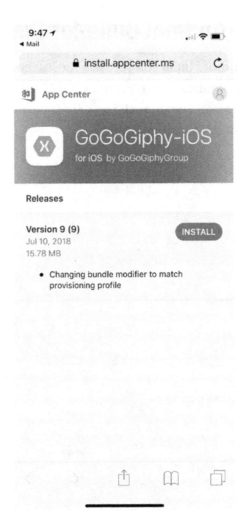

Figure 3-56. *Installing the app*

Configuring the Android Build for Distribution

Now let's return to your Android build you set up in the last chapter and configure it for distribution. Mimic the settings shown in Figure 3-57. You will distribute a Debug version of the build, set it to build the branch on every code push, and increment the build number using the Build ID.

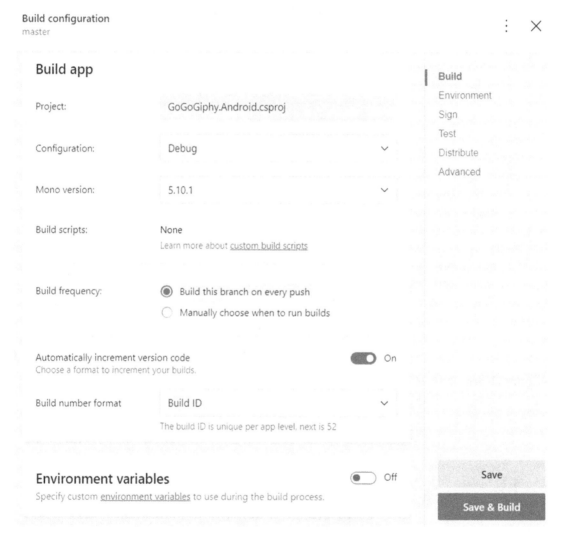

Figure 3-57. *Configuring the Android build for distribution*

Scroll down the build configuration. Refer to Figure 3-58. Upload the keystore file you created in the prior section. Type the keystore password, key alias, and key password that you configured when you set up your keystore. Set the distribution group to your Developers group.

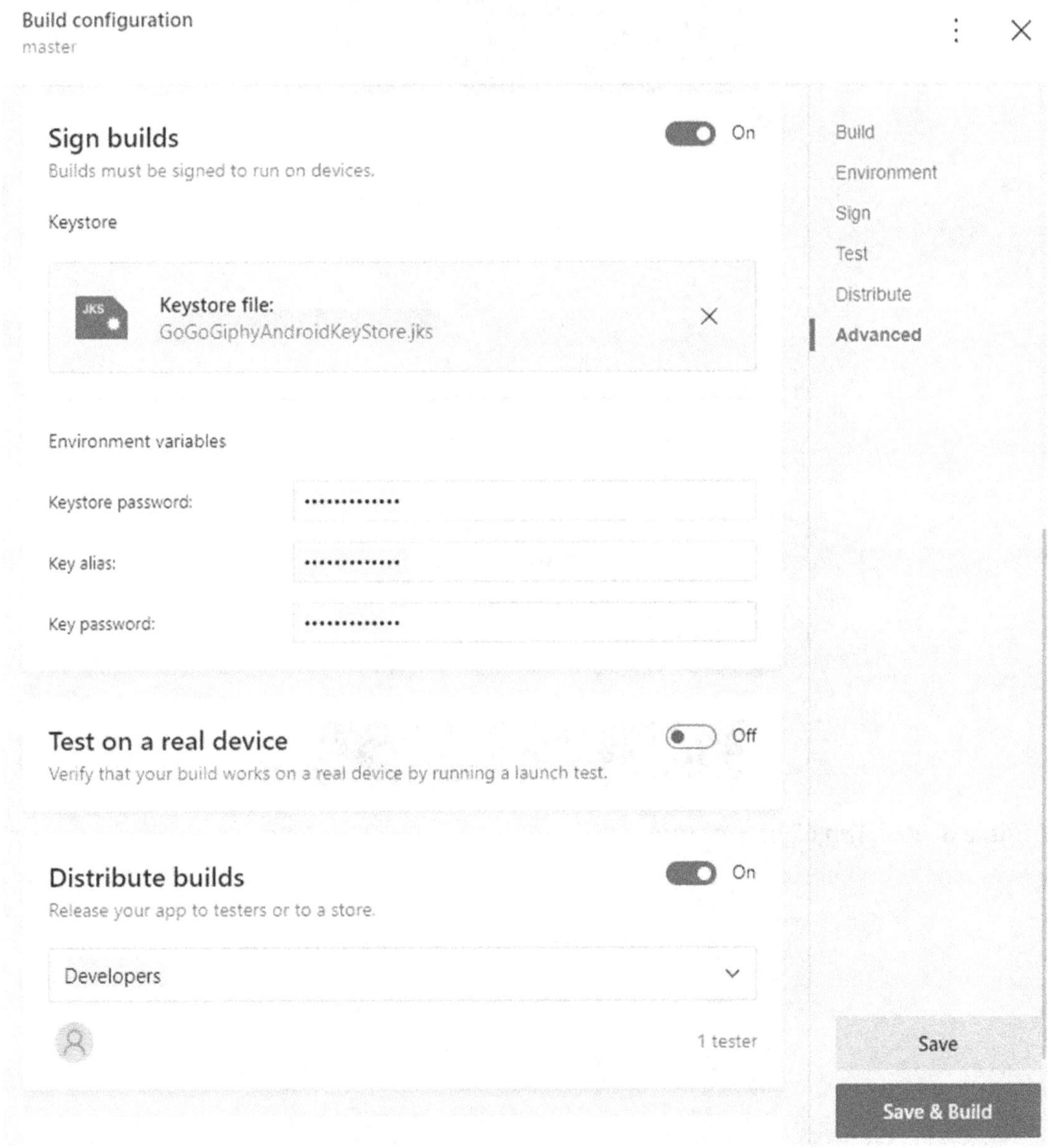

Figure 3-58. *Uploading the keystore file and entering passwords*

Click the Save & Build button in Figure 3-58. Once the build has finished, if everything was configured correctly, the service will send an invitation to the members in your Developers group. Figure 3-59 shows a sample email. Click the Install button to begin the download (Figure 3-60).

Figure 3-59. *App Center email*

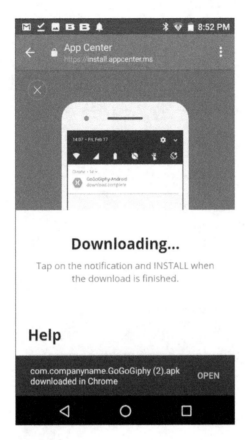

Figure 3-60. *Installing the app*

In your Android device, before installation, your device will prompt you to trust unknown sources before it starts installing. Go to Settings ➤ Security. Check Unknown sources to allow App Center to install the app for you. Refer to Figures 3-61 and 3-62.

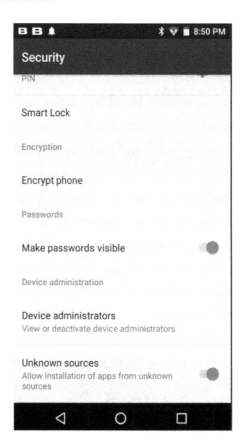

Figure 3-61. *Enabling unknown sources*

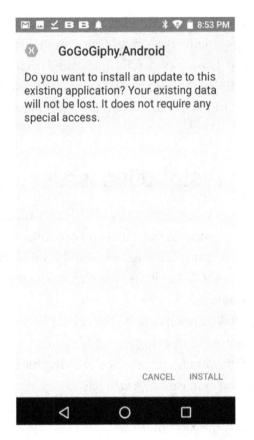

Figure 3-62. *Installing the app*

Note   Before committing your code, verify that Use Shared Runtime is disabled in
Android Options. Right-click the Android project, select Android Options, and verify
the setting under Packaging properties. If you hover over the setting, Visual Studio
will give you a useful tip about its purpose. Even though the setting decreases
your app package size so it is faster to deploy, the setting was never designed
to be used when deploying to physical devices. Your app will launch but will not
show any content. You can verify it yourself by checking the setting and deploying
to a physical device yourself. That is why the setting is disabled by default in the
Release configuration.

Congratulations! Give yourself a pat on the pack because you completed the significant step of continuous delivery as part of your mobile DevOps journey. If everything goes well, you will now have a fully automated cycle of distributing apps to your phone. If everything did not go well, consult the next section, "Troubleshooting Distribution Issues," where I show you a few common troubleshooting steps to help you figure out your issues.

Troubleshooting Distribution Issues

I include this section because in my effort to troubleshoot various iOS distribution issues, I came up with some common steps that you can follow to help you in your quest to troubleshoot similar distribution issues. You will undoubtedly find Android distribution much easier than iOS distribution, which is why this section is devoted to iOS distribution troubleshooting.

If you open the drop-down options on the Download button, you will notice the three options shown in Figure 3-63. Saving the build locally and inspecting the data within it gives you a lot of insight into the application identifier, device IDs, etc. that App Center collects and uses. You can use these artifacts to inspect and investigate between App Center and the Apple Developer Portal in case you included the wrong App ID or the wrong device ID. I will show you how now.

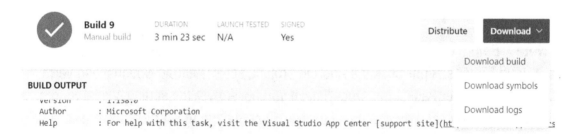

Figure 3-63. *Downloading the build artifacts*

Save the build to a local folder. Right-click the build folder that was downloaded and extract to the same folder. You will see the IPA file that is distributed to your iOS device. This IPA file is more than simply the application that gets installed on your iOS device. It is an archive file that includes all the binaries that get installed to your iOS device. You can extract this file using a common archive application like WinZip, WinRAR, or 7-Zip. Upon extracting the contents, you will see a Payload folder, as shown in Figure 3-64.

Name	Type	Size
Payload	File folder	
GoGoGiphy.iOS.ipa	iOS App	16,155 KB

Figure 3-64. *Inspecting the extracted build artifacts*

Open the Payload folder, browse through the contents, and locate the file called embedded.mobileprovision. This file contains several pieces of important information that become useful when debugging and troubleshooting issues (Figure 3-65).

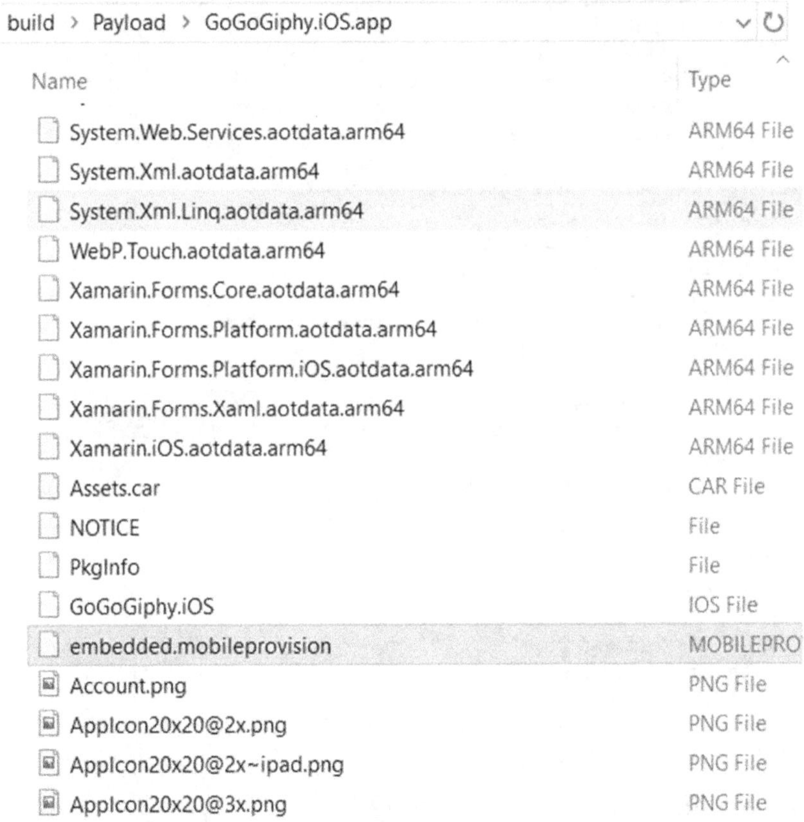

build > Payload > GoGoGiphy.iOS.app

Name	Type
System.Web.Services.aotdata.arm64	ARM64 File
System.Xml.aotdata.arm64	ARM64 File
System.Xml.Linq.aotdata.arm64	ARM64 File
WebP.Touch.aotdata.arm64	ARM64 File
Xamarin.Forms.Core.aotdata.arm64	ARM64 File
Xamarin.Forms.Platform.aotdata.arm64	ARM64 File
Xamarin.Forms.Platform.iOS.aotdata.arm64	ARM64 File
Xamarin.Forms.Xaml.aotdata.arm64	ARM64 File
Xamarin.iOS.aotdata.arm64	ARM64 File
Assets.car	CAR File
NOTICE	File
PkgInfo	File
GoGoGiphy.iOS	IOS File
embedded.mobileprovision	MOBILEPRO
Account.png	PNG File
AppIcon20x20@2x.png	PNG File
AppIcon20x20@2x~ipad.png	PNG File
AppIcon20x20@3x.png	PNG File

Figure 3-65. *Opening the mobileprovision file*

153

Apple intended users to open this file on a Mac device. However, you can open this file on Windows using a special text editor application like NotePad++ or TextPad. Although some parts of this file will be unreadable, you can still identify the important pieces, shown in Figure 3-66.

```
embedded.mobileprovision  ×
        <key>Entitlements</key>
        <dict>
                <key>keychain-access-groups</key>
                <array>
                        <string>J333CKB8Y9.*</string>
                </array>
                <key>get-task-allow</key>
                <true/>
                <key>application-identifier</key>
                <string>J333CKB8Y9.com.sunny.gogogiphy</string>
                <key>com.apple.developer.team-identifier</key>
                <string>J333CKB8Y9</string>
                <key>aps-environment</key>
                <string>development</string>
        </dict>
        <key>ExpirationDate</key>
        <date>2019-07-10T01:49:30Z</date>
        <key>Name</key>
        <string>GoGoGiphyDevelopmentProfile</string>
        <key>ProvisionedDevices</key>
        <array>
                <string>413ea956908739a16b7c04fb          </string>
                <string>b51661ef958f687c9e52e06b          /string>
        </array>
        <key>TeamIdentifier</key>
        <array>
                <string>J333CKB8Y9</string>
        </array>
        <key>TeamName</key>
        <string>Arindam Mukherjee</string>
        <key>TimeToLive</key>
        <integer>365</integer>
        <key>UUID</key>
        <string>afb8e829-8967-4d7b-aec1-a1e6d9138e0b</string>
        <key>Version</key>
```

Figure 3-66. *Reading the mobileprovision file*

The App ID and the name of the provisioning profile are highlighted. Typical causes of distribution problems are usually the following:

- Mismatch of application identifier in your entitlements and your provisioning profile

- Incorrect device identifiers registered in the Apple Developer Portal

Setting Up the QA Branch for Build Scripts

In Chapter 2, you set up multiple branches in your Azure DevOps repository. You finally arrive at the reason for your change from the last chapter. In this section, you are going to set up the QA branch for building and distribution based on the concepts you learned in Chapters 2 and 3. The whole point of setting up an entirely new branch is for the purpose of using build scripts later in this chapter. If you remember, I mentioned in the last chapter that it is not good practice to include key values and secret values directly in the source code. You will avoid this scenario with the QA branch.

For the purpose of this chapter, I will explain configuring the Android QA branch. If you are interested in repeating the same steps for iOS, follow the steps I explained earlier in this chapter for App IDs, signing requests, developer certificates, and provisioning profiles.

Let's set up the QA branch now.

- Go to the GoGoGiphy-Android app in App Center.

- Click Build.

- Locate the QA branch and click the gear icon on the far right of the page.

- Configure the new build as follows. If you forgot the steps, please revisit Chapter 2 where I show you how to set up a new build and the earlier sections in this chapter where I walk you through each topic, such as distribution.

  - Select Debug for the configuration.

  - Select the appropriate Android SDK version (Figure 3-67).

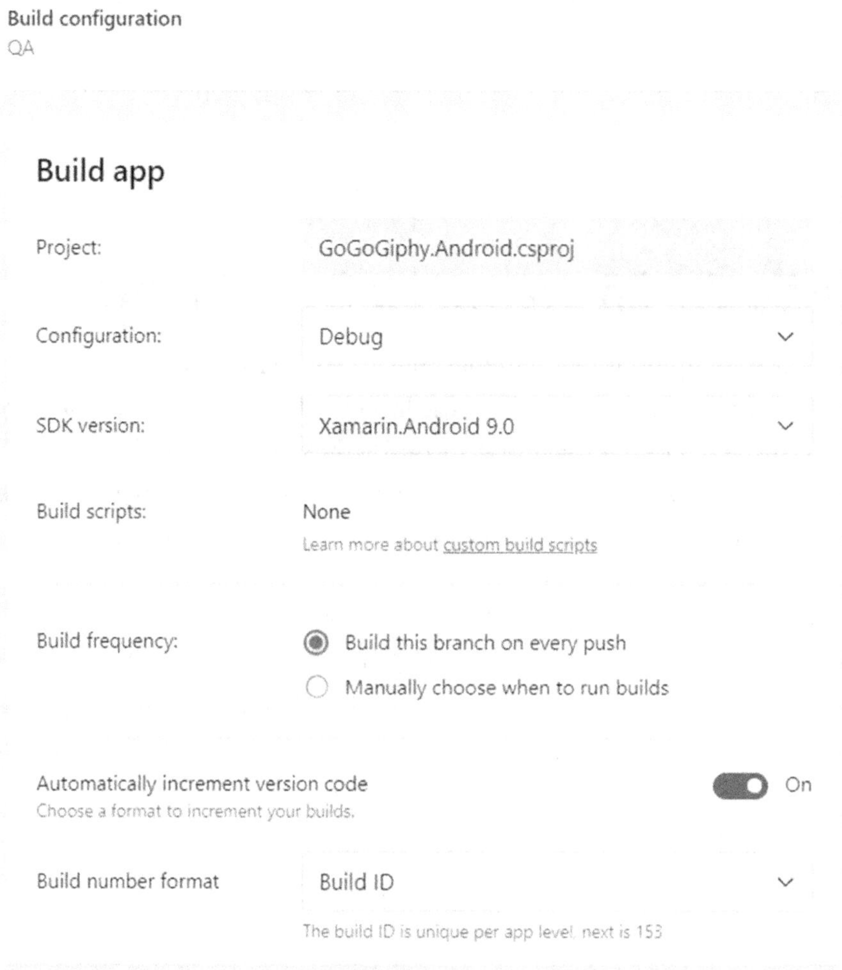

Build configuration
QA

Build app

Project: GoGoGiphy.Android.csproj

Configuration: Debug   ⌄

SDK version: Xamarin.Android 9.0   ⌄

Build scripts: None
                            Learn more about custom build scripts

Build frequency: ⦿ Build this branch on every push
                            ◯ Manually choose when to run builds

Automatically increment version code   🔘 On
Choose a format to increment your builds.

Build number format   Build ID   ⌄
                           The build ID is unique per app level. next is 153

Figure 3-67. *Setting the Android build configuration settings*

- Set the environment variables as shown in Figure 3-68. You can ignore the AppCenterToken variable for now because I have that set from a later chapter.

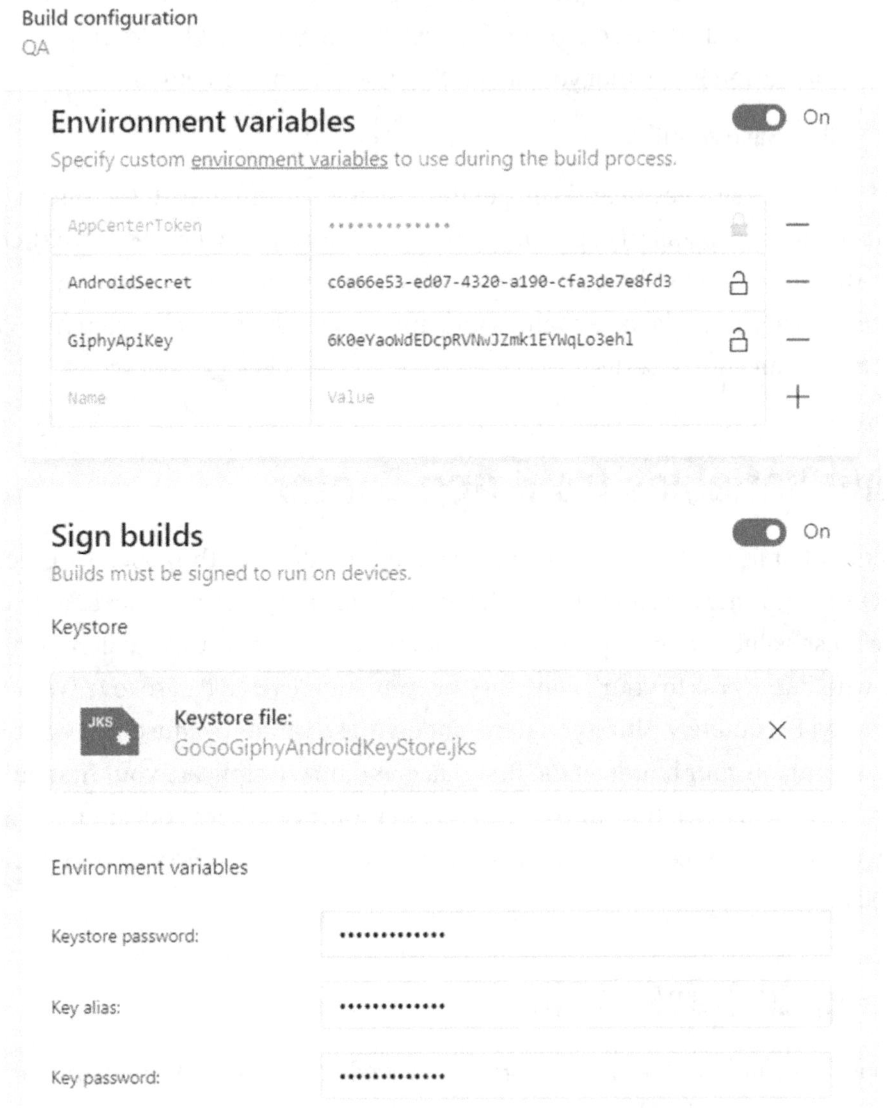

Build configuration
QA

Environment variables   ⬤ On

Specify custom environment variables to use during the build process.

AppCenterToken	••••••••••••••	🔒	—
AndroidSecret	c6a66e53-ed07-4320-a190-cfa3de7e8fd3	🔓	—
GiphyApiKey	6K0eYaoWdEDcpRVNwJZmk1EYWqLo3ehl	🔓	—
Name	Value		+

Sign builds   ⬤ On

Builds must be signed to run on devices.

Keystore

JKS   **Keystore file:**   ✕
      GoGoGiphyAndroidKeyStore.jks

Environment variables

Keystore password: ••••••••••••••

Key alias: ••••••••••••••

Key password: ••••••••••••••

Figure 3-68. *Setting the environment variables and sign builds*

- Reupload the Android Keystore file, reenter the keystore password, reenter the key alias, and reenter the key password, as shown in Figure 3-68.

- Set Distribute builds to On.

- Set your distribution group to Developers. Ideally, you want to have a separate distribution group for Testers. But you set it to Developers now so you know that you are getting the distribution email.

- Click Save & Build.

If your build is successful and you get the distribution email with the Install button from which you can install the app locally on your Android device, you have successfully set up your QA branch for the upcoming sections where I will show you how to use post-clone build scripts to replace key values and app secrets dynamically from App Center and not from your source code.

Setting Variables from App Center

If you remember from Chapter 1, you hard-coded the values for the `AppCenterSecretiOS`, `AppCenterSecretAndroid`, and the `ApiKey` variables. This practice is never a good one because these values are now part of your source control repository, which means anyone who has access to your Git history or your source code can recover your secret values easily! Fortunately, since you hard-coded these values because you wanted to practice setting up your builds in the first place and not complicate your first build setup, you have reached a point now in your App Center journey where you can replace these variable values dynamically during the build process in App Center itself. How do you accomplish this?

Ignoring Git Tracked Files

The first action you must take is to ignore the tracked Settings.cs file where the variables are stored. Why? In the ideal world, even in your Development branch, you want to save the values into the local `Settings.cs` file in order to run the app in your local simulator but avoid committing and pushing your changes to your remote Git repository and have App Center dynamically replace the values in the Settings.cs just before the build. Since I did not want to complicate the build steps from the earlier chapters so you could understand the basic concepts faster, I saved this section until now. Remember that you have already forked your Git repository or cloned my Git repository into your Azure DevOps account. In either case, since it uses the Git implementation, all the files are tracked already in your local repository. I will now show you how to untrack the tracked Settings.cs file.

- Open Windows Explorer.

- Navigate to the root of your folder where your solution file or your .gitignore file is located.

- Open a command prompt. Type cd or change directory into the root of your project path.

  - Tip: Select the breadcrumb where the network path is shown. Delete the highlighted path and type cmd.

- In the terminal window, type the following command. This command updates the staging index to ignore changes to the Settings.cs at the following path:

  git update-index --assume-unchanged GoGoGiphy/GoGoGiphy/Settings.cs

- Make any changes to the Settings.cs file.

- Return to your command prompt. Type git status. Verify the Settings.cs does not show up as "modified."

You are now untracking the Settings.cs file so you can use the secret values and API values locally to run the app on your simulator. If you are interested in tracking your file again, you can type the following command:

git update-index --no-assume-unchanged GoGoGiphy/GoGoGiphy/Settings.cs

You can type git status again to verify that the file is being tracked once more.

Working with App Center Variables

Before diving into build scripts, you must first learn about App Center variables. I will repeat this section again in the final chapter for the UI tests.

The App Center team has created several important variables that you can utilize in your Bash or PowerShell script files. These variables expose key locations on the server for your scripts to reside. The most relevant App Center variables are the following:

`APPCENTER_SOURCE_DIRECTORY:`	Location of the source code on the build machine
`APPCENTER_OUTPUT_DIRECTORY:`	Location where the build results are stored
`BUILD_REPOSITORY_LOCALPATH:`	Location where the repository is cloned

App Center provides more system variables; read about them at `https://docs.microsoft.com/en-us/appcenter/build/custom/scripts/`.

The final point to keep in mind is that any build script can reference these App Center variables when it is run on the App Center servers. They are referenced in the Bash code with the $ character. I will show you examples as you construct the post-clone script.

Setting Up Post-Build Scripts

Now you'll learn about the different types of build scripts before writing your first script. Build scripts are scripts that run on the App Center cloud servers at different stages of the build process. App Center provides three different build scripts. You will revisit build scripts again in the final chapter of the book when you set up your UI tests. The following are the definitions of the different scripts at different points of the build process:

- **Post-Clone**: The script that runs after the code repository is cloned but before the build runs

- **Pre-Build**: The script that runs before the build starts but after dependencies like NuGet packages are installed

- **Post-Build**: The script that runs after the build finishes and the artifacts are copied to the output folder

You can find more information about build scripts at `https://docs.microsoft.com/en-us/appcenter/build/custom/scripts/`. Microsoft also maintains a public GitHub repository offering helpful examples of build scripts at `https://github.com/Microsoft/appcenter-build-scripts-examples`. But I will show you how to set up your first build script.

Setting Up Your Post-Clone Build Script

I will show you how to replace any string value in any file in your repository theoretically. For the purpose of replacing these variable values, you will use the post-clone build script that will run immediately after the Git repository is cloned on the App Center server and will replace the three variable values in the `Settings.cs` file so you do not have to hard-code those values.

These build scripts are written in the Bash programming language. Do not worry if you have never programmed in Bash before because neither had I when I first started learning App Center. I will walk you through the process of writing the Bash commands.

You created your QA branch earlier in this chapter purely for the purpose of simulating a real-life scenario of commit development changes into your master branch, merging your changes into the QA branch with pull requests, and not committing any key values or secrets into the source code history in the QA branch. Your Git commit log already contains key values and app secrets from your master branch. In a real-life scenario, you would ideally commit development values for your keys and secrets into your master branch, which is your development branch, and commit production values for your keys and secrets into your QA or Staging branches. Your QA branch is the branch that will make use of the post-clone scripts to replace keys and secrets from values stored in App Center and not store these key values and secret values within the source code itself. Those keys and secrets are stored securely within App Center.

Two final concepts to keep in mind are the actual filename of the post-clone script and the location of the script within the source code repository. First, the filename must be `appcenter-post-clone.sh` because App Center will identify this file as a post-clone script based on the filename and the file extension. Second, the file location is crucial because you will need to create two separate post-clone scripts, one for the iOS project and the second for the Android project.

Note   Verify that the filename is exactly `appcenter-post-clone.sh`. Otherwise, the App Center build will not detect the file.

Let's begin your setup.

- Open Visual Studio.

- Switch to the QA branch from within Visual Studio. By this point, you should still be in your master branch since you have never checked out a different branch. I will repeat the steps from Chapter 2 in case you forgot how to switch branches.

  - Open Team Explorer. If it is not already open, you can find it from View ➤ Team Explorer.

  - Select Branches. The master branch should be checked out locally to you.

  - Expand remotes/origin to explore the remote branches on your Azure DevOps repository. You should see the QA branch that you created earlier.

  - Double-click the branch to check out the branch locally on your machine. Your Team Explorer should appear like Figure 3-70. You can peruse the source code and see that the files are identical to the master branch when you first created your repository.

- Open the GoGoGiphy solution file.

- Locate the two post-clone build script files. I included the files for you but with a file extension of .rename because I did not want either your iOS or Android builds to detect this script when you set up your build from Chapter 1. It would have run this build script if the file extension was .sh.

  - appcenter-post-clone.rename is located in the Solution Items folder at the root of the solution. This file is located on the root of the solution because it is the post-clone script needed for the iOS build.

  - appcenter-post-clone.rename is the other file located in the GoGoGiphy.Android project. This second file is the post-clone script for the Android build.

- Rename both file extensions from .rename to .sh.

- Open either the iOS or the Android post-build script in Visual Studio. Your script will look like the following. I am showing the iOS post-clone build script because the Android script is nearly identical. I will walk you through the individual commands. The relevant commands that will set the variable values have been **highlighted**.

```
#!/usr/bin/env bash

echo "***********************************************************"
echo "Post Clone Script"
echo "***********************************************************"

echo "Post Clone Script"
echo "Updating AppCenterSecretiOS in Settings"

echo "AppCenterToken value: $AppCenterToken"
echo "iOSSecret value: $iOSSecret"

#echo "BUILD_REPOSITORY_LOCALPATH Contents"
#ls -R $BUILD_REPOSITORY_LOCALPATH
```

 # Updating AppCenterSecretiOS

SettingsFile=$BUILD_REPOSITORY_LOCALPATH/GoGoGiphy/GoGoGiphy/Settings.cs

sed -e " "s,iOSSecret,$iOSSecret,g" $SettingsFile
sed -e " "s,GiphyApiKey,$GiphyApiKey,g" $SettingsFile

 # Print out file for reference
cat $SettingsFile

```
echo "Updated AppCenterSecretiOS!"
```

- Here are explanations for the common commands and keywords in Bash:

  - # is used to comment out commands.

  - echo is used to write commands as output to the screen or a log file. Every echo command that you see in the script file will be written to the App Center output and the Post Clone Script. txt file. I will show you later how to view this file on your local machine.

- I include the following command for testing purposes. You can uncomment this code by removing the # character for the `ls` command. If you have trouble locating the `Settings.cs` file in the `BUILD_REPOSITORY_LOCALPATH`, uncomment the `ls` command to list out all the files and subfolders recursively as indicated by the `-R` flag. I will show you later how to save this script and include it in your iOS build.

```
#echo "BUILD_REPOSITORY_LOCALPATH Contents"
#ls -R $BUILD_REPOSITORY_LOCALPATH
```

- Let me explain the first relevant command.

  - The first line is a comment.

    ```
    # Updating AppCenterSecretiOS
    ```

  - The second line references an App Center variable called `BUILD_REPOSITORY_LOCALPATH`. These variables are available only when the script runs on App Center itself. You will explore App Center variables in greater detail in the final chapter when you learn about UI testing. This command saves the entire content of the Settings.cs file into a variable called `SettingsFile`.

    ```
    SettingsFile=$BUILD_REPOSITORY_LOCALPATH/GoGoGiphy/
    GoGoGiphy/Settings.cs
    ```

- The third and fourth commands are the same command. The `sed` command is also known as a Stream Editor or a non-interactive line editor from the Linux world. It receives text input, either from stdin or from a file, performs a certain set of operations on each line in the file, and outputs the result to stdout or to another file. This command is used for pattern-matching on strings.

- Now I will explain each of the flags in the command.

  - The `-e` argument indicates the next string as an editing instruction.

  - The `s` is the substitute flag indicating the command will replace one string with another string.

- The iOSSecret is the first string to replace. This is the initial value of the AppCenterSecretiOS variable.

- $iOSSecret is the referenced App Center variable from which you will retrieve the string value that you will replace.

- The g flag indicates that it performs this substitution globally throughout the file.

- $SettingsFile stores the entire contents of the SettingsFile, so the sed command performs the string substitution globally through the entire file content.

  You can find more information about the sed command from www.gnu.org/software/sed/manual/sed.html.

  ```
  sed -e " "s,iOSSecret,$iOSSecret,g" $SettingsFile
  sed -e " "s,GiphyApiKey,$GiphyApiKey,g" $SettingsFile
  ```

- The cat command prints out the new SettingsFile to the App Center output during the build process, so you can see if the post-clone script ran the sed command successfully.

  ```
  # Print out file for reference
  cat $SettingsFile
  ```

- Save the file. Commit the changes in your repository.

- Return to App Center and the iOS build. Verify that you see the following highlighted icon in the Build scripts section. App Center should now see the post-clone script because you renamed the file type to .sh (Figure 3-69).

Figure 3-69. *Saving the post-clone build script into the iOS Build*

- Save the build once so the build will include the post-clone script as part of the build process.

- Finally, you need to enter your App Center variables and their values that you use in the script for string substitution.

    - Go to environment variables and enable it to On.

    - Enter the GiphyApiKey variable and paste the value from your Giphy account. Refer back to Chapter 1 to access your Giphy account.

    - Enter the iOSSecret variable and paste the value from the App Center Secret value for iOS. Refer back to Chapter 2 to remember how to get this value. Your environment variables should look similar to Figure 3-70. (I have obfuscated my key and secret values.)

Figure 3-70. *Saving the environment variables*

- Click Save & Build on the build definition

- After the build completes and sends you the email notification, install
  the app on your physical device and verify that you can access the
  gifs. If you can see the gifs, you know the post-clone build script is
  substituting the key and secret values correctly in order to access the
  Giphy API, so congratulations!

- If you want to verify truly that the post-clone script is working as expected,
  now I will show you how to verify within the log file itself. Return to App
  Center and the iOS build, go to the Build section, click the last successful
  build where you used the post-build script, open the Download combo-
  box, and click Download Logs, as shown in Figure 3-71.

Figure 3-71. *Downloading the build logs*

- Download the zip file to a local folder. Extract the contents.

- Open the Job subfolder within the extracted contents. Locate the
  `Post-Clone Script.txt` file.

- Open the text file. Inspect the contents of the `Settings.cs` file that is written by the `cat` command in the post-clone script. Finally, verify whether the string substation worked correctly or not.

Whew! I know that was a lot of steps. I included all of the steps that you need in order to get dynamic variable replacement working on App Center and avoid hard-coding these variable values directly in your source code. I will leave it up to you to repeat the above steps for the Android build. Do not worry because the steps are nearly identical. You just need to edit the post-clone build script in the GoGoGiphy.Android project.

Summary

Congratulations on reaching the end of this chapter! This chapter had a lot of material about automating the entire distribution part of the cycle. I hope you learned a lot, both from the material in this chapter and from the mistakes you made along the way. The mistakes you make are your best teachers.

I'll summarize what you learned in this chapter:

- How to create your iOS App ID

- How to register your Apple device

- How to create a certificate signing request

- How to create a developer certificate

- How to create an iOS provisioning profile

- How to register devices in App Center

- How to create distribution groups

- How to configure builds for developer distribution

- How to set up the QA branch for build scripts

- How to set variables from App Center

- How to set up your post-clone build script

In the coming chapters, now that you can use and test the sample app on a physical device, you will dive into crash reporting and analytics as you use the app on a real device.

CHAPTER 4

Reporting Analytics and Crashes

Welcome back! In Chapter 2, you learned how to set up continuous builds. In Chapter 3, you learned how to set up continuous deployment to development and test devices. You now have the fundamentals of a proper continuous integration/continuous deployment pipeline for your Xamarin Forms app.

You can now get started on integrating crash reports and analytics into your sample app. You will go through this app and make several code changes in different areas. You will build your code locally, commit and push the changes back up to the remote master branch, and test your changes on your physical devices.

Here is what you will learn in this chapter:

- How to add the App Center SDK for analytics and crashes

- How to simulate a test crash

- How to handle several App Center crash events

- How to add your own custom events

- How to set up continuous export of analytics and crashes to Azure

Covering the Basics

Before you dive into the details, let's cover the basics first. What is crash reporting? Visual Studio App Center provides the ability for your app to report crash events automatically back up to App Center where they can be stored and analyzed. These crash events happen unexpectedly and are not handled gracefully in your code.

© Sunny Mukherjee 2019
S. Mukherjee, *Learn Microsoft Visual Studio App Center*, https://doi.org/10.1007/978-1-4842-4382-4_4

You might be thinking, unhandled exceptions? They do not happen to me. Well, App Center is here to capture those awkward moments so you can give a friendlier experience to your user so they know that you do care about their experience.

What are custom events? Custom events are a way for a developer to program in specific events that can be reported back up to App Center for analytical purposes. For example, you can use custom events to analyze how your user is using the app, what pages in the app they are using the most, what pages they are using the least, and what they are searching for. You will go through the process of setting up all of these features in the sample app.

Adding the App Center SDK for Crashes and Analytics

Let's begin first by adding the App Center SDK for crashes and analytics.

1. Open the Xamarin Forms solution. Right-click the solution and click the Manage NuGet Packages for Solution option.

2. Open Visual Studio and the GoGoGiphy solution file. Search for Microsoft.AppCenter.Crashes and check the projects on the right pane, as in Figure 4-1. Visual Studio will install the NuGet packages in the selected projects.

Figure 4-1. *Microsoft.AppCenter.Crashes NuGet Package*

3. Repeat the above steps to install the Microsoft.AppCenter. Analytics package in the same projects, as shown in Figure 4-2.

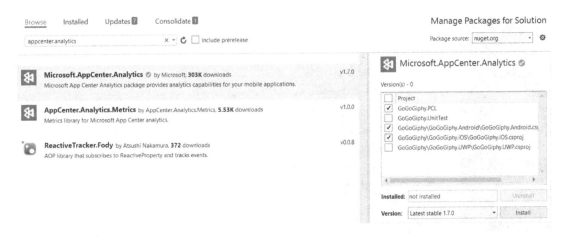

Figure 4-2. *Microsoft.AppCenter.Analytics NuGet package*

4. If you are not a fan of using the UI, you can use the following PowerShell commands in the Package Manager Console. You can find this console in View ➤ Other Windows ➤ Package Manager Console.

```
Install-Package Microsoft.AppCenter.Crashes
Install-Package Microsoft.AppCenter.Analytics
```

5. Now you will reference the packages you just added so you can use the packages from your code. Add the following using statements to App.xaml.cs and HomeViewModel in the shared project:

```
using Microsoft.AppCenter;
using Microsoft.AppCenter.Analytics;
using Microsoft.AppCenter.Crashes;
```

Next, App Center must be able to identify your app from the thousands of other apps out there. How does it accomplish this? App Center assigns a unique Guid to your app when you create your Xamarin.Forms iOS or Android app.

6. Return to App Center. Go to the Settings page of each app. You will see the App Secret at the top of the page, as in Figures 4-3 and 4-4.

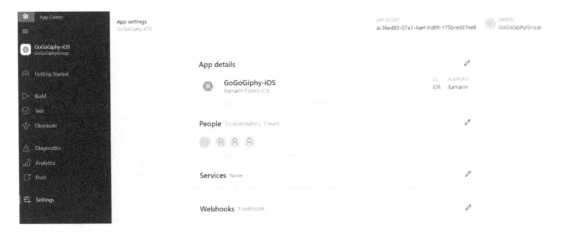

Figure 4-3. *App Center iOS App Secret*

Figure 4-4. *App Center Android App Secret*

7. Copy the Guids for each app. Return to `Settings.cs` in the Core project. Add the appropriate Guid to the appropriate variable, as shown in Listing 4-1.

Listing 4-1. Settings.cs

```
internal static string AppCenterSecretiOS { get; set; } = "";

internal static string AppCenterSecretAndroid { get; set; } = "";
```

8. Finally, open App.xaml.cs. Add the code shown in Listing 4-2 at the end of the InitializeAppCenter() function.

Listing 4-2. App.xaml.cs ➤ InitializeAppCenter() Function

```
// Initialize AppCenter SDK
AppCenter.Start
(
 String.Format
 (
  "ios={0};android={1};"
  , Settings.AppCenterSecretiOS
  , Settings.AppCenterSecretAndroid
 )
 , typeof(Analytics)
 , typeof(Crashes)
);
```

The code is how you identify your Xamarin Forms iOS and Android apps for App Center by passing in the Guids you pasted in the Settings file.

Note   Remember to add the AppCenter.Start(..) code at the end of the function. You will add several event handlers prior to the call to this Start(..) function. Adding the event handlers after the Start(..) function will not trigger the events.

Adding Custom Events

The App Center SDK provides the ability to raise custom events in the app. Why is this useful? You can analyze how your user is using the app when it is used publicly.

You are going to add your own custom event to report back to App Center what your users are searching. The HomeViewModel class has a searchCommand that is bound to the search bar in HomePage.xaml.cs. When the user searches for a string in the search bar, the code triggers this command. Add the code snippet highlighted in **bold** in Listing 4-3 into the action expression of the Command object.

Listing 4-3. HomeViewModel ➤ SearchCommand

```
_searchCommand = new Command<string>
(
    (text) =>
    {
        var searchEvent = new Dictionary<string, string>
        {
            {"SearchString", text }
        };

        Analytics.TrackEvent("Giphy searched", searchEvent);
        Search();
    }
)
```

Let's evaluate what is happening in this code. It creates a Dictionary object and adds one key-value pair called SearchString and adds the text variable containing the search string that you typed in the search bar. The key in this Dictionary object is vital because the key is used later organize events in the App Center Events page, which I will show you later. In the next line, it passes in the name of the event, which is Giphy searched, and the Dictionary object. In addition, you can add more dictionary keys and values, such as date, user id, session id, etc. All the keys and values will be wrapped inside the same dictionary and reported back to App Center as part of the same event.

You can add such a custom event example to anywhere in your code where you want to monitor how your users are using the app. Be careful to use it intelligently through your app and not everywhere through your app. Keep in mind you are raising events and sending them to App Center, so tracking more events means sending more data to App Center. In an upcoming section, you will wire up the custom events to export to Azure Application Insights. Again, the more events you send to App Center means the more data is exported to Azure, which means higher data usage on Azure. Use this feature wisely.

Figure 4-5 shows what you would see after the "Giphy searched" event is logged in App Center.

Figure 4-5. *Events*

Let me explain what you will see in the Events page. First, notice that the custom event that you just raised from your code called "Giphy searched" is located at the top left of the screen. Second, notice the four highlighted items in the SearchString table at the bottom of the page. App Center does a wonderful job of organizing your events based on the dictionary keys that you send to App Center. Notice how I searched for "World cup," "Avengers," and "Iron man" in the search bar of the sample app in order to generate the events you see above. Lastly, the top two tables show you the number of events raised per user and the number of events per session. Of course, you can customize your searches based on the combo-boxes at the top-right corner of the page where you can filter by Version and Time.

Now click the Log Events on the left-hand panel. Figure 4-6 shows the Log flow section and the individual search strings that I searched for when testing the app. This view is a textual view of the same representation above except the above tabular view is more organized based on your dictionary keys.

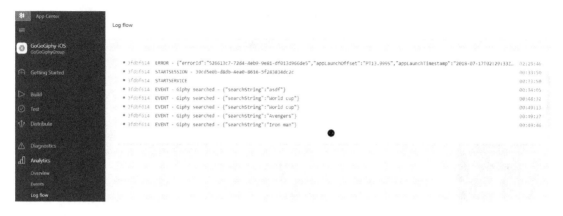

Figure 4-6. *Log flow*

Adding a `Dictionary` object to the `TrackEvent(..)` function is entirely optional. It is
only one of the overloaded functions of `TrackEvent()`. You can easily call `TrackEvent()`,
as shown in Listing 4-4. Keep in mind you just will not log the value of the event in the
Log Flow section.

Listing 4-4. HomeViewModel ➤ SearchCommand ➤ No Dictionary Object
Parameter

```
_searchCommand = new Command<string>
(
    (text) =>
    {
        var searchEvent = new Dictionary<string, string>
        {
            {"SearchString", text }
        };

        Analytics.TrackEvent("Giphy searched");
        Search();
    }
)
```

Simulating a Test Crash

In this section, you will learn how to simulate a test crash so you can report it to App Center. Luckily, App Center provides an API function called GenerateTestCrash(). This function works only with Debug configurations of the build. If you remember, you set up the continuous build in Chapter 2 using the Debug configuration. This test crash will work on a simulator and a physical device. When you finish testing, you will comment out the code.

Let's begin! You will simulate a test crash when the user searches for a query string in the search bar.

Open HomeViewModel.cs and open searchCommand again. Add the code highlighted in **bold** in Listing 4-5 prior to the Analytics.TrackEvent(..) call.

Listing 4-5. HomeViewModel ➤ searchCommand

```
private ICommand _searchCommand;

_searchCommand = new Command<string>
  (
     (text) =>
     {
        var searchEvent = new Dictionary<string, string>
        {
              {"SearchString", text }
        };

        Crashes.GenerateTestCrash();
        Analytics.TrackEvent("Giphy searched");
        Search();
     }
  )
```

Remember to add the using references for the Crashes SDK to the top of the class.

Build the iOS app. If it builds successfully, run the app in the simulator. Search for anything in the search bar. You should see the app crash in the simulator.

Return to App Center. Go to the iOS app and go to Crashes. At first, you will notice App Center saying that it is still collecting data, as shown in Figure 4-7.

Figure 4-7. *App Center iOS App Crashes page*

Be patient. Sometimes it takes a few minutes for App Center to collect the crash data from your app and report it on the dashboard. Press refresh. You should soon see your crash data, as shown in Figure 4-8.

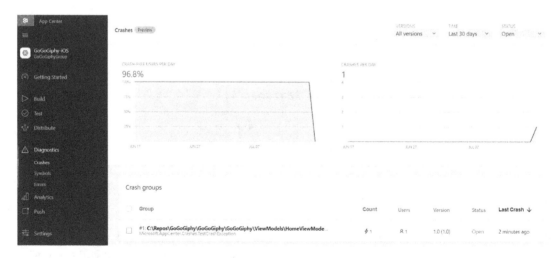

Figure 4-8. *App Center iOS crash data*

Go to the Crash groups section shown in Figure 4-8. Click the first crash group. You will now be able to see the detailed stack trace shown in Figure 4-9. App Center does a wonderful job of showing the stack trace line by line so you can troubleshoot and determine exactly in what function your app crashed.

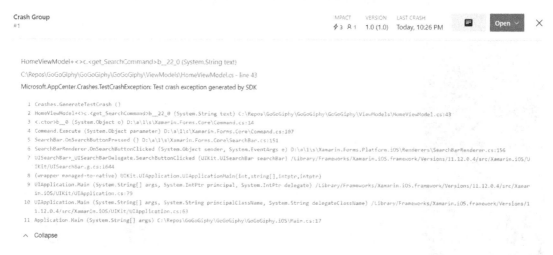

Figure 4-9. *iOS crash group*

Scroll further down and you will see the crashes grouped according to the device. I deployed the app to both my developer and tester devices and repeated the steps above to see the crash reports shown in Figure 4-10. You can click one device at a time to view when and where the crash occurred in the code.

Figure 4-10. *Crash reports*

If you were able to follow along with the steps and images above, you should now be able to replicate the same steps for Android. As an assignment, integrate the crash reports for Android. If you are successful, you should see screens similar to the ones below.

Figure 4-11 shows the Crashes page just before it reports any crash data.

Figure 4-11. *App Center Android Crashes page*

Figure 4-12 shows the same test crash exception on an Android device that you generated for iOS earlier.

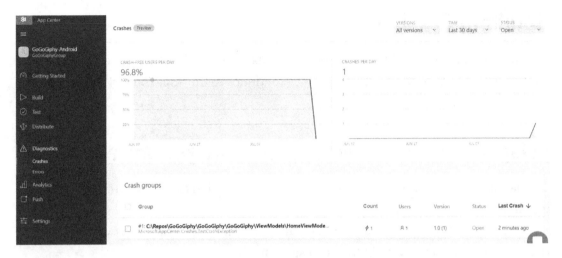

Figure 4-12. *App Center Android crash data*

Figure 4-13 shows the stack trace after you drill into the test crash exception.

Figure 4-13. *Android crash group*

You will conclude this section by committing and pushing your changes to the remote master branch. Go ahead and commit your code. You will need this simulated test crash in the coming sections to handle the crashes.

Handling Crashes

The App Center SDK provides a number of events out of the box that you can handle in your code to give your user a more elegant experience in the app. You will go through each of the events one by one.

Using the HasCrashedInLastSessionAsync Value

The easiest ways for your app to know whether it crashed in the last session is by making use of two easy snippets of code.

The code in Listing 4-6 returns a Boolean value when used with the await keyword, thus indicating a crash event in the prior session.

Listing 4-6. Crashes SDK HasCrashedInLastSessionAsync()

```
bool didAppCrash = await Crashes.HasCrashedInLastSessionAsync();
```

If you want to do something useful with the code in Listing 4-6 instead of just getting a return value, refer to the code in Listing 4-7. You can drop the await keyword and get a Task<bool> object from the call to the HasCrashedInLastSessionAsync() function. Next, you can use the ContinueWith(..) function that will execute asynchronously upon completion of this target task.

See Listing 4-7 and add the code to the InitializeAppCenter() function but before the call to AppCenter.Start(..).

Listing 4-7. App.xaml.cs ➤ InitializeAppCenter() ➤
HasCrashedInLastSessionAsync() Subsequent Task

```
Crashes.HasCrashedInLastSessionAsync().ContinueWith((arg) =>
{
 Xamarin.Forms.Device.BeginInvokeOnMainThread(() =>
 {
    try
    {
       Task<bool> didAppCrash = Crashes.HasCrashedInLastSessionAsync();

       if (didAppCrash.Result)
       {
```

```
            Current.MainPage.DisplayAlert("Oops", "You noticed the app
            crashed on you. Sorry for the inconvenience.", "Ok");
        }
    }
    catch (Exception exception)
    {
        Debug.WriteLine(exception.Message);
    }
});
});
```

This code invokes an action on the Main UI thread. It calls the Crashes.
HasCrashedInLastSessionAsync() again to get the value. It queries the interior
Result property in the object. And it displays an alert to the user apologizing for the
inconvenience.

Follow the steps below to simulate the crash and test your new alert box:

1. Build the project.

2. Run it in the simulator.

3. Search for a test string in the search bar.

4. Wait for the app to crash.

5. Relaunch the app from the phone desktop.

If all goes well, you will see the display alerts in Figures 4-14 and 4-15 in both the
Android and iPhone simulators.

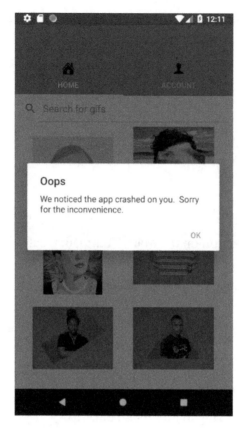

Figure 4-14. *Android crash message*

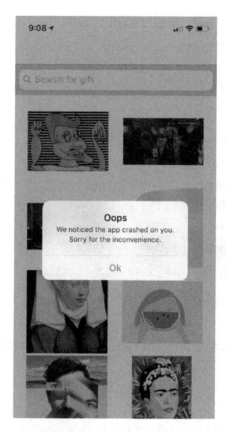

Figure 4-15. *iPhone crash message*

Before going further, comment out the code you just added as the asynchronous task on the Main UI thread because you will add more code in coming sections to give a more interactive experience to the user.

Handling the ShouldAwaitUserConfirmation Event

The App Center SDK exposes another callback event, ShouldAwaitUserConfirmation, that you can attach a handler in order to give your user the opportunity to send a crash report or not. This callback event is powerful because it gives the user the chance to make three distinct actions. And you can handle each of the actions and instruct App Center crashes accordingly.

Remember to comment out the code you added in the last section to handle HasCrashedInLastSessionAsync() because the code should not prompt the user twice. Add the callback handler in Listing 4-8 to InitializeAppCenter(..) but before the call to AppCenter.Start(..).

Listing 4-8. App.xaml.cs ➤ InitializeAppCenter() ➤ Crashes.
ShouldAwaitUserConfirmation

```
Crashes.ShouldAwaitUserConfirmation = () =>
{
 Xamarin.Forms.Device.BeginInvokeOnMainThread(() =>
 {
   Current.MainPage.DisplayActionSheet("Uh Oh. Sorry I crashed. Do you want
   to send a crash report?", "Cancel", null, "Send", "Always Send", "Don't
   Send").ContinueWith((arg) =>
   {
       var answer = arg.Result;
       UserConfirmation userConfirmationSelection;

       if (answer == "Send")
       {
           userConfirmationSelection = UserConfirmation.Send;
       }
       else if (answer == "Always Send")
       {
           userConfirmationSelection = UserConfirmation.AlwaysSend;
       }
       else
       {
           userConfirmationSelection = UserConfirmation.DontSend;
       }

   Crashes.NotifyUserConfirmation(userConfirmationSelection);
   });
 });

 return true;

};
```

Let's analyze what is happening in this handler. Once more, the code is invoking an action on the Main UI thread. It is displaying an action sheet that will show a friendly message to the user and give the user three options to choose from. It has a ContinueWith(..) action with arg as the state object that contains the user's response. The Result property on the state object contains the user's response. The code compares what type of action the user has chosen, sets the UserConfirmation object, and calls Crashes.NotifyUserConfirmation(..) with the UserConfirmation object.

If the user chooses Send or Always Send, you will see the crash log in App Center. If the user chooses Always Send and if another crash happens again, this callback event will not trigger again.

Follow these steps in order to simulate the crash and see the new code in action:

1. Build the project.

2. Run it in the simulator.

3. Search for a test string in the search bar.

4. Wait for the app to crash.

5. Relaunch the app from the phone desktop.

6. Choose one of the three options.

If all goes well, you will see the display prompts in the Android and iPhone simulators (Figures 4-16 and 4-17).

Figure 4-16. *Android user response*

Figure 4-17. *iPhone user response*

Handling the SendingErrorReport Event

The App Center SDK exposes three more callback events that allow your app to know what is happening during and after the crash reporting events. Why are they important? For example, if your app experiences a slower than normal Internet connection, it may take a while for your app to send the crash report. It makes sense to inform that the user this action is happening.

The first callback event, SendingErrorReport, allows your app to know when it is sending a crash report. Add the callback handler in Listing 4-9 to the InitializeAppCenter(..) function but before the call to AppCenter.Start(..). Wait on the testing because you will implement the SentErrorReport event first.

Listing 4-9. App.xaml.cs ➤ InitializeAppCenter() ➤ Crashes.
SendingErrorReport

```
Crashes.SendingErrorReport += (sender, e) =>
{
 AppCenterLog.Info(AppName, "Sending error report");

 var args = e as SendingErrorReportEventArgs;
 ErrorReport report = args.Report;

 if (report.Exception != null)
 {
   AppCenterLog.Info(AppName, report.Exception.ToString());
 }
 else if (report.AndroidDetails != null)
 {
   AppCenterLog.Info(AppName, report.AndroidDetails.ThreadName);
 }

  // Show modal page displaying status of crash report.
 Xamarin.Forms.Device.BeginInvokeOnMainThread(() =>
 {
   Tuple<string, bool> values = new Tuple<string, bool>(message, true);
    FreshBasePageModel pageModel = GetCurrentPageModel();
   pageModel.CoreMethods.PushPageModel<ModalActivityViewModel>(values, true);
 });
};
```

Let's evaluate what is happening in this code. The first part of the code snippet is
extraneous because the code is logging some useful data about what is happening. If
the report has an exception, the code logs this data as well. But the important part of
this snippet is toward the bottom where it invokes the action on the Main UI thread. In
this action, the code calls GetCurrentPageModel() in order to access the CoreMethods
object in the FreshMvvm framework. The code invokes PushPageModel(..) with a
Tuple object containing the message to display and a Boolean variable to control the
ActivityIndicator on the ModalActivityPage.xaml.

You can follow the same steps from the prior section to rebuild the app, generate a test crash, and watch for this friendly message on the modal page. But instead, skip to the next section where you will replace the user message on the modal page after the crash report is sent.

Handling the SentErrorReport Event

The App Center SDK exposes this callback event to indicate that a crash report was sent successfully. Add the callback handler in Listing 4-10 to `ModalActivityViewModel` > `InitializeEvents()`.

Listing 4-10. ModalActivityViewModel ➤ InitializeEvents() ➤ Crashes. SentErrorReport

```
Crashes.SentErrorReport += (sender, e) =>
{
 var args = e as SentErrorReportEventArgs;
 ErrorReport report = args.Report;

 Message = "Successfully sent error report. You can close this dialog";
 IsActivityRunning = false;
 IsActivityVisible = false;
};
```

Let's evaluate what is happening in this code. At this point when the app is running, the user sees the modal page already with the `ActivityIndicator` running. In reality, this operation happens so fast that the user never really sees the ActivityIndicator running because the crash report is sent in less than a second. Open and inspect the code in the `ModalActivityPage.xaml`. The code already has the `IsActivityRunning` and `IsActivityVisible` properties bound to the `ActivityIndicator` view control. Therefore, this code disables and hides the `ActivityIndicator` view control after the crash report is sent.

Add the code in Listing 4-11 to the `InitializeAppCenter(..)` function but before the call to `AppCenter.Start(..)`.

191

Listing 4-11. App.xaml.cs ➤ InitializeAppCenter() ➤ Crashes.SentErrorReport

```
Crashes.SentErrorReport += (sender, e) =>
{
 AppCenterLog.Info(Settings.AppName, "Sent error report");

 var args = e as SentErrorReportEventArgs;
 ErrorReport report = args.Report;

 if (report.Exception != null)
 {
   AppCenterLog.Info(Settings.AppName, report.Exception.ToString());
 }
 else
 {
   AppCenterLog.Info(Settings.AppName, "No system exception was found");
 }

 if (report.AndroidDetails != null)
 {
   AppCenterLog.Info(Settings.AppName, report.AndroidDetails.ThreadName);
 }
};
```

Follow these steps to simulate a crash again and show the modal page:

1. Build the project.

2. Run it in the simulator.

3. Search for a test string in the search bar.

4. Wait for the app to crash.

5. Relaunch the app from the phone desktop.

6. Choose one of the three options.

7. Wait for the modal page to appear, showing that the crash report was sent successfully.

8. Click the X button at the top right to close the modal page (Figures 4-18 and 4-19).

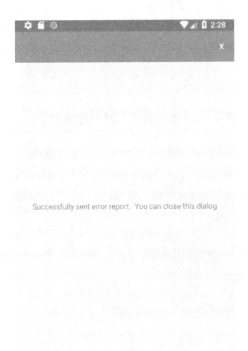

Figure 4-18. *Android modal page*

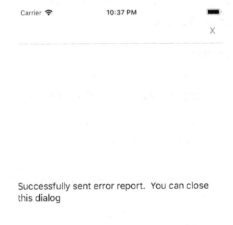

Figure 4-19. *iPhone modal page*

Of course, you can always make the above modal pages more beautiful with better styles. But I kept the code as minimal as possible to give you an idea of how everything works.

Handling the FailedToSendErrorReport Event

The App Center SDK exposes one more event that you will handle. If the event the crash report can't be sent because the device loses network connectivity, the app can display a helpful message to the user. Add the event handler in Listing 4-12 to InitializeAppCenter() again.

Listing 4-12. App.xaml.cs ➤ InitializeAppCenter() ➤ Crashes. FailedToSendErrorReport

```
Crashes.FailedToSendErrorReport += (sender, e) =>
{
 string message = "Failed to send error report";
 AppCenterLog.Info(Settings.AppName, message);

 var args = e as FailedToSendErrorReportEventArgs;
 ErrorReport report = args.Report;

 if (report.Exception != null)
 {
   AppCenterLog.Info(Settings.AppName, report.Exception.ToString());
 }
 else if (report.AndroidDetails != null)
 {
   AppCenterLog.Info(Settings.AppName, report.AndroidDetails.ThreadName);
 }

 if (e.Exception != null)
 {
   AppCenterLog.Info(Settings.AppName, "There is an exception associated
   with the failure");
 }
```

```
// Show modal page displaying status of crash report.
Xamarin.Forms.Device.BeginInvokeOnMainThread(() =>
{
  Tuple<string, bool> values = new Tuple<string, bool>(message, false);
   FreshBasePageModel pageModel = GetCurrentPageModel();

   pageModel.CoreMethods.PushPageModel<ModalActivityViewModel>(values, true);
});
};
```

Let's examine what's happening. The callback handler is similar to the prior ones. The code toward the bottom invokes the Action on the Main UI thread again. It calls the same `ModalActivityPage` and displays the message to the user and does not show the `ActivityIndicator` on `ModalActivityPage.xaml`.

Setting Up Continuous Export to Azure

Now that you have walked through all the steps of setting up analytics and crashes and handling the App Center crash events appropriately, keep in mind that App Center allows developers the option of storing analytics and crashes on a more persistent and secure data storage service like Azure so developers can return to the data months later, analyze the data, and even create reports from it. But will App Center store the analytics and crash data indefinitely? No! I will show you in the first part of this section how to query the retention period of data using the App Center API.

Querying Data Retention Settings

As you go through the various chapters, you will visit the App Center API from time to time because the API exposes more information than what you can find on the website. This is your first attempt at querying something from the API. I will show you all the steps necessary to query the retention settings.

The App Center API is available at `https://openapi.appcenter.ms`. The Retention Settings API (Figure 4-20) is available further down the same page at `https://openapi.appcenter.ms/#/errors/errors_getRetentionSettings`.

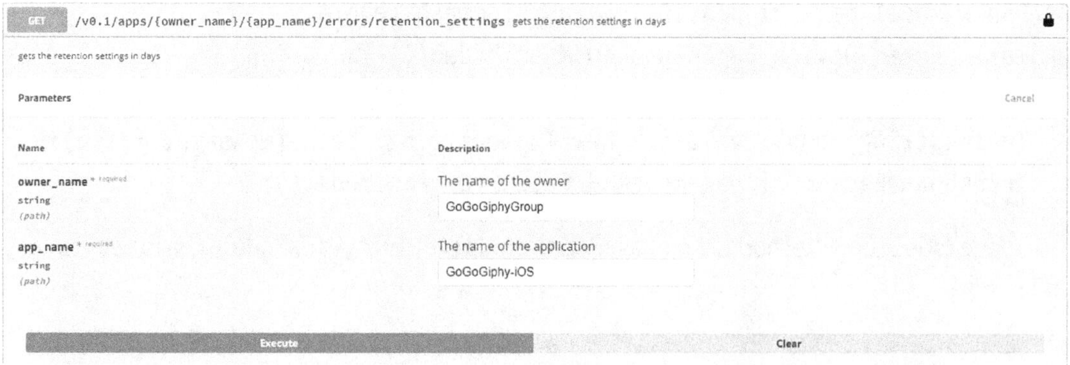

Figure 4-20. *The Retention Settings API*

In Figure 4-20, App Center allows you the option of trying out the API on the page itself. But it needs some data first before it can start. Let's gather the necessary information for this API call.

Click the Lock icon at the top right of Figure 4-20. It will ask for an APIToken (Figure 4-21). In this image, the App Center API asks for authorization from the App Center Portal to make sure you are authorized to use the API.

Figure 4-21. *Authorization*

Return to App Center. Go to Settings. Click API Tokens and then click the New API token button shown in Figure 4-22.

Figure 4-22. *API Tokens*

Give your token a useful description and set it for full access, as shown in Figure 4-23.

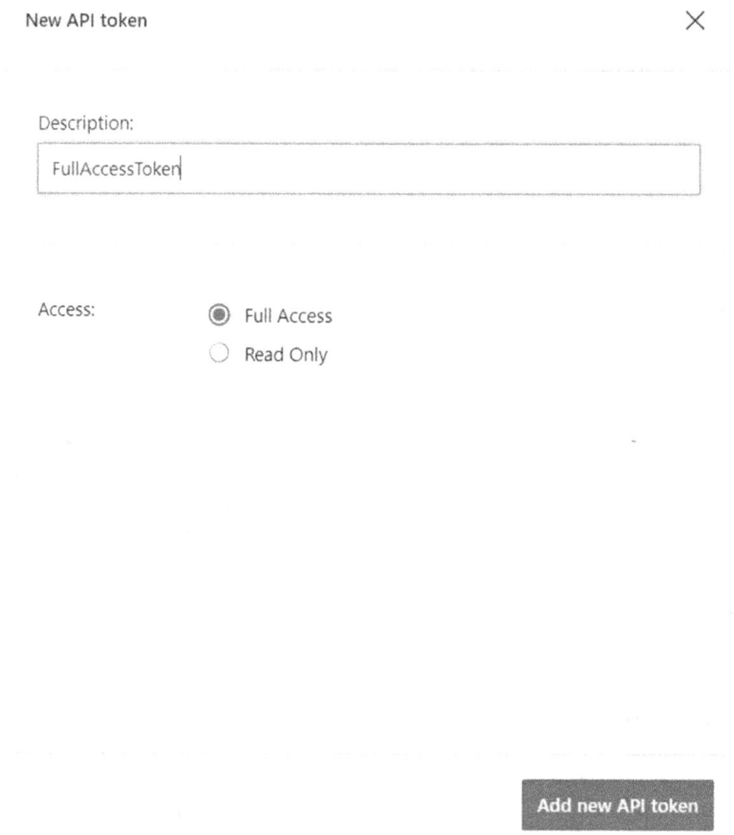

New API token   ✕

Description:

FullAccessToken

Access: ⦿ Full Access
                       ○ Read Only

[Add new API token]

Figure 4-23. *New API token*

The next prompt will show you the new API token you just created. Be sure to save this token in a safe place. After closing this prompt, you will not be able to view the token again. If you forget or lose the token, your only recourse is to delete it from App Center and recreate it.

Copy and paste the API token into the prompt shown in Figure 4-24.

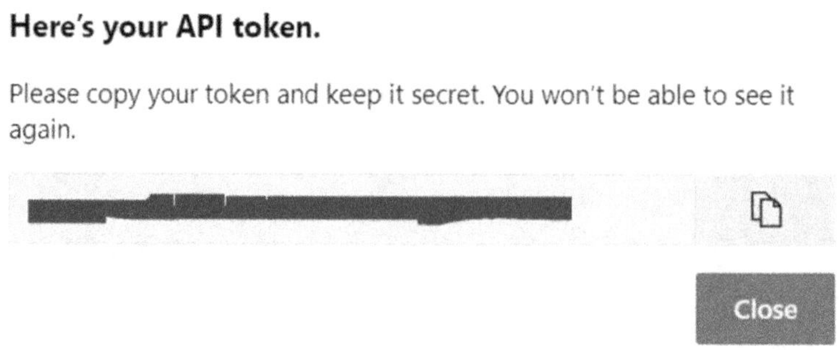

Here's your API token.

Please copy your token and keep it secret. You won't be able to see it again.

                                                                      [Close]

Figure 4-24. *Token prompt*

In case the App Center UI has changed since the time of this writing, you can find the Owner name another way. Go to the Overview page of either the Android or the iOS app. Refer to the URL. The app URL should be one of the following:

```
https://appcenter.ms/users/{owner-name}/apps/{app-name}
```

```
https://appcenter.ms/orgs/{owner-name}/apps/{app-name}
```

Simply find your Owner name from your URL based on your matching URL signature.

The old way of finding the Owner Name is shown below, but the UI may have changed since the time of this writing. You can return to App Center. Click the iOS app. Go to Settings. The top of the page should appear like Figure 4-25. The highlighted text is the owner name.

Figure 4-25. *Owner name*

The same page has the name of the application. Click the App Details or the Pencil icon to view the details. Copy the app name (Figure 4-26).

App settings
GoGoGiphy-iOS

App details

App name:

GoGoGiphy-iOS

Icon:

Description:

Xamarin Forms iOS

GoGoGiphy-iOS

App details

Collaborators

Services

Webhooks

Export

Email notifications

OS: iOS

Platform: Xamarin

Editing OS and Platform will be supported soon.

Azure's subscription: Visual Studio Enterprise: BizSpark

Save changes

Figure 4-26. *App name*

If you gathered all the right information and configured it correctly, click Execute and you should see the data shown in Figure 4-27.

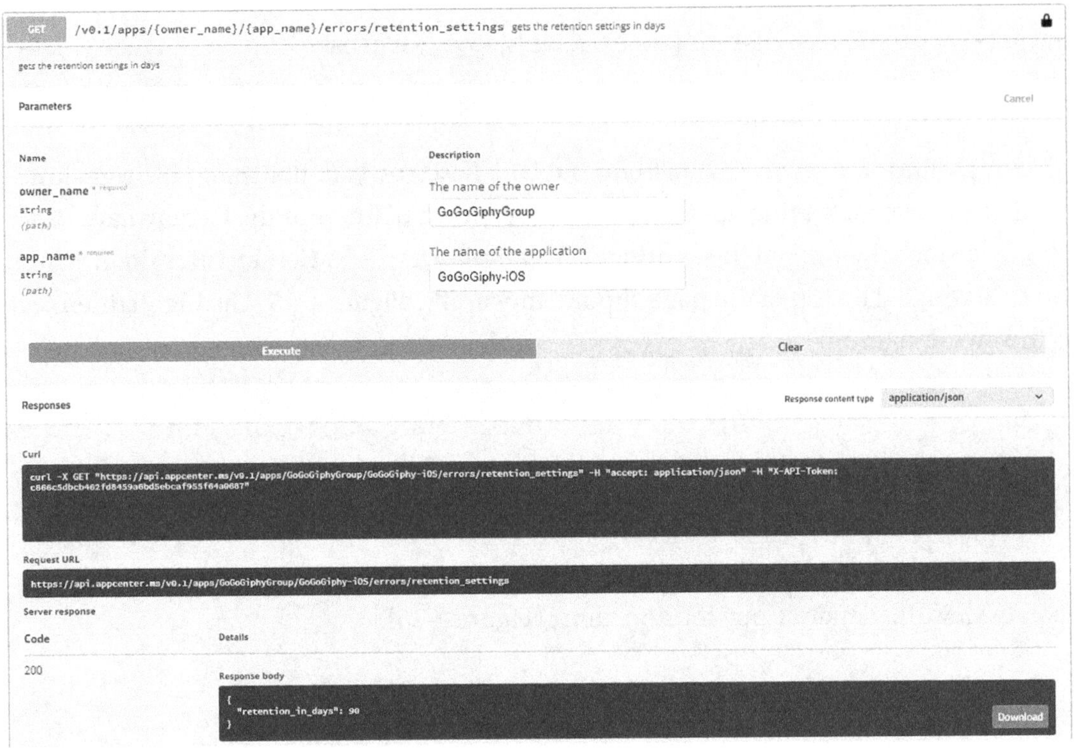

Figure 4-27. Retention Settings API request

Notice that the data returned from the API request has a retention period of 90 days. As you can see, App Center only retains your errors and crash data for a temporary period of time, which emphasizes the importance of exporting your data to a more persistent storage medium like Azure.

The above steps were only a small sample of the full potential of the App Center API.

Moreover, in case the App Center team decides to change their API since the time of this writing, you can find the retention period a far more easier way. Simply go to either your Android or iOS app, click on Settings, and click on Data. You will notice a combo-box next to Diagnostics allowing you to select either 28 days or 90 days.

You might be thinking. Why did you not show me the easy way in the first place? Well, now you know how to use the App Center CLI because we went through this simple exercise!

Exporting Analytics to Application Insights

In this section, I will show you the steps necessary to set up continuous export of analytics to Azure Application Insights. If you do not have an Azure account, please revisit Chapter 1 to sign up for an account.

What is Application Insights? It is a feature of Azure originally created for web developers to collect telemetry about their apps and services, diagnose issues, and analyze the performance and usage. You want to set up Application Insights Export for your app because you just verified App Center's data retention period is 90 days or less and you want to store your custom events indefinitely on Azure for future analysis. I will not go into great detail about Application Insights in this section because it is beyond the scope of this chapter, but if you want to learn more about this feature, go to Microsoft's documentation site at `https://docs.microsoft.com/en-us/azure/azure-monitor/app/app-insights-overview`.

Let's begin setting up your data export. There are actually two ways to set up data export. The first is the standard export option where App Center does the heavy lifting for you by creating your Azure resource, creating your resource group in Azure, and assigning the resource to the resource group. The second is the customize export option where you set up the Azure resource first and then return to App Center to link your Azure resource to App Center.

Since I like knowing how a Lego figure is built piece by piece so I can build it again later if it falls apart, I will explain the custom export option. First, log into your Azure portal. Click the Create a resource option at the top left of the left pane. Search for Application Insights in the search bar. Click the Create button. You should see the screen shown in Figure 4-28.

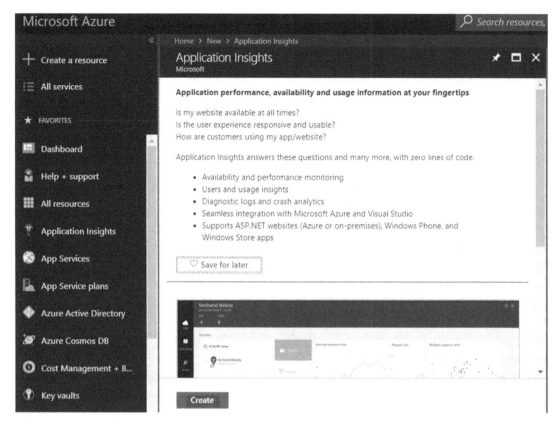

Figure 4-28. *Azure Application Insights*

Type in the following values from Figure 4-29:

- You may need to use a different name for your application because it may be taken.

- Use App Center application for the application type.

- I used my BizSpark account. The subscription should be automatically set for you using the same subscription when you first set up your Azure account.

- Create a new resource group called AppCenterResourceGroup because you will use this resource group to organize all Azure resources going forward.

- Choose the datacenter physically closest to your location.

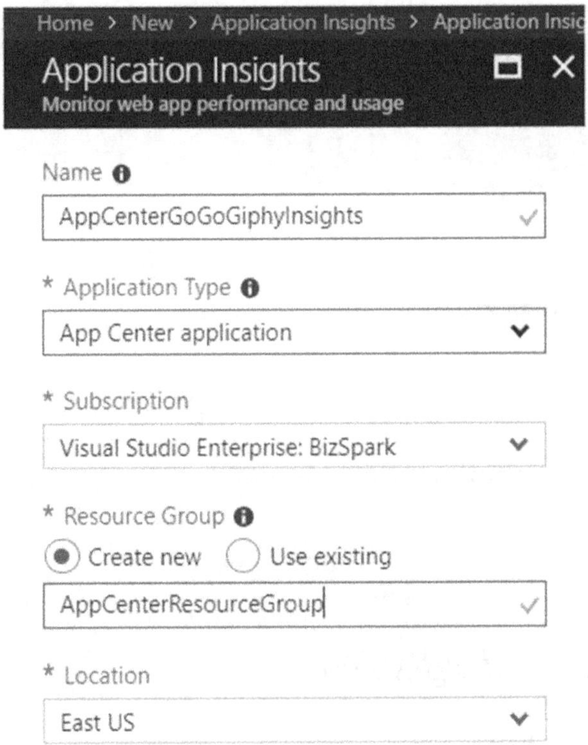

Home > New > Application Insights > Application Insig

Application Insights

Monitor web app performance and usage

Name ❶

AppCenterGoGoGiphyInsights   ✓

* Application Type ❶

App Center application   ⌄

* Subscription

Visual Studio Enterprise: BizSpark   ⌄

* Resource Group ❶

◉ Create new   ◯ Use existing

AppCenterResourceGroup   ✓

* Location

East US   ⌄

Figure 4-29. Applicaton Insights setup

After you click Create, give Azure a few minutes to provision your new service. When it is set up, you should see a screen like Figure 4-30. (I redacted my Subscription ID but highlighted the Instrumentation Key because you will need this key for App Center to link to your Application Insights resource.)

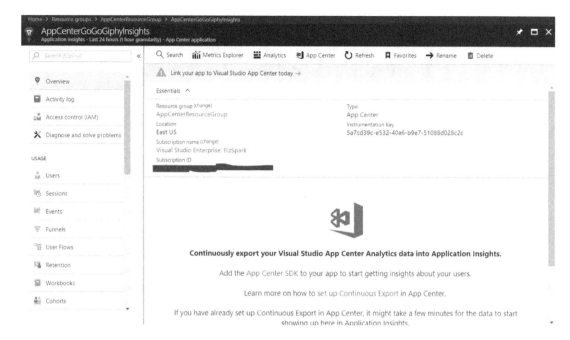

Figure 4-30. *Application Insights overview*

Now you will set up the Azure connection on the App Center side. Go into your App Center Organization, click Manage, and click Azure, as shown in Figure 4-31. Initially, your subscriptions will be empty. You will add your Azure subscription link now.

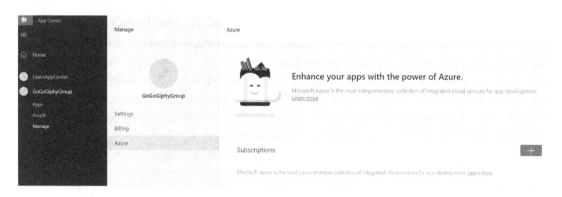

Figure 4-31. *App Center Azure subscriptions*

Click the + button shown. If you are already logged into Azure on a different browser tab, you will see the prompt shown in Figure 4-32. Please log into Azure using the appropriate account prior to this step. Once you see this prompt, click the Connect button.

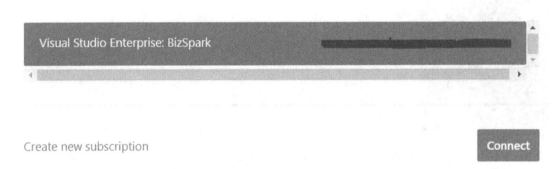

Figure 4-32. *Azure Subscription connect prompt*

Return to App Center again. You will see your Azure subscription linked, as shown in Figure 4-33.

Figure 4-33. *App Center Azure subscriptions*

Now you will set up continuous export to Azure. Return to your app, go to Settings, click Export, and click New Export (Figure 4-34).

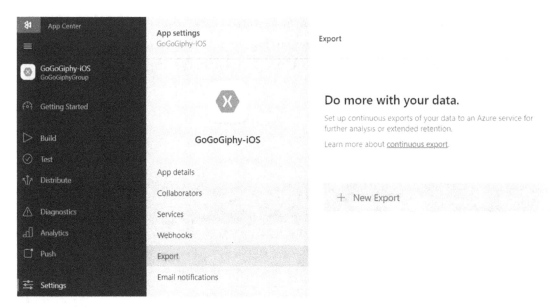

Figure 4-34. *App Center Azure continuous export*

A panel will slide out from the right, as shown in Figure 4-35. Click the Application Insights and Customize boxes.

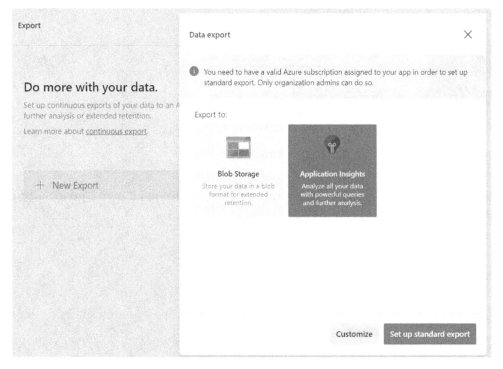

Figure 4-35. *Application Insights data export*

Finally, paste the Instrumentation Key you copied from the first step into the textbox, as shown in Figure 4-36.

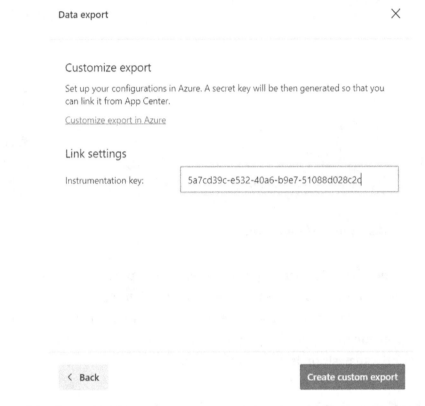

Figure 4-36. *Data export setup*

At this point, App Center will automatically export all custom events you may have stored in App Center up until now.

Return to Application Insights, as shown in Figure 4-37. Click Events. Open the combo-box named "Who used". You can select your custom event in the list of available selections to filter and show only your custom events.

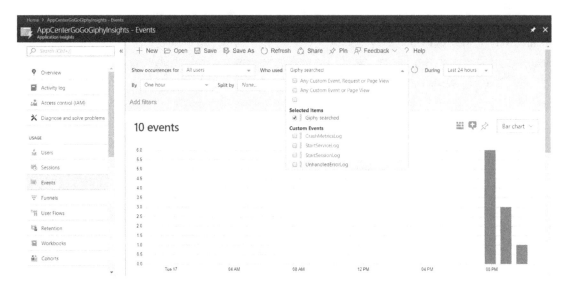

Figure 4-37. Application Insight events

Great job! You now have Application Insights set up to export your custom events continuously from your users as they use your app. You can now imagine the possibilities. You can learn how your users use your app, how long they use it, and what parts of your app are the most popular. Moreover, this data is now persisted on Azure and you can perform analysis on it from within Azure.

Setting Up Export of Crashes to Blob Storage

In this section, you will walk through the steps of setting up continuous export of your crash data to Azure Blob Storage. Unfortunately, at the time of this writing, App Center does not support continuous export of crash data to Azure Application Insights. That is why only the Blob Storage feature is available. Of course, you can create your own custom solution to set up crash data to an Azure SQL database. But let's look at continuous export to Blob Storage since it is supported out of the box.

What is Blob Storage? It is another feature in Azure that allows applications to store unstructured data like text, binary, or file data on a highly secure, durable, and scalable data storage system. Since the details of Blob Storage are beyond the scope of this chapter, you are welcome to learn more about Blob Storage from `https://docs.` `microsoft.com/en-us/azure/storage/blobs/storage-blobs-overview`.

Just like in the previous section, you have the option of setting up a standard export or a custom export. Let's begin setting up your Blob Storage on Azure using the custom export option to go through the manual steps. Log into your Azure portal. Click Storage and click the Storage account - blob, file, table, queue option shown in Figure 4-38.

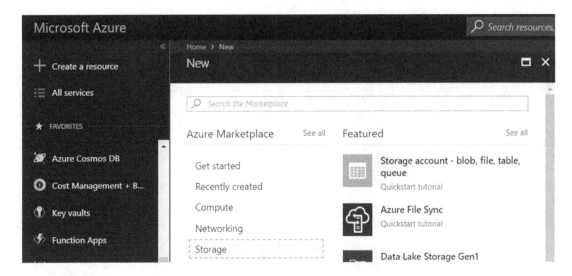

Figure 4-38. *Azure Blob Storage*

Next, copy the values into the fields shown in Figures 4-39 and 4-40.

- Give your Blob Storage resource a unique name.

- Click Resource Manager.

- Choose the datacenter physically closest to your location.

- Keep the Performance and the Secure Transfer Required field default values.

- The Azure subscription should be selected by default.

- Choose the AppCenterResourceGroup you created in the prior section.

- Leave the remaining options as the default values.

- Click Create.

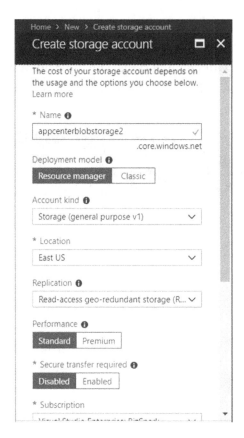

Figure 4-39. *Creating Blob Storage*

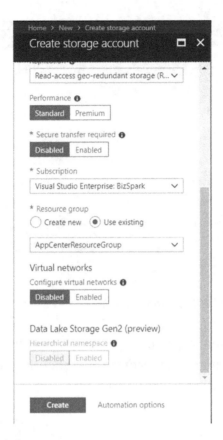

Figure 4-40.   *Creating Blob Storage*

Give Azure a few minutes to create and provision your new Blob Storage account. Once it is created, click Access keys, as shown in Figure 4-41. Copy the Connection string value.

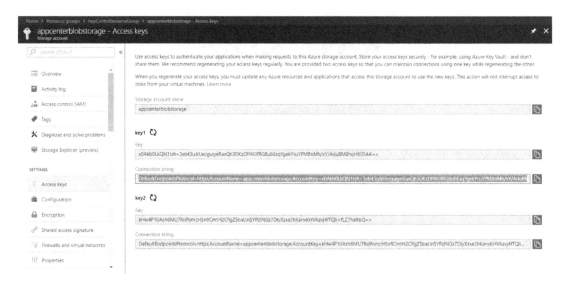

Figure 4-41. *Azure Blob Storage access keys*

As in the previous section, return to App Center, go to your app, go to Settings, click Export, click New Export, choose Blob Storage, and click Customize. Figure 4-42 shows the setup of Blob Storage for the Android app.

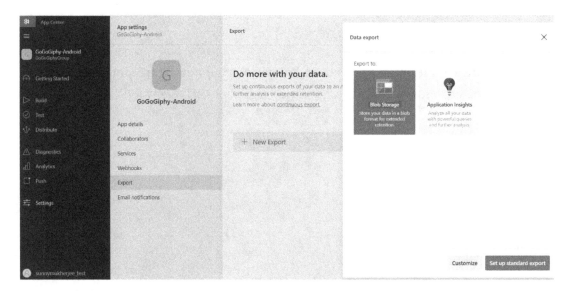

Figure 4-42. *App Center Blob Storage data export setup*

Paste the connection string you copied in the previous step (Figure 4-43).

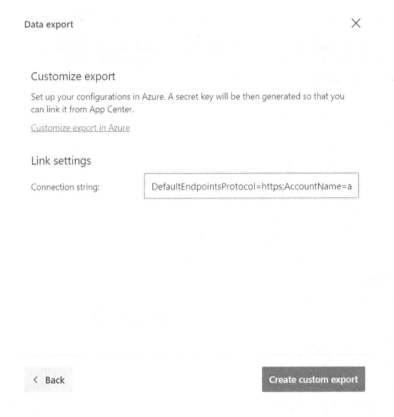

Figure 4-43. *App Center data export*

Now you are ready! Give App Center a few minutes to upload crash data to Azure. Return to Azure, click Storage Explorer, and click Archive under Blob Containers. Drill down through the subfolders and you will see your crash data automatically uploaded in the respective files (Figure 4-44).

Figure 4-44. *Azure Blob Storage Explorer*

You can download one of the data files to your local system. You should see data like that shown in Listing 4-13. You can see how important data like AppId, AppVersion, OsVersion, etc. are stored on a persistent data storage system like Azure Blob Storage. It will open your mind to a world of possibilities you can do with this data. For example, you can analyze how frequently crashes are happening on different devices and if you see a spike in crashes after the release of a new version of your app.

Listing 4-13. Crash Data File

```
[
  {
    "AppBuild":"21",
    "AppId":"049e7128-8937-4511-bad9-79d5460875aa",
    "AppNamespace":"com.sunny.gogogiphy",
    "AppVersion":"21",
    "CarrierCountry":"us",
    "CarrierName":"AT&T",
    "CorrelationId":"edc6ada4-570b-4cee-bb87-0630009dfdcb",
    "CountryCode":"us",
    "EventId":"",
    "EventName":"",
    "IngressTimestamp":"2018-07-25T03:24:10.664Z",
    "InstallId":"4f1bff37-6681-4541-a34b-7aaf583505b8",
    "IsTestMessage":"False",
    "LiveUpdateDeploymentKey":"None",
    "LiveUpdatePackageHash":"None",
    "LiveUpdateReleaseLabel":"None",
    "Locale":"en_US",
    "MessageId":"634c009a-1693-4b99-bba7-d68db10da773",
    "MessageType":"StartServiceLog",
    "Model":"iPhone10,6",
    "OemName":"Apple",
    "OsApiLevel":"None",
    "OsBuild":"15G77",
    "OsName":"iOS",
    "OsVersion":"11.4.1",
```

```
  "Properties":"[\"Crashes\",\"Analytics\"]",
  "ScreenSize":"2436x1125",
  "SdkName":"appcenter.ios",
  "SdkVersion":"1.7.1",
  "SessionId":"00000000-0000-0000-0000-000000000000",
  "Timestamp":"2018-07-25T03:24:06.195Z",
  "TimeZoneOffset":"-PT4H",
  "WrapperRuntimeVersion":"11.2.0",
  "WrapperSdkName":"appcenter.xamarin",
  "WrapperSdkVersion":"1.7.0"
},
{
  "AppBuild":"21",
  "AppId":"049e7128-8937-4511-bad9-79d5460875aa",
  "AppNamespace":"com.sunny.gogogiphy",
  "AppVersion":"21",
  "CarrierCountry":"us",
  "CarrierName":"AT&T",
  "CorrelationId":"2492c104-625a-49a4-845d-027d6fb32a11",
  "CountryCode":"us",
  "EventId":"",
  "EventName":"",
  "IngressTimestamp":"2018-07-25T03:24:10.19Z",
  "InstallId":"4f1bff37-6681-4541-a34b-7aaf583505b8",
  "IsTestMessage":"False",
  "LiveUpdateDeploymentKey":"None",
  "LiveUpdatePackageHash":"None",
  "LiveUpdateReleaseLabel":"None",
  "Locale":"en_US",
  "MessageId":"7a01c01e-115c-4411-b787-652751345386",
  "MessageType":"StartSessionLog",
  "Model":"iPhone10,6",
  "OemName":"Apple",
  "OsApiLevel":"None",
  "OsBuild":"15G77",
```

```
    "OsName":"iOS",
    "OsVersion":"11.4.1",
    "Properties":"",
    "ScreenSize":"2436x1125",
    "SdkName":"appcenter.ios",
    "SdkVersion":"1.7.1",
    "SessionId":"56d829e4-c563-4296-906e-428c145e3ac1",
    "Timestamp":"2018-07-25T03:24:06.188Z",
    "TimeZoneOffset":"-PT4H",
    "WrapperRuntimeVersion":"11.2.0",
    "WrapperSdkName":"appcenter.xamarin",
    "WrapperSdkVersion":"1.7.0"
  }
]
```

Summary

Congratulations! If you were able to hang with me through this chapter and go through all the above sections, you achieved a lot in this chapter. Let's reflect on what you learned before continuing further. You did the following:

- Set up the App Center SDK for analytics and crashes

- Set up custom events in the code

- Simulated a test crash in the code

- Set up multiple event handlers for App Center crashes to make the app experience friendlier for the user

- Set up continuous export of analytics and crashes to Azure

App Center provides a lot of features out of the box that you as a developer can leverage and make the app more robust and friendly for your users.

In the next chapter, you will go through the steps of setting up push notifications for your iOS and Android apps.

CHAPTER 5

Sending Push Notifications

Are you still excited to learn more about App Center? In the last chapter, you learned how to capture analytics and crash events from your users. In this chapter, you will get into more fun stuff. I will introduce you to the concept of push notifications.

Be aware that App Center is only one service provider out there that abstracts and automates the process of sending push notifications. When I say abstract, I mean it provides a consistent experience or look-and-feel, either with the UI or the API, over the individual platform notification providers. The other service out there that provides similar functionality is Azure Notification Hubs. Of course, you can always use Apple Push Notification Service (APNS) or Firebase Cloud Messaging separately. Although I will not contrast App Center Push with the other providers, just keep in mind that they exist and App Center providers a layer of abstraction above them so you as a developer can worry about simply sending a notification to App Center while App Center handles the communication with the other providers.

Here is what you will learn in this chapter:

- How to configure Apple Push Notification Service

- How to configure Firebase Cloud Messaging

- How to set up push notifications on Xamarin

- How to send push notifications

- How to handle push notifications

- How to define notification audiences

- How to send silent push notifications

217

© Sunny Mukherjee 2019
S. Mukherjee, *Learn Microsoft Visual Studio App Center*, https://doi.org/10.1007/978-1-4842-4382-4_5

- How to send custom data to your users

- How to summarize all concepts in a real-life example

- How to send the same real-life notification using the App Center API

Introducing Push Notifications

What are push notifications? Think of them as a way for a provider to broadcast or send messages directly to your device so you can interact with your users directly or alert your users of an event or news. Push notifications involve the following components:

- Company server

- Push notification service

- User's device

- App running on user's device

Typically, the life of a push notification starts from a company's server. The server generates a notification and the unique device identifiers. The push notification service receives the request. It broadcasts the notification to all the devices specified in the notification. If the app is installed on the user's device, the device receives the notification. If you are familiar with the Publisher-Subscriber design pattern, then you will recognize immediately that push notifications follow this pattern. In this pattern, you have a single publisher who publishes or broadcasts a message to all subscribers who are listening for messages. These messages are "pushed" in real time to the subscribers rather than the subscribers polling the publisher intermittently for new messages.

As of now, you have a sample app running on a physical device. All you need to do now is enable push notifications offered by both Apple Push Notification Service and Firebase Cloud Messaging for Android. I will show you how to connect App Center with these individual providers so you can send the notifications from a single portal instead of each provider separately.

In iOS, you can send and receive both local and remote notifications. What are local notifications? They are a feature in iOS to let apps communicate with other apps on a local physical device based on a set of conditions, such as the location or the time of day.

You might be thinking, "Why would one app talk to another app?" For example, you can have one app set reminder alerts for another app. Or you can trigger an alert to a user based on his/her location using GPS. Even though I will not cover local notifications in this chapter, I want you to be aware of this feature. This chapter is about remote notifications only.

You may be wondering, "When would I use a remote notification?" Here are some examples where remote push notifications are powerful:

- For a news app, you can send an alert when news is trending or breaking during the day or the week.

- For a shopping app, you can send an alert when a product goes on sale, when others are buying it, when a merchant offers a coupon, etc.

- For a finance app, you can send an alert when a transaction is posted to your credit card account, when a stock price changes, when funds are deposited to your savings account, etc.

Even within remote notifications, iOS provides two different types. One is user-facing where the user is alerted to a notification with an audible sound and a visual cue, such as a banner, toast, and/or a badge number on the app. For iOS users, a badge number is the number that you see on the top-right corner of the app icon when the app is minimized. The second is a silent remote notification that gives your service the ability to wake up your app running in the background and perform some action. The user may or may not be aware of this event, hence the name "silent."

In this chapter, for the purpose of learning with your sample GoGoGiphy app, first you will learn how to send test push notifications, then how to let your users interact with your notifications, and finally how to send silent notifications. You will wrap up by sending a more realistic example of a push notification by alerting the user when certain gifs are trending and popular among the community. You will send notifications to physical devices on each platform service.

You have a lot to cover in this chapter. Please feel free to explore one section at a time without taking in the entire chapter in a single stride. Let's begin!

Configuring the Apple Push Notification Service

You will begin be setting up your Apple Push Notification Service. Unsurprisingly, like Chapter 3 where you had more steps to follow with signing certificates and provisioning profiles in Apple, the Apple Push Notification (APN) service has more steps to configure than Firebase. I will start this section with APN.

1. Go to the Apple Developer portal. Go to Certificates, Identifiers, & Profiles. You should see the webpage shown in Figure 5-1. Click the Keys section. Click the + button to create a new key. Give the key a name and enable Apple Push Notification service, as shown in Figure 5-1.

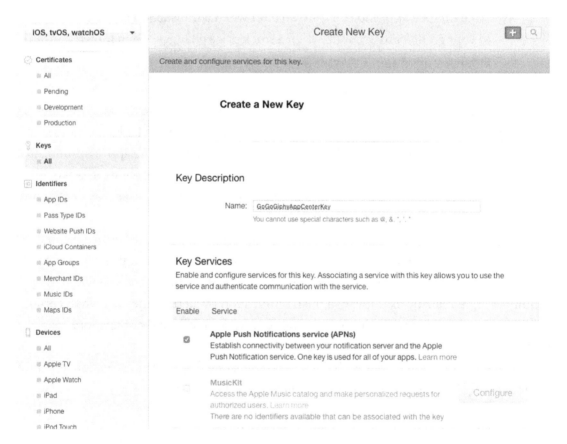

Figure 5-1. *Apple keys*

2. After clicking the Continue button and setting up the key, download the key and save it to your desktop, as shown in Figure 5-2. (I redacted the Key ID of course.)

Your key is ready.

Download and Back Up

After downloading your key, it cannot be re-downloaded as the server copy is removed. If you are not prepared to download your key at this time, click Done and download it at a later time. Be sure to save a backup of your key in a secure place.

Name: GoGoGiphyAppCenterKey

Key ID:

Services   Apple Push Notifications service (APNs)

Download

Figure 5-2. Key download

3. Open the key in a text editor, as shown in Figure 5-3. You will need to copy and paste the key in a later section when configuring push notifications on App Center.

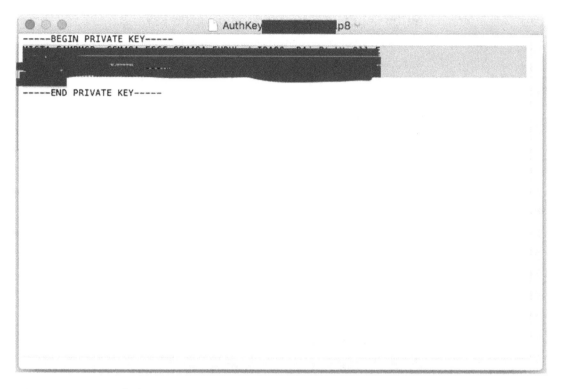

Figure 5-3. *Apple key*

    4.   You will see your new key listed in the Keys section, shown in Figure 5-4.

Figure 5-4. *Keys*

    5.   Now let's revisit the App ID in the Identifiers section. If you
          remember, you configured an App ID for the GoGoGiphy app and
          enabled push notifications. Refer to Figure 5-5.

Figure 5-5. *GoGoGiphy App ID*

6. Scroll down the webpage through the list of application services until you see push notifications. You will see it is set as Enabled but still Configurable, meaning you still need to configure it, as shown in Figure 5-6. Click the Create Certificate button under Development SSL Certificate. You will create a new push notification development certificate.

Push Notifications
● Configurable

Apple Push Notification service SSL Certificates
To configure push notifications for this iOS App ID, a Client SSL Certificate that allows your notification server to connect to the Apple Push Notification Service is required. Each iOS App ID requires its own Client SSL Certificate. Manage and generate your certificates below.

Development SSL Certificate	
Create an additional certificate to use for this App ID.	Create Certificate

Production SSL Certificate	
Create an additional certificate to use for this App ID.	Create Certificate

Figure 5-6. *Push notifications configuration*

You will repeat the same set of steps you performed in Chapter 3 when you configured your developer certificate by signing it with your certificate signing request (CSR) file. You should still have this CSR file saved on your desktop from Chapter 3.

1. If you need a refresher on how to create a CSR file, Apple gives you a set of instructions, shown in Figure 5-7.

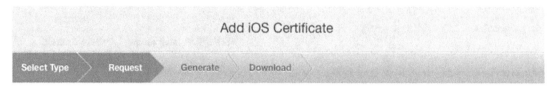

About Creating a Certificate Signing Request (CSR)

To manually generate a Certificate, you need a Certificate Signing Request (CSR) file from your Mac. To create a CSR file, follow the instructions below to create one using Keychain Access.

Create a CSR file.
In the Applications folder on your Mac, open the Utilities folder and launch Keychain Access.

Within the Keychain Access drop down menu, select Keychain Access > Certificate Assistant > Request a Certificate from a Certificate Authority.

- In the Certificate Information window, enter the following information:
    - In the User Email Address field, enter your email address.
    - In the Common Name field, create a name for your private key (e.g., John Doe Dev Key).
    - The CA Email Address field should be left empty.
    - In the "Request is" group, select the "Saved to disk" option.
- Click Continue within Keychain Access to complete the CSR generating process.

Figure 5-7. *CSR instructions*

2. Click the Continue button in Figure 5-7. The next page will ask you to locate the CSR file to sign the APNS developer certificate. Either click the Choose File button or drag the CSR file from your desktop to the webpage shown in Figure 5-8.

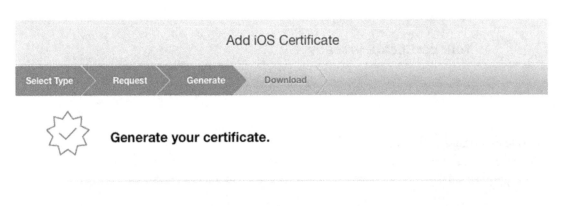

When your CSR file is created, a public and private key pair is automatically generated. Your private key is stored on your computer. On a Mac, it is stored in the login Keychain by default and can be viewed in the Keychain Access app under the "Keys" category. Your requested certificate is the public half of your key pair.

Upload CSR file.
Select .certSigningRequest file saved on your Mac.

Figure 5-8. *Signing the APNS certificate with CSR file*

3. Click the Continue button again. Your APNS developer certificate is now ready for use (Figure 5-9). You can download the certificate to your desktop if you want. It is only needed for APNS but not for App Center.

Your certificate is ready.

Download, Install and Backup

Download your certificate to your Mac, then double click the .cer file to install in Keychain Access. Make sure to save a backup copy of your private and public keys somewhere secure.

Documentation

For more information on using and managing your certificates read:

Create certificates

Figure 5-9. *APNS developer certificate*

4. Now you will complete the App Center configuration of APNS. Return to App Center. Go to the Push section and set up the APNS. At this step, you will copy the Key ID you set up in the Apple Developer portal and the Authentication Token you saved to your desktop. Refer to Figure 5-10 where all the fields are filled out and the Key ID and Authentication Token are redacted. Repeat the steps shown in Figure 5-10.

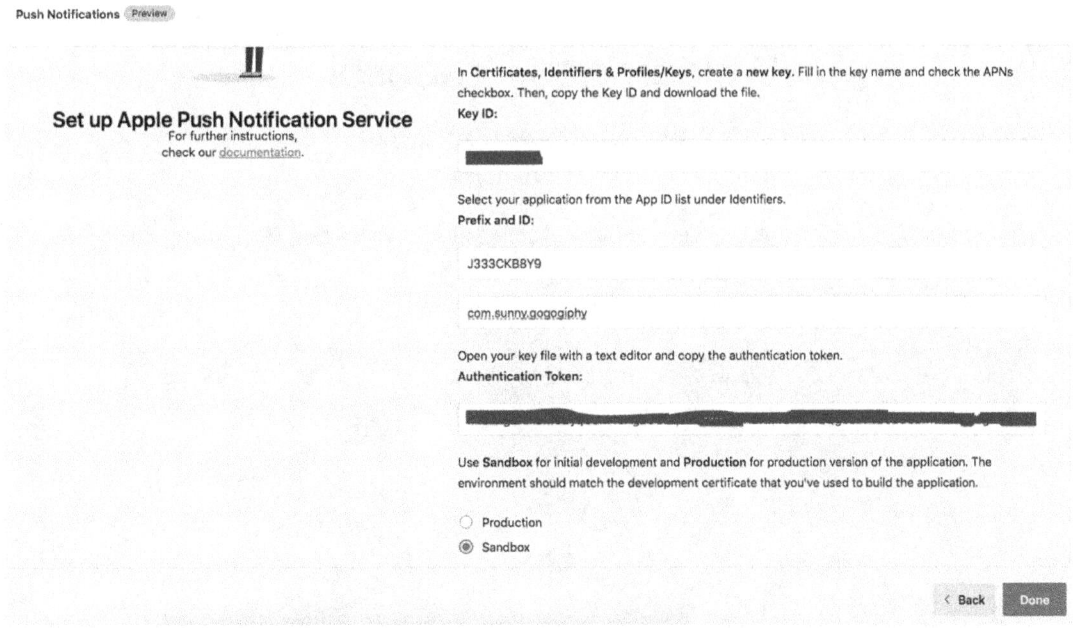

Push Notifications Preview

Set up Apple Push Notification Service
For further instructions,
check our documentation.

In **Certificates, Identifiers & Profiles/Keys**, create a new key. Fill in the key name and check the APNs checkbox. Then, copy the Key ID and download the file.
Key ID:

Select your application from the App ID list under Identifiers.
Prefix and ID:

J333CKB8Y9

com.sunny.gogogiphy

Open your key file with a text editor and copy the authentication token.
Authentication Token:

Use **Sandbox** for initial development and **Production** for production version of the application. The environment should match the development certificate that you've used to build the application.

○ Production
◉ Sandbox

‹ Back   Done

Figure 5-10. *Setting up the Apple push notification service*

Believe it or not, you have completed the most difficult part of this chapter. Everything is downhill from here. Now you will configure Firebase.

Configuring Firebase Cloud Messaging

In this section, you will configure Firebase Cloud Messaging so you can send push notifications to your Android devices. Just like the previous section, App Center will forward all notifications to Firebase, which will then forward these notifications to the registered devices.

1. Go to the following URL:

    ```
    https://console.firebase.google.com/
    ```

2. Sign in with your Google email address and password. You will see the Welcome Page shown in Figure 5-11.

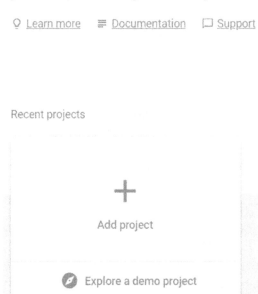

Figure 5-11. *Welcome page*

3. Click the + button to add a project. Refer to Figure 5-12. Enter a project name. Google will assign a Project ID automatically. Click the I accept checkbox to accept the terms and conditions. Click the Create project button.

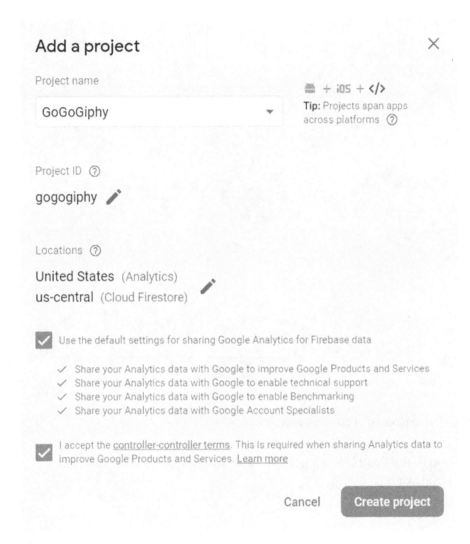

Figure 5-12. Adding a project

Your new project should now be ready, as shown in Figure 5-13.

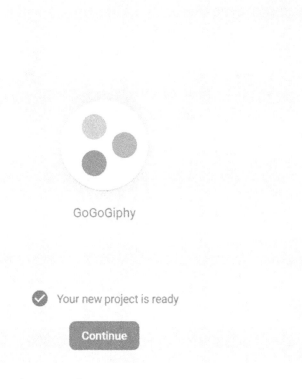

Figure 5-13. *Successful project creation*

4. Go to the Project Settings of your newly created project, shown in Figure 5-14.

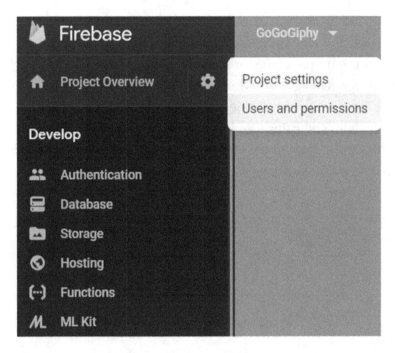

Figure 5-14. *Project settings*

5. Click the Cloud Messaging tab as shown in Figure 5-15. You will see the Server Key information that you will need when configuring the push notifications on App Center. (I redacted a part of my Server Key.) You will need the Sender ID when configuring the App Center Push SDK in your code.

Settings

General   **Cloud Messaging**   Integrations   Service accounts   Data privacy   Users and permissions

Project credentials

Add server key

Key	Token
Server key	AAAAQH1O7Dw:APA91bHqIGzs7dlAnE_jA7wq0gH9BTipmd85rxbEHmqQF5h0zxll-YbnhZNky_8iuXO3 Q7ax-hviX2G410eQduLb1W50W284fqqVSB_aKSfSw4I-kfrGR2uYd96CNYAKRU3z2TmmnR-s_3knxo2lv
Legacy server key ⑦	AIzaSyCJ_QfwXBmBpo1aVqebCzkcVBn_tlS2p2E
Sender ID ⑦	
276980231228	

Figure 5-15. *Project Settings*

6. Return to App Center. Go to the Push section for the Android app and begin the setup process. You should see the webpage shown in Figure 5-16. You can ignore the instructions given by App Center about integrating Firebase to your application because these instructions are pertinent for a Xamarin Android app since you are integrating Push Notifications for a Xamarin Forms Android app. The steps for a Xamarin Forms app are easier. Of course, if you are working on a Xamarin Android app, please feel free to follow the instructions shown below. Click the Next button.

Figure 5-16. *Setting up Firebase Cloud Messaging*

7. Now App Center will ask you for the Server Key from Firebase. Copy and paste the Server Key from Firebase into the textbox, as shown in Figure 5-17.

Figure 5-17. *Adding a Server Key*

That's it! You are done setting up push notifications for Firebase with App Center.

Setting Up Push Notifications on Xamarin

Now you will begin integrating the Push SDK with your Xamarin Forms sample app. The Push SDK is needed in order to register your sample app as the receiving or subscription point of the push notifications that App Center broadcasts using either the Key ID and authentication token with Apple PNS or the Server Key with Firebase.

The first step of the integration is to add the App Center Push NuGet package to all the relevant projects. Keep in mind that the sample app will have the NuGet packages installed already. All you need to do is update the existing packages. However, if you want to start from scratch, follow these steps:

- Open Visual Studio and the GoGoGiphy solution.

- Right-click the solution file and select the Manage NuGet Packages for Solution option.

- Search for microsoft.appcenter in the search bar.

- Click the relevant projects where the NuGet package will be installed. Your actions should be the same as Figure 5-18.

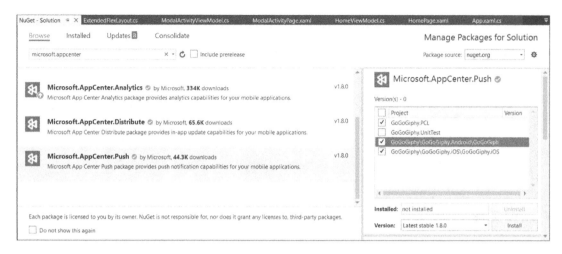

Figure 5-18. *Adding the Microsoft.AppCenter.Push NuGet package to projects*

If you prefer the command-line option, click the View menu ➤ Other windows ➤ Package Manager Console. Click the appropriate project from the combo-box and enter the following command (remember you have to repeat the following command for all the projects one by one as opposed to Figure 5-18):

```
Install-Package Microsoft.AppCenter.Push
```

After adding the NuGet package, add the SDK to your code. Open the `App.xaml.cs` file. Add the following reference to the top of the file:

```
using Microsoft.AppCenter.Push
```

Locate the SDK registration at the bottom of the `InitializeAppCenter()` function in the `App.xaml.cs`. Add the code highlighted in **bold** in Listing 5-1.

Listing 5-1. Add Caption

```
// Initialize AppCenter SDK
AppCenter.Start
(
      String.Format
      (
            "ios={0};android={1};"
            , Settings.AppCenterSecretiOS
            , Settings.AppCenterSecretAndroid
```

234

```
    )
    , typeof(Analytics)
    , typeof(Crashes)
    , typeof(Push)
);
```

Next, you need to enable the iOS project to enable push notifications. Open the `Entitlements.plist` file in the project. Click the Push Notifications section and check the Enable Push Notifications checkbox shown in Figure 5-19.

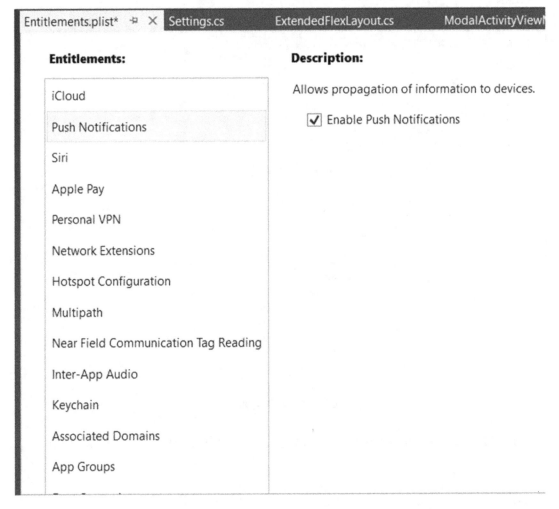

Figure 5-19. *Enabing push notifications for the iOS project in Entitlements.plist*

You need to repeat a similar set of steps for the Android project. Right-click the Android project and select Properties. Click Android Manifest. Scroll down the Required Permissions list or search for BROADCAST_WAP_PUSH and RECEIVE_WAP_PUSH permissions. Enable both of them (Figures 5-20 and 5-21).

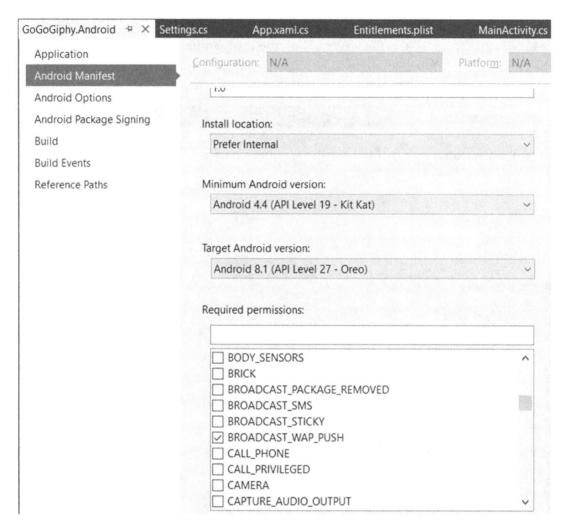

Figure 5-20. *Enabling the BROADCAST_WAP_PUSH permission in the Android project*

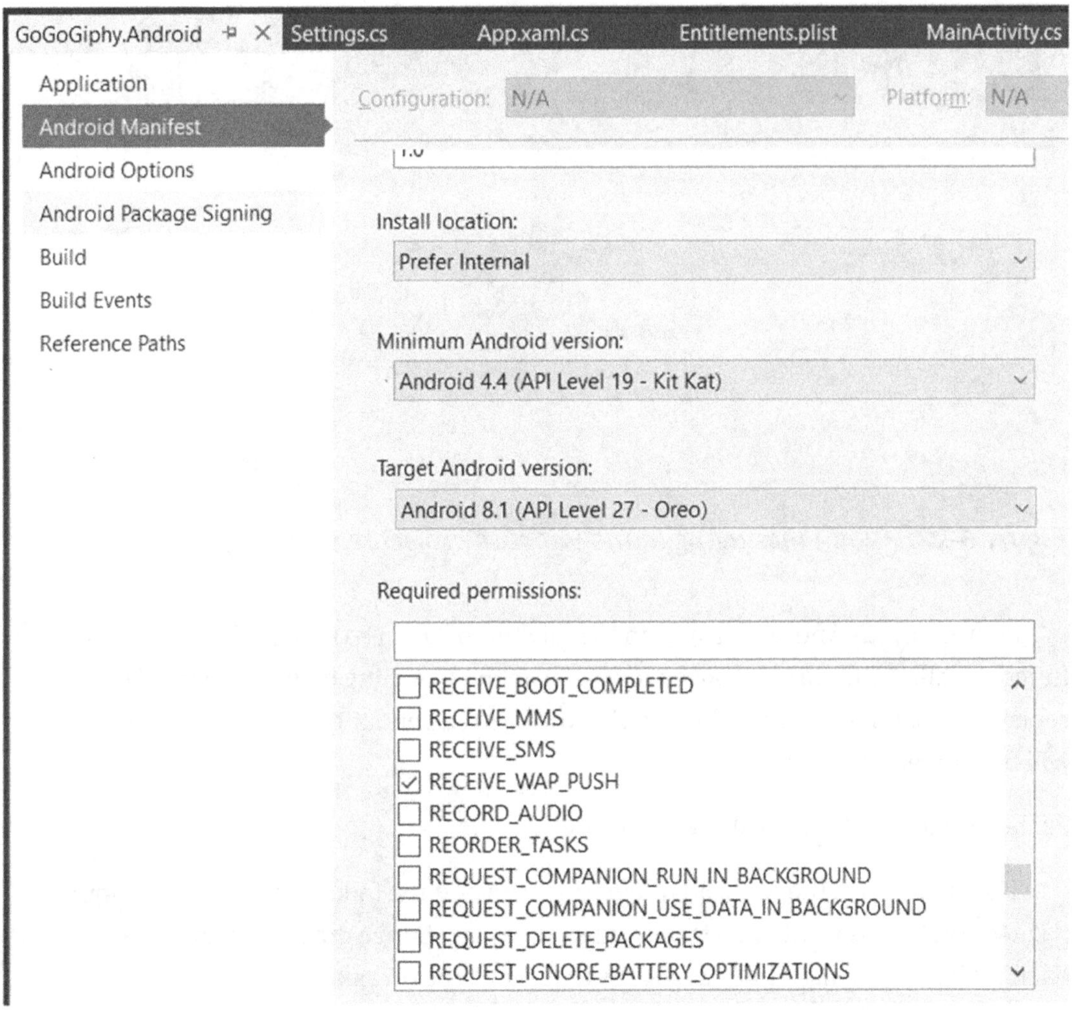

Figure 5-21. *Enabling the RECEIVE_WAP_PUSH permission in the Android project*

You now need to copy and paste the Sender ID from the Cloud Messaging tab in the Firebase project settings. Let's pause for a moment to think about what is happening underneath the hood. App Center uses the Server Key to forward the notifications from either the Web or the API to Firebase. Firebase uses the Sender ID to locate the appropriate project as the receiving point of the notifications. Since you are registering this Sender ID with the App Center Push SDK, this is how App Center knows how to collect the notifications from Firebase and forward them back to your Xamarin Forms app (Figure 5-22).

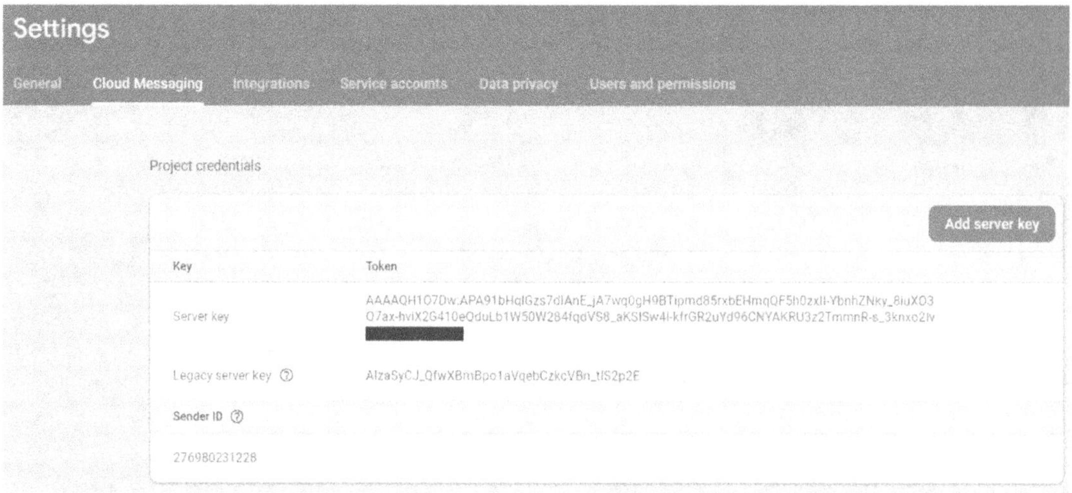

Figure 5-22. *Cloud messaging in the Firebase project settings*

Return to your Android project in Visual Studio. Open `MainActivity.cs`. Locate a function called `InitializeAppCenter()`. Paste the following code in there. Of course, replace the Sender ID shown below with your actual Sender ID from Firebase since it will be different than mine:

```
Push.SetSenderId("276980231228");
```

The final step of the Android integration is to add the following function to your `MainActivity` class. This step is needed in case you change the `launchMode` of the `MainActivity` to `singleTop`, `singleInstance`, or `singleTask`:

```
protected override void OnNewIntent(Intent intent)
{
    base.OnNewIntent(intent);
    Push.CheckLaunchedFromNotification(this, intent);
}
```

You have integrated the App Center Push SDK with both the iOS and Android projects.

Sending Push Notifications

Now you will utilize what you configured by sending your first test notification! Return to App Center, go to the iOS GoGoGiphy app, and the Push section. Click the Send notification button. You will see a panel slide out from the right.

Fill out the Campaign Name, Title, and Message fields, as shown on the left of Figure 5-23. Leave silent push disabled and no values entered in custom data. I will go over where and why silent push and custom data should be used in a later section. After filling out the relevant details, click the Next button.

In the second page of the Send Notification wizard, leave the default option of All registered devices selected because you are only sending push notifications to all registered developer devices connected to your provisioning profile.

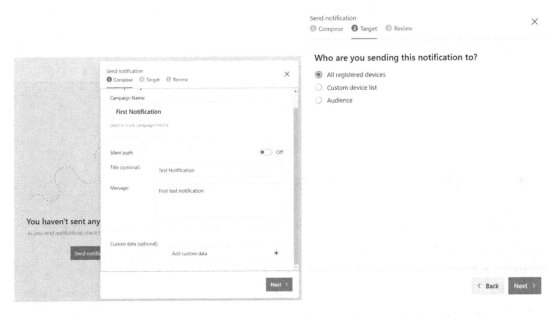

Figure 5-23. *The Send Notification wizard (first and second pages)*

Review the summary of changes in this push notification in the third page of the Send Notification wizard. Do NOT click the Send notification button yet (Figure 5-24). You have one more step to verify.

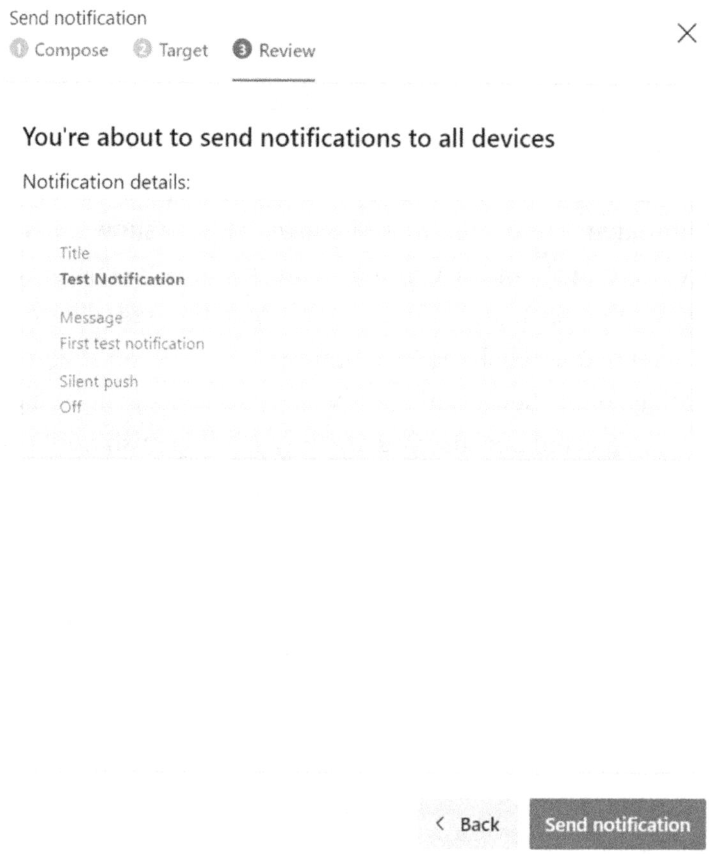

Send notification

① Compose   ② Target   ❸ Review   ✕

—————

You're about to send notifications to all devices

Notification details:

Title
Test Notification

Message
First test notification

Silent push
Off

⟨ Back   Send notification

Figure 5-24. *The Send Notification wizard (third page)*

If you were not prompted before, after installing the GoGoGiphy app on your iOS device from the email from App Center and after launching the app, you should see the prompt asking for your permission to allow it to send notifications, as shown in Figure 5-25. I show you how it appears on both my iPhone X and iPhone 6 Plus devices. Click the Allow button.

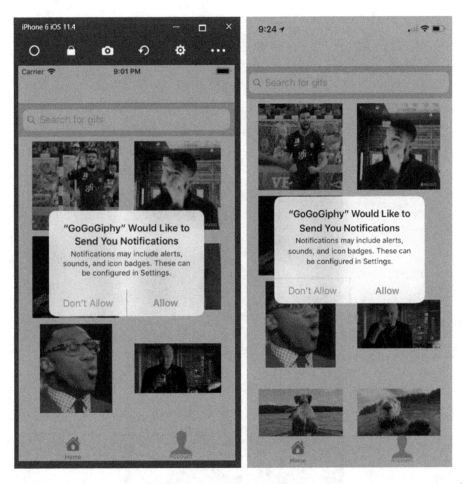

Figure 5-25. *Allow notifications prompt: iPhone X (left) and iPhone 6 Plus (right)*

Return to the third page in the Send Notification wizard and click the Send notification button. If your app is collapsed or not running, you will see your notification come through on you iOS device as shown in Figure 5-26.

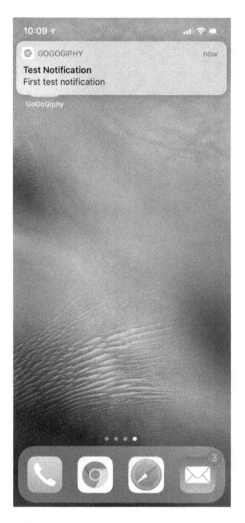

Figure 5-26. *iOS test notification*

Repeat the same set of steps on App Center to send a push notification to your Android device; the steps are identical in Android. Remember to go into your Android app and the Push section. If everything goes successfully, after launching the app on your Android device, your notification should appear similar to Figure 5-27.

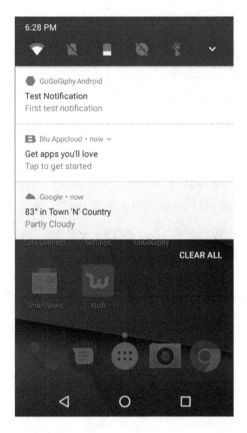

Figure 5-27. *Android test notification*

Up until now, you have configured APNS and Firebase and sent a test notification to your devices on both platforms. But you have not done anything interesting with this feature yet. You will get into the interesting stuff in the coming sections. But you need to configure a few more things and learn a few more concepts before you get there.

Handling Push Notifications

Push notifications are good on their own. But they are even more powerful if you let the user interact with the notification and handle this interaction in your code.

Reopen the `App.xaml.cs`. Locate the `InitializeAppCenter()` function. Add the code in Listing 5-2 to the bottom of the function but above the `App.Start(..)` call or the registration of the various App Center SDKs.

Listing 5-2. Add Caption

```
Push.PushNotificationReceived += (sender, e) =>
{
     Xamarin.Forms.Device.BeginInvokeOnMainThread(() =>
     {
          // Summarize the notification title and message.
          StringBuilder summary = new StringBuilder
               ("Push Notification Received \n\tNotification Title:
               " + e.Title + "\n\tMessage: " + e.Message);

          // If receiving custom data, add to the summary.
          if (e.CustomData != null)
          {
               summary.AppendLine("\nCustom Data:");

                    foreach(KeyValuePair<string, string> value in
                    e.CustomData)
                        {
                            summary.AppendLine("\t" + value.Key +
                            "\t" + value.Value);
                        }
          }

     Current.MainPage.DisplayAlert("Push Notification Received", summary.
     ToString(), "Ok");
     });
};
```

Let's evaluate what is happening in this code. The App Center Push SDK exposes an
event called PushNotificationReceived. You attach a delegate to this event. Inside this
delegate, you invoke BeginInvokeOnMainThread() to indicate that the code within the
enclosing block should execute on the Main UI thread. Then you build a StringBuilder
object with the Title, Message, and CustomData that was sent in the notification in the
Send Notification wizard. Even though you have not sent any custom data yet from App
Center, in the If block you iterate through the values in the e.CustomData dictionary and
appending the key-value pairs in the StringBuilder object on separate lines. You end
the enclosing block by calling DisplayAlert(..) and show the user the notification that
was received from App Center.

Of course, this is only test code. In a realistic app, you will not show a display alert to the user every time a notification is received. But this proves to you that the interaction between the user and the notification is working and it shows you the contents of the notification too.

After adding the above code, rebuild the solution and recommit your code. Wait for your continuous build to finish building. After getting the email from App Center, install and launch the app. Repeat the steps from Figures 5-23 and 5-24. If everything goes successfully, you will see the display alerts shown in Figure 5-28.

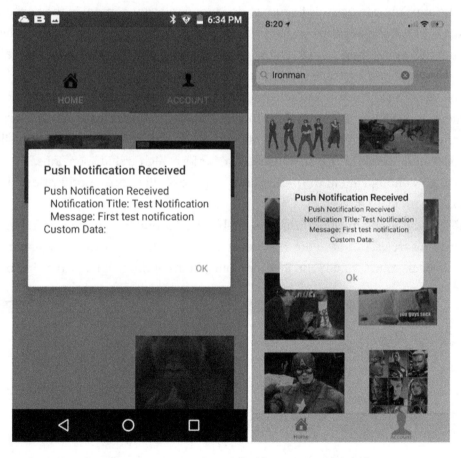

Figure 5-28. *Test notification in Android (left) and iOS (right)*

Sending Silent Push Notifications

Silent remote notifications are the second type of remote notifications, as mentioned in the introduction. This feature was introduced in iOS 7. Android accomplishes the same behavior by allow the app to not show the notification but instead handles the event of the notification. Consequently, this section will only cover the iOS project to show you specifically how to send silent push notifications.

What are silent notifications exactly? They are a powerful way for your service to wake up your app in the background without alerting the user and perform an operation within the app. You can use this feature to download relevant content in the background when the user is not using the app. When the user opens the app again, they receive the latest content without having to fetch the data from your servers, thus reducing waiting time and improving your user experience.

Upon receiving a silent background notification, iOS gives your app up to 30 seconds to do whatever is necessary in your app. During this time, for example, it can download relevant content from your server. Please do remember this limited time window when using silent push notifications because they are not meant to perform high-traffic operations.

Okay, now enough about the nature and purpose of silent push notifications. Let's get into the action already!

The first action you must perform is to enable remote notifications in your `Info.plist` file. Open the `Info.plist` file at the top level of the project. Open the Capabilities tab. Check the Enable Background Modes and Remote Notifications options, as shown in Figure 5-29.

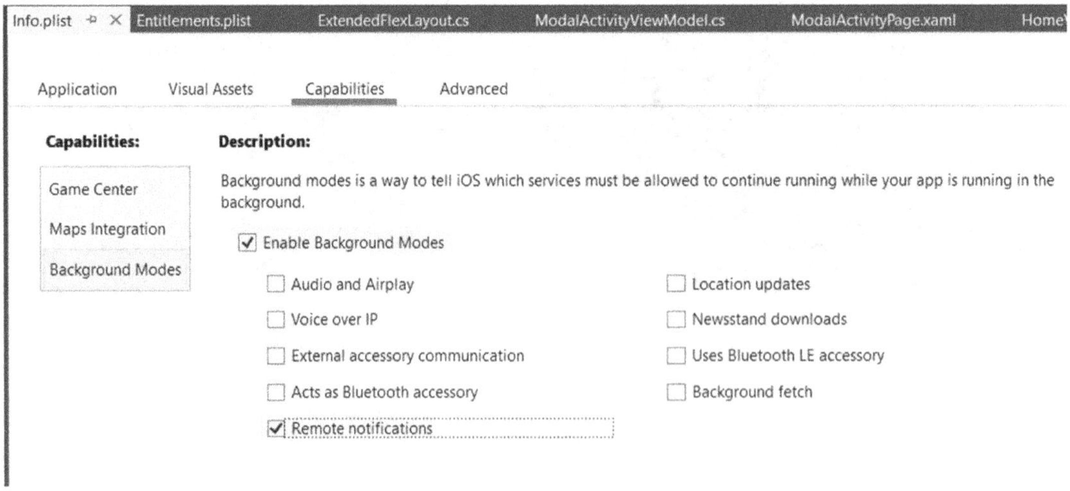

Figure 5-29. *Enabling background modes and remote notifications in Info.plist*

Next, you will perform a simple operation of setting the badge number of your app to 1 when it receives a silent notification. Fortunately, iOS exposes an event handler called DidReceiveRemoteNotification(..) that handles remote notifications specifically. You can read more about this handler at https://developer.apple.com/documentation/uikit/uiapplicationdelegate/1623013-application.

Keep in mind that remote notifications are handled in the same PushNotificationReceived handler of the App Center Push SDK. I just show an alternative, platform-specific way of handling the same event in the iOS class. You will remove the testing code in this event handler at the end of this section.

Now open the AppDelegate.cs. Copy and paste the code in Listing 5-3 into the class.

Listing 5-3. Add Caption

```
public override void DidReceiveRemoteNotification(UIApplication
application, NSDictionary userInfo, Action<UIBackgroundFetchResult>
completionHandler)
{
        UIApplication.SharedApplication.ApplicationIconBadgeNumber = 1;
}
```

Save and build the project. Commit your changes to the master branch. Wait for the build to finish. Install the app again from the App Center email before moving further ahead in this section.

Now return to App Center and go to the Push section. Click the Send Notification button again. At this time, enable the Silent Push toggle button, as shown in Figure 5-30. Notice how Title and Message become optional settings in this pane. Do NOT enter any values; leave them blank. Otherwise, it will not be a silent push and it will not trigger the above event handler. In fact, it will transform into a normal, user-facing remote notification so the user will get alerted by the notification.

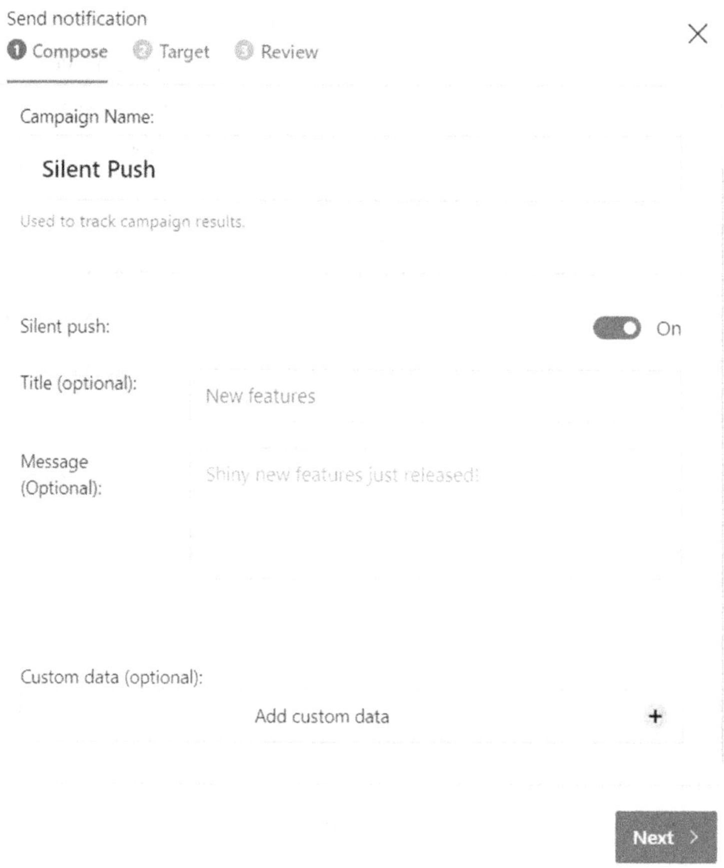

Send notification

① Compose   ② Target   ③ Review   ✕

Campaign Name:

Silent Push

Used to track campaign results.

Silent push: ⬤◯ On

Title (optional):   New features

Message
(Optional):   Shiny new features just released!

Custom data (optional):

Add custom data   +

Next >

Figure 5-30. *Sending a silent push remote notification*

Click the Next button shown in Figure 5-30. If you coded everything correctly, you should now see the badge number of your app set to number 1. Congratulations! You just sent your first test silent notification.

Before moving ahead, you must keep a few things in mind about silent push notifications. APNS declares a JSON key called `content-available` and sets it to 1 as part of the JSON payload sent from the server. This alerts your app that content is available for download. But the simple act of enabling silent push on the App Center panel is the equivalent of setting `content-available` to 1, thus making it unnecessary to include this value in the Custom Data payload. If you use the App Center API and not the website and if you want to send a silent remote notification, then you need to set `content-available` to 1. Later you will explore some useful key-value pairs you can send in the Custom Data payload.

> **Note**   One very important fact about testing with silent remote notifications is that they only work when the app is running in the background or foreground. **Running** is the keyword here. Do **not** force quit your app. When you force quit the app and send a silent notification, your app will never get the event.

Before moving on to the next section, return to the DidReceiveRemoteNotification(..) handler and remove the code within since it was only testing code. You can leave an empty function stub in there for future use.

Defining Notification Audiences

This section is fairly short. You will go through the steps of defining an audience for a push notification and then sending a notification to that audience. First, you need to understand when and why to use audiences. Audiences become powerful when you want to target specific users of your app based on their location, device type, language, etc. You can find more information at https://docs.microsoft.com/en-us/appcenter/push/audiences.

For example, you may want to send push notifications to your users based on their region (country or language) or you may want to send custom notifications based on users who use a certain type of device (device model or screen size).

Return to App Center and click the Audiences link, shown in Figure 5-31.

Figure 5-31.   *Push audiences*

Click the New Audience button. Mimic the settings shown in Figure 5-32. Since both of my iOS devices are registered in the United States, my audience is both of my devices. That is the reason why it says "You're targeting 100% of your users." In a realistic scenario, if I had more devices to test with, this would be a smaller percentage. If you are located in another region of the world, replace the country value with the name of your country in the filter. Click the Save button when finished.

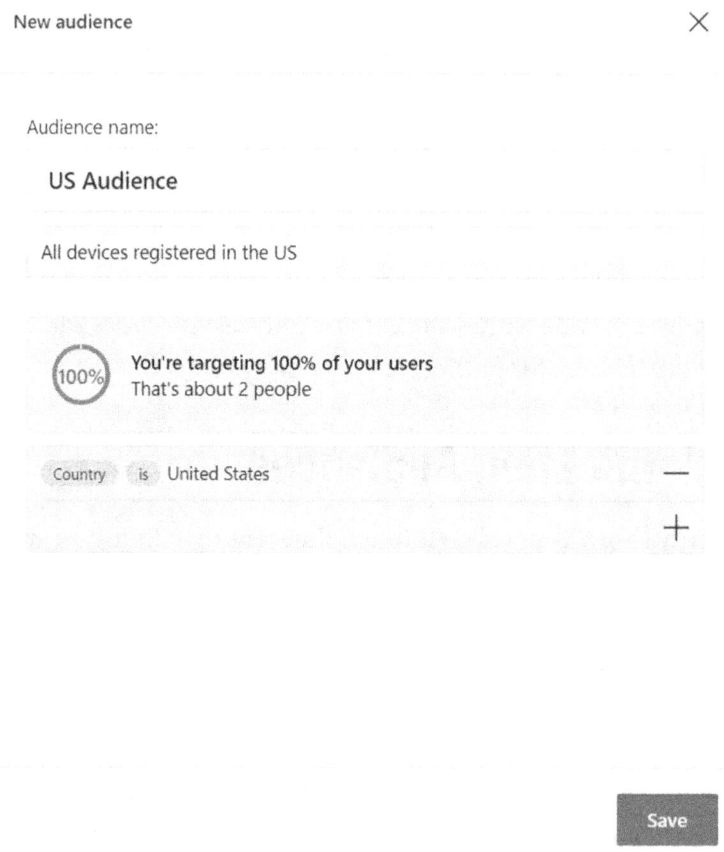

New audience   ✕

Audience name:

US Audience

All devices registered in the US

(100%) **You're targeting 100% of your users**
        That's about 2 people

Country   is   United States   —

                                                                 +

Save

Figure 5-32. *New Audience panel*

Return to the Push section and repeat the steps you followed in the previous section to send a test notification. On the Target page of the Send Notification wizard, you selected the All registered devices option up until now. Click the Audience option and select US Audience or the audience that you defined for your country (Figure 5-33). Click Next and you should still see your test notification come through because you are part of your own audience.

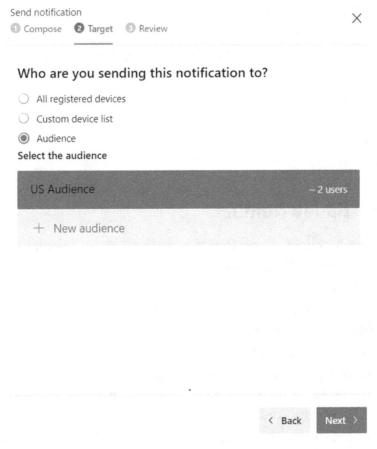

Figure 5-33. *Target page of the Send Notification wizard*

Sending Custom Data

In this section, you will quickly run through the individual topics and test each feature
at a time from App Center. You will wrap everything together in a realistic scenario at the
end of this chapter.

If you remember when you pasted the code into the PushNotificationReceived
handler in App.xaml.cs, the code had an If condition that checked for the CustomData.
What is custom data exactly? And when and why should it be used?

Custom data is a way for App Center to customize the push notification for additional
functionality like setting the application badge number or playing a sound. For example,
you may want to set the application badge number on a silent remote notification so the
user knows notifications are waiting for the user. Or you may want to play a sound for

a more important notification. In addition, you can even send your own custom data as long as it does not conflict with one of the keywords from iOS or Android. At the end of the day, the custom data collection is nothing but a collection of key-value pairs in a JSON payload.

You can read more about using custom data for Xamarin Forms at `https://docs.microsoft.com/en-us/appcenter/sdk/push/xamarin-forms#custom-data-in-your-notifications`.

Let's get started.

Setting the Badge Number

In an earlier section, you already set the platform-specific way of setting the badge number. In this section, I will show you how to set the badge number to any number you wish instead of simply incrementing by 1. Why would you need to do this? For example, if you are making a news app and if you want to push 10 silent notifications to your reader in the background, you can alert your user that you have 10 unread news notifications waiting for your reader to read. In iOS, if you set the badge number to 0, it will clear the badge number and not display anything.

Before you set the badge number from App Center, you need to give your app the ability to reset the badge number to 0 when the user opens it (thus clearing the notifications). iOS exposes an event handler called `OnActivated(..)` that you can leverage for this purpose. Open the `AppDelegate.cs` file. Paste the code in Listing 5-4 into it. As you can see, the code is simple and sets the `ApplicationIconBadgeNumber` property to 0.

Listing 5-4. Add Caption

```
public override void OnActivated(UIApplication uiApplication)
{
     UIApplication.SharedApplication.ApplicationIconBadgeNumber = 0;

     base.OnActivated(uiApplication);
}
```

Now return to the Push section in App Center. Set the properties to match those in Figure 5-34. Notice the inclusion of a key called badge with a value of 1 in the custom data collection. Click Next. You should see the badge number on the app icon shown on the right.

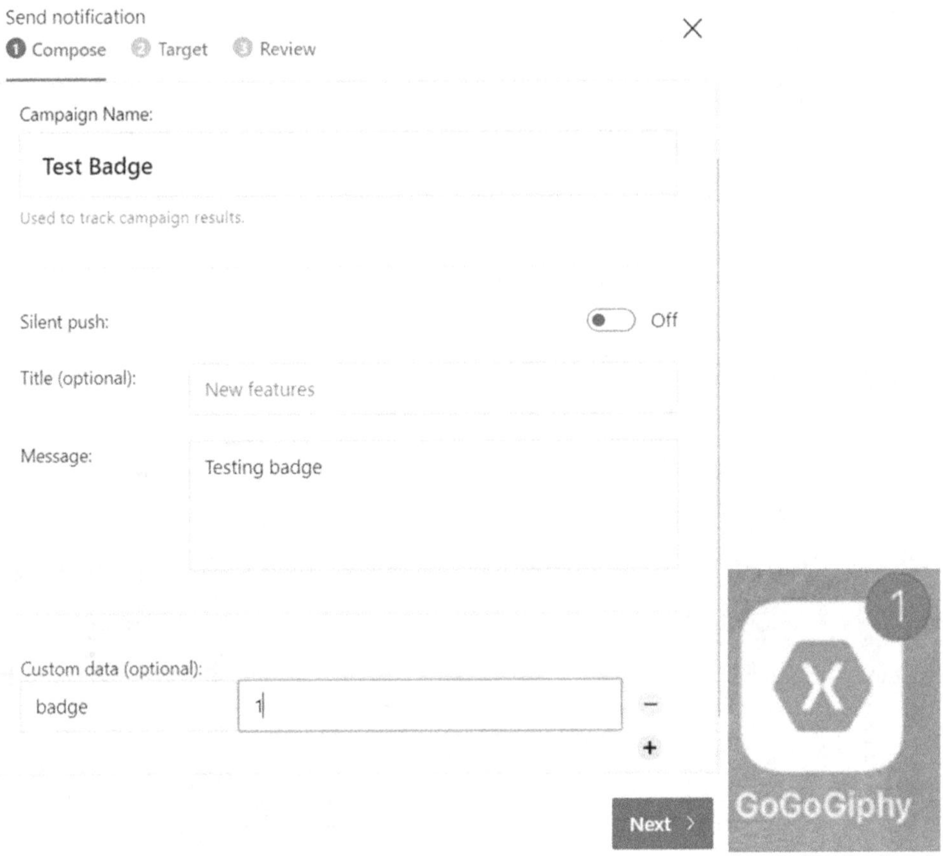

Send notification

① Compose   ② Target   ③ Review   ✕

Campaign Name:

Test Badge

Used to track campaign results.

Silent push: (●⎯) Off

Title (optional):   New features

Message: Testing badge

Custom data (optional):
    badge | 1 | —
                                      +

                              Next ›

Figure 5-34. *Setting the badge number to 1*

Now let's set the same badge number to an amazingly high number, like 9999, but this time you will send a silent notification. This mimics a situation where you send a number of notifications since the user last opened the app, such as in a news app.

Open the Send Notification Panel again. Match the settings in Figure 5-35 and click Next. You should see the badge number on the app icon shown on the right.

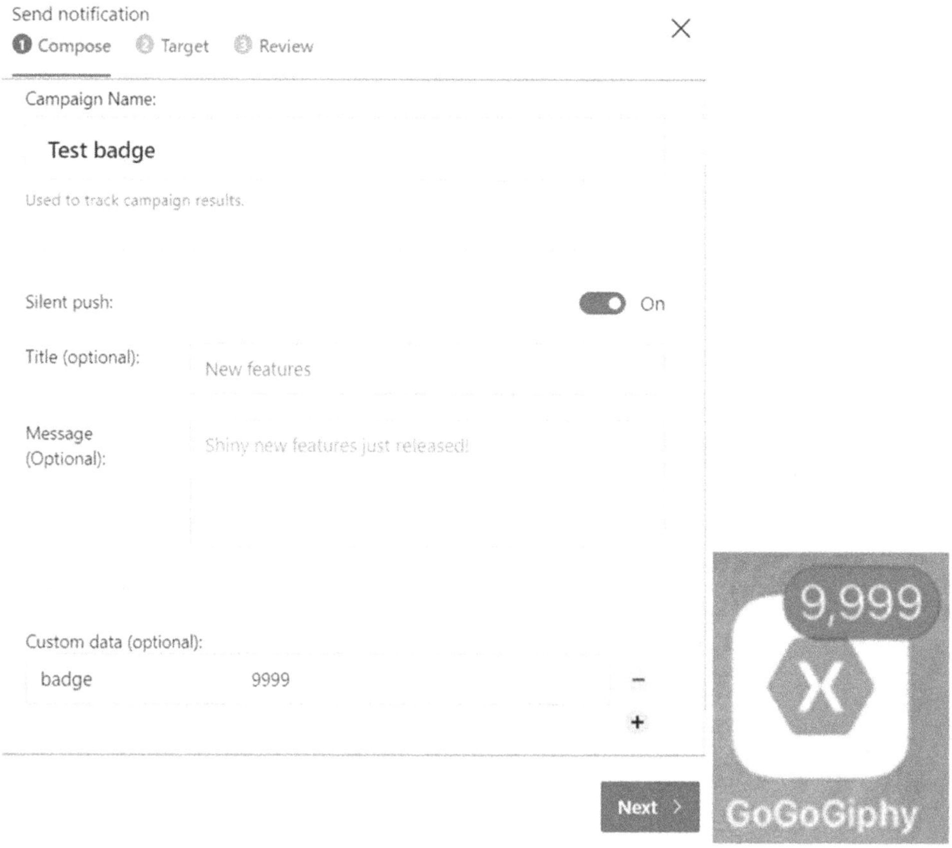

Figure 5-35. *Setting the badge number to 9999 with a silent notification*

Playing a Sound

In this section, you will play a sound to alert the user that a notification was received. You will play the default system sound. You have the ability to play your own custom sound, but that is beyond the scope of this chapter. You can read more about using your own sound file in the custom data at https://docs.microsoft.com/en-us/appcenter/push/#custom-data-in-your-notifications.

Open the Push section and the Send Notification panel again. Copy the settings in Figure 5-36. Notice the addition of a sound property to the custom data with a value of default. Click Next. You should see the visual notification and hear the system sound.

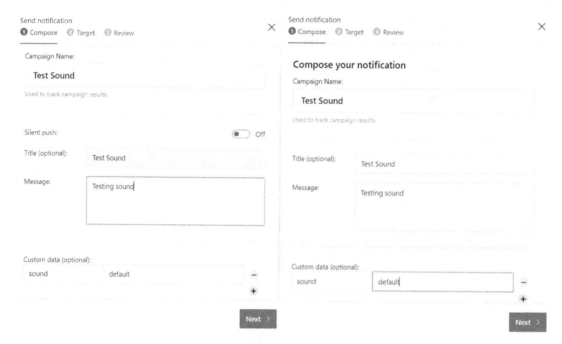

Figure 5-36. *Testing a sound on iOS (left) and Android (right)*

You can repeat the same sound alert with a silent notification on iOS only, as shown in Figure 5-37.

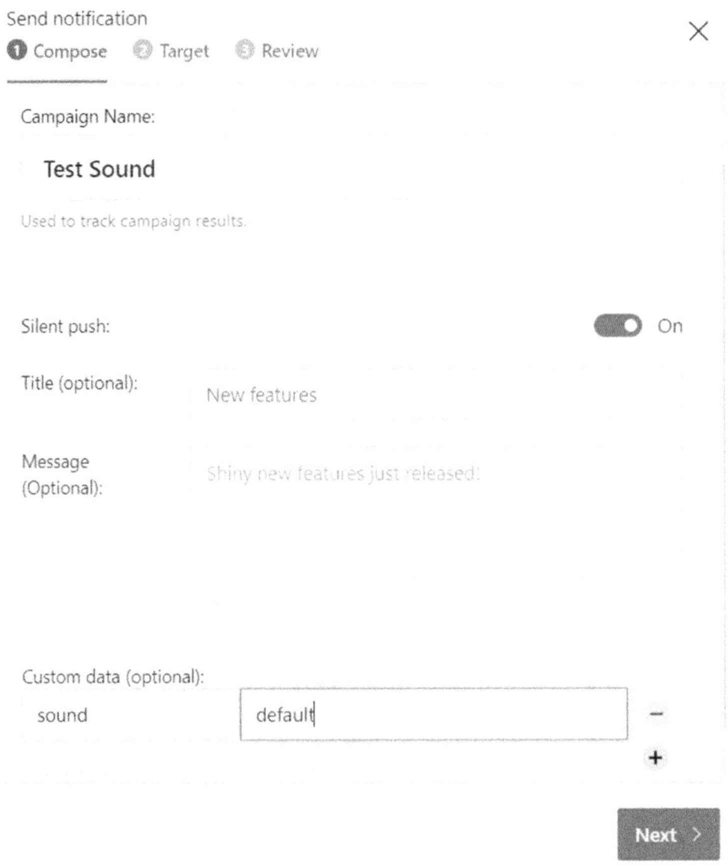

Figure 5-37. *Testing a sound with a silent notification*

Full Example

In this section, you will combine all the concepts you learned in the previous sections and utilize them in a realistic example. In the real-life scenario, you will send a user-facing notification alerting the user that certain gifs are trending among the community. When the user clicks the notification, it will perform a search for the trending gifs as if the user was searching in the app itself. Finally, you will repeat the same action by initiating a background search when the user is not using the app by utilizing a silent remote notification. Let's begin!

Your first code change will be to add a function in the GiphyService class to communicate with the Giphy Service. Open GiphyService.cs. Add the code in Listing 5-5.

Listing 5-5. Add Caption

```
internal async Task<Giphy> SearchGifsAsync(string searchText)
{
     Giphy giphy = new Giphy();

     try
     {
          if(!String.IsNullOrEmpty(searchText))
          {
                    string searchUrl = String.Format(Settings.
                    SearchUrl, Settings.ApiKey, searchText, Settings.
                    LimitCount, Settings.Rating);

               HttpResponseMessage responseMessage = httpClient.
               GetAsync(searchUrl).Result;
               string jsonString = responseMessage.Content.
               ReadAsStringAsync().Result;
               giphy = JsonConvert.DeserializeObject<Giphy>(jsonString);

          }
     }
     catch (Exception exception)
     {

     }

     return giphy;
}
```

Let's review what is happening in this code. It is instantiating a new Giphy model object. It checks if the searchText parameter is empty or null. It formats the searchUrl string based on the ApiKey from the Settings class, the searchText parameter, the LimitCount property, and the Rating property. It makes a call using the HttpClient class and passes in the searchUrl string. It receives a responseMessage back from this call, from which it reads the JSON string. It finally deserializes the JSON string into the Giphy class.

You will now make use of this SearchGifsAsync(..) function in the HomeViewModel class to populate the TrendingImages collection.

Add the Search(..) function in Listing 5-6 to HomeViewModel.

Listing 5-6. Add Caption

```
private void Search(string searchText)
{
       Analytics.TrackEvent("Search: " + searchText);

       try
       {
             GiphyServiceObj = GiphyService.GetInstance();

             Giphy = GiphyServiceObj.SearchGifsAsync(searchText).Result;

             if (Giphy != null)
             {
                           TrendingImages.Clear();

                    foreach (Datum datum in Giphy.Data)
                    {
                         TrendingImages.Add(datum);
                    }
             }
       }
       catch (Exception exception)
       {

       }
}
```

Let's review what is happening above. The code makes a call to the App Center
Analytics SDK to call the TrackEvent(..) function to log what users are searching
manually for from the search bar or when App Center pushes a notification down to
the app. Next, it calls the SearchGifsAsync(..) function you created to get the Giphy
object. If the Giphy object is already set, it clears the TrendingImages collection and
iterates through the data collection in the Giphy object to add them one at a time to the
TrendingImages collection. Remember that this TrendingImages collection is bound to
the ExtendedFlexLayout control in HomePage.xaml.

Verify that the SearchCommand has the implementation to call the Search(..)
function. If it does not, add the code in Listing 5-7.

Listing 5-7. Add Caption

```
public ICommand SearchCommand => _searchCommand ??
 (
      _searchCommand = new Command<string>
      (
          (text) =>
          {
                  var searchEvent = new Dictionary<string, string>
              {
                  {"SearchString", text }
              };

              //Crashes.GenerateTestCrash();
              Search(text);
          }
      )
 );
```

Next, you need the ability to handle the custom search string in your PushNotificationReceived event handler. See Listing 5-8.

Listing 5-8. Add Caption

```
Push.PushNotificationReceived += (sender, e) =>
{
    Xamarin.Forms.Device.BeginInvokeOnMainThread(() =>
      {
          // Summarize the notification title and message.
          StringBuilder summary = new StringBuilder
          ("Push Notification Received \n\tNotification Title:
           " + e.Title + "\n\tMessage: " + e.Message);

          bool isContentAvailable = false;
          string searchText = String.Empty;

          // If receiving custom data, add to the summary.
          if (e.CustomData != null)
          {
```

```
            summary.AppendLine("\nCustom Data:");

foreach(KeyValuePair<string, string> value in
e.CustomData)
{
    summary.AppendLine("\t" + value.Key + "\t" +
    value.Value);

     switch(value.Key)
     {
         case "content-available":

         isContentAvailable = Convert.
         ToBoolean(value.Value);
                 break;

         case "SearchText":

                 searchText = value.Value;
                 break;
     }
}

if (!String.IsNullOrEmpty(searchText))
{
    FreshBasePageModel freshBasePageModel =
    GetCurrentPageModel();

    if (freshBasePageModel is HomeViewModel)
     {
         HomeViewModel homeViewModel =
         freshBasePageModel as HomeViewModel;
         homeViewModel.SearchCommand.
         Execute(searchText);
     }
}
}
```

```
        //Current.MainPage.DisplayAlert("Push Notification Received",
        summary.ToString(), "Ok");
    });
};
```

Let's review what is happening above. (I will only explain what is happening in code that is highlighted above.) Remember that your CustomData collection is simply a key-value collection formatted in JSON. You will send a key-value pair from App Center titled SearchText eventually. The code iterates through the collection until it sees two keys, one named content-available and the other named SearchText. The code saves the value when the key value is SearchText. It verifies if the value of searchText is neither null nor empty, gets the current page model, casts it as a HomeViewModel, and calls the SearchCommand with the searchText parameter, which invokes the Search(..) function you defined above. This code effectively repeats what happens when a user searches for a string in the search bar and allows App Center to pass in a SearchText key and value.

Finally, verify that the XAML in HomePage.xaml is coded properly. This code should be available from when you cloned the repository. Just in case, verify that the code is the same as shown in Listing 5-9. I highlight the line of code where the binding is set between the TrendingImages collection and the ExtendedFlexLayout control.

Listing 5-9. Add Caption

```
<ScrollView Orientation="Vertical">

    <controls:ExtendedFlexLayout x:Name="TrendingImagesPanel"
        Direction="Row"
            Wrap="Wrap"
        JustifyContent="SpaceEvenly"
        ItemsSource="{Binding Path=TrendingImages, Mode=TwoWay}"
        >
        <controls:ExtendedFlexLayout.ItemTemplate>
                <DataTemplate>
                <forms:CachedImage HorizontalOptions="Center"
                    VerticalOptions="Center"
                    DownsampleToViewSize="True"
                    HeightRequest="150"
                    WidthRequest="150"
```

```
                            Margin="2"
                            Source="{Binding Path=Images.Original.
                            Url, Converter={StaticResource
                            Key=UrlToPathConverter}}"
                >
                    <forms:CachedImage.GestureRecognizers>
                        <TapGestureRecognizer
                                Command="{Binding
                                Path=TappedCommand}"
                                 CommandParameter="{Binding
                                 Path=.}"
                                 Tapped="TapGestureRecognizer_
                                 Tapped"
                                 NumberOfTapsRequired="1"
                        />
                    </forms:CachedImage.GestureRecognizers>
                </forms:CachedImage>
            </DataTemplate>
        </controls:ExtendedFlexLayout.ItemTemplate>
    </controls:ExtendedFlexLayout>
</ScrollView>
```

Rebuild the solution. Run the app locally on the iOS and Android simulators. On the home page, type any popular search string in the search bar. You should see the home page populate based on your search.

Commit and push your code to the repository. Next, you will test your new search feature from a remote push notification. Return to App Center, go to the iOS app, and go to the Push section. Click the Send Notification button. I will show the results of the iOS app below and not the Android app because the steps in App Center are identical.

Keep in mind the user will see the visual notification. Since Marvel superheroes are all the rage at the time of this writing, you will use Hulk (one of my favorite characters) as your first trending notification. Mimic the settings in Figure 5-38 to send your first user-facing notification. Add the sound key with the value of default to get the user's attention when the notification comes in. Click the Next button. Choose the US Audience option or the country you defined earlier. Send the notification.

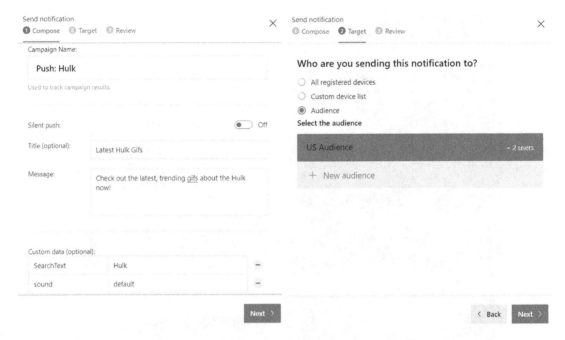

Figure 5-38. *Sending a push notification: SearchText as Hulk and sound as default (left) and target page selecting US audience (right)*

If you coded everything correctly above, you should see the notification in Figure 5-39. After clicking the notification, you should see the collection populate with gifs about the Hulk.

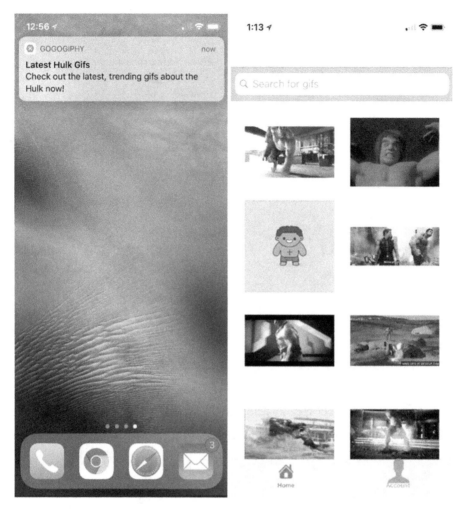

Figure 5-39. *Notification: Hulk (left) and results (right)*

Now keep the app running. Do **NOT** force quit the app. You can leave the app running in the foreground or the background. You will send a silent notification with a SearchText value of Spiderman Homecoming, a film about my other favorite Marvel character. Mimic the settings in Figure 5-40 in App Center. Enable silent push and leave the Title and Message fields blank. And add a badge key with a value of 1 to alert the user that a silent notification was sent if the user had the app collapsed or running in the background. Click Next. Select the US Audience option or your country audience in the Target page. Click Next again to send the silent notification (Figure 5-41).

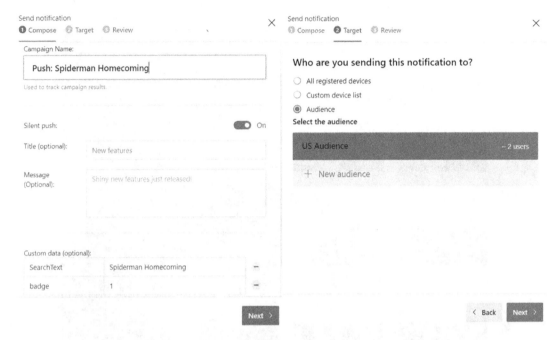

Figure 5-40. *Silent notification: SearchText as Spiderman Homecoming and badge as 1 (left) and target page selecting US audience (right)*

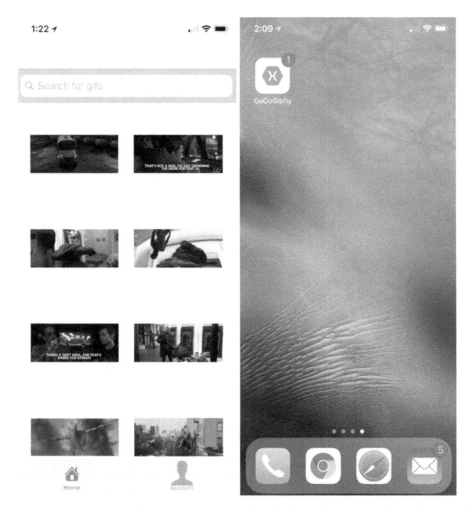

Figure 5-41. *Spiderman homecoming results (left) and app with badge number (right)*

Congratulations! If you coded everything correctly and followed the steps exactly above, you now have the basic workings of an app integrated with App Center to use push notifications in a real-life scenario.

Automating Notifications with API

You might be wondering by now, "Do I have to come into the UI every time I want to send a notification to my users?" Of course not! That is where the App Center API comes in. The API sends all traffic in JSON format, so the Web UI is simply abstracting that layer for you. If you remember from Chapter 4, you used the App Center API in order to get the retention period of how long App Center would retain your analytics and crash data. App Center has a similar API endpoint for push. The Push API can be found at `https://openapi.appcenter.ms/#/push`.

You will only touch upon the API that sends notifications using the POST Http verb:

`https://openapi.appcenter.ms/#/push/Push_Send`

Your first action is to verify if you created an API token in the first place. You should already have an API token in place from when you used it in Chapter 4. But if you skipped that section, please refer back to Chapter 4 on how to create an API token. The API token will be visible at the page shown in Figure 5-42. You can click New API Token if you have not created one yet. Remember to save the API token to a safe place because it only displayed once.

Figure 5-42. *App Center API token*

Next, you must authorize your API to use the token from the previous chapter. Click the Lock icon on the far right on the API after going to `https://openapi.appcenter.ms/#/push/Push_Send`.

After authorizing the API, copy the settings exactly as shown in Figure 5-43. I highlighted the owner_name and the app_name values because they need to be pasted from the Settings of the app. If you forgot how to do it, refer back to Chapter 4 for a refresher. I use the iOS app for the app_name below.

Figure 5-43. *App Center Push_Send API*

The code in the JSON payload is shown in Listing 5-10 so it is easier to read. Let's review what is happening. You set the name of the Push Notification Campaign to `API Push: Ironman`, set the title of the notification to `Check out new Ironman gifs`, set the body of the message to `New Ironman gifs trending online now!`, and set the sound, badge number, and the SearchText keys in the Custom Data collection. The best part about this approach is that you can save this code, repeat it for different custom notifications, and automate the whole process!

Listing 5-10. Add Caption

```
{
  "notification_content": {
    "name": "API Push: Ironman",
    "title": "Check out new Ironman gifs",
    "body": "New Ironman gifs trending online now!",
    "custom_data" : {"sound" : "default", "badge" : "1", "SearchText" : "Ironman"}
  }
}
```

If you want to try out the custom audience that you had set up to send notifications only to within your country, replace the JSON code with code in Listing 5-11. Notice the addition of the notification_target with its values in the payload.

Listing 5-11. Add Caption

```
{
  "notification_target" : {
    "type" : "audiences_target",
    "audiences" : ["US Audience"]
  },
  "notification_content": {
    "name": "API Push: Ironman",
    "title": "Check out new Ironman gifs",
    "body": "New Ironman gifs trending online now!",
    "custom_data" : {"sound" : "default", "badge" : "1", "SearchText" : "Ironman"}
  }
}
```

If you set up everything correctly, you will see a Code 202 response message back from the server indicating that the notification sent request was received successfully (Figure 5-44).

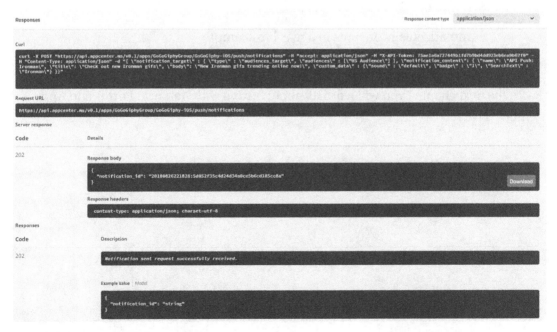

Figure 5-44. *App Center API server response*

And you should have received a notification on your iOS or Android device, depending on the app_name you chose.

Summary

If you followed along through the course of the entire chapter, bravo on a remarkable accomplishment in learning about push notifications using App Center! Here is a quick summary of everything you learned and your accomplishments:

- Configured Apple Push Notification Service

- Configured Firebase Cloud Messaging

- Set up push notifications on Xamarin

- Sent a first test and handled push notifications

- Defined notification audiences

- Learned about the differences between silent and user-facing notifications

- Sent and handled silent push notifications

- Sent custom data to your users

- Summarized all concepts in a real-life example

- Sent the same real-life notification using the App Center API

In the next chapter, you will learn all about testing with Xamarin Forms and App Center.

CHAPTER 6

Running Tests

You are now into the home stretch of this book. If you have kept up with me thus far, you should have set up push notifications for both iOS and Android builds in the last chapter. In this chapter, I will show you how to run UI tests and view the results on actual physical devices in the cloud!

Are you excited yet? You should be because this chapter is not just about UI testing; it is about saving you money! If you are single developer creating an app or an enterprise with a team of developers and testers, after designing, developing, and distributing your app, every developer or team will reach the last phase of the DevOps cycle: testing.

Nevertheless, I do want to make one point clear before jumping into this chapter. I am not going to sugar-coat the challenges lying ahead for you. This chapter by far is the most difficult chapter in this entire book. Be prepared to configure a lot of settings—and try and fail multiple times. To be honest, I did not keep count, but I think I may have tried and failed close to 100 times before I got the UI tests to work successfully for the first time! Don't worry. We will get through this chapter together. Be mentally prepared for multiple trials and mistakes, but hopefully, my repeated trials and mistakes with UI testing will save you from several hours of trying the wrong things.

Here is what you will learn in this chapter:

- How to configure projects for Xamarin.UITest

- How to set up device sets in App Center

- How to configure the CLI command in the post-build script

- How to use App Center variables

- How to set up post-build scripts to run in App Center

- How to save the access token into an environment variable

- How to get the UITest command template

271

© Sunny Mukherjee 2019
S. Mukherjee, *Learn Microsoft Visual Studio App Center*, https://doi.org/10.1007/978-1-4842-4382-4_6

- How to configure the iOS `UITest` command to test in App Center

- How to configure the Android `UITest` command to test in App Center

- How to run UI tests asynchronously in App Center

- How to use REPL to make writing UI tests easier

Why Choose App Center for UI Testing?

The ultimate goals of any mobile developer are user adoption and user retention of an app. You want your app to appeal to your market audience, and you want your users to keep using your app. How can you know for sure that your app will work and behave as expected on hundreds of devices and dozens of form factors in the market? As a single developer or a team, you only have three choices for UI testing.

- Door #1: Test on simulators. Publish it to the app stores, and hope that it works on every configuration out there.

- Door #2: Buy the most common or popular devices on the market currently and test on those devices before publishing. If it works on the best devices, hope that it works on older devices.

- Door #3: Pick a cloud provider like App Center that maintains almost every possible phone on the market and stays current and relevant with upcoming phones and operating system releases. Even though a cloud provider will charge you a monthly fee, it will save you money in the long run because you do not have to keep buying phones. And you can be confident these UI tests are run on actual physical devices and not just simulators.

It should be fairly obvious what door should be the least risky and least expensive for you, but I will break down the logic for you. If you pick door #1, you cannot know with 100% certainty if your app will behave as expected on every phone and every phone factor. If you risk it and your app misbehaves, you risk the chance that one errant UI design like a button too small for pressing or a panel not showing will give your users a bad experience. Bad experience means bad reviews and fewer downloads. Bad reviews can be a death sentence for a mobile app. Door #1 is a foolish choice.

Door #2 is viable but not a wise choice either because it is expensive to own and manage multiple physical phones. In order to develop the app I wrote for this book, I personally own two iPhones, an Android and an iPad Mini. Clearly, I could not possibly purchase every device, especially Android devices, which is why I had to rely on App Center to test on most flavors of Android on the market now. And do not forget you will rack up costs because phone devices go obsolete quickly because manufacturers release new phones into the market constantly.

Door #3 is the clear and logical choice here. Just look at how much power you get from a single website:

- Pick and choose phones across years, operating systems, or physical form factors and organize them into device sets.

- See your test runs on clear and beautiful dashboards.

- See actual screenshots of your app running on physical devices in the cloud.

- View test results and logs to understand where and why your app failed on a device.

Before you dive in to the actual configuration and UI testing, let's get a couple of important concepts out of the way.

Pricing

Let's get the bad news out of the way first. Nothing is free forever! Microsoft wants to give you a taste of how App Center UI testing works. You get unlimited free tests on a single concurrency for the first 30 days, meaning you can run UI tests on one device at a time, so go wild with as many UI tests as you want during this time. Hopefully, if you follow my instructions in this chapter, you can shave off a significant number of repeated attempts to get it working right, thus giving you more of the trial period to write your own UI tests.

Let's cover the pricing briefly. All of the pricing and billing information is in the App Center site itself. Go to the GoGoGiphy organization, click Manage, and click Billing on the left. Your webpage should look similar to Figure 6-1. Keep in mind the page itself may change since App Center updates the site often.

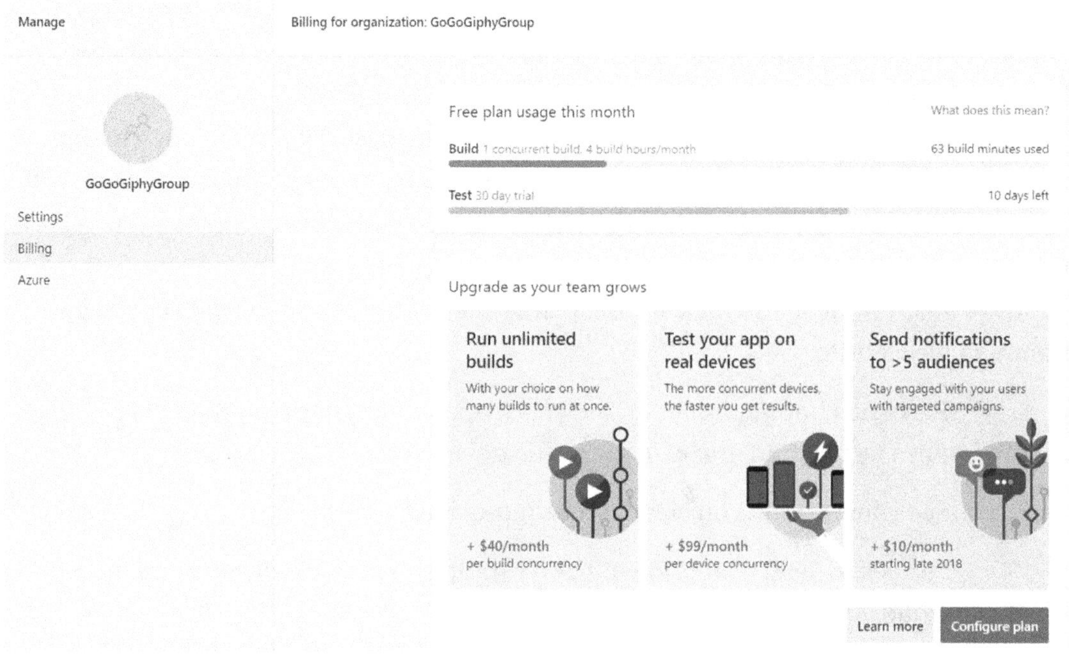

Figure 6-1. *Billing and pricing information*

You can click the Learn more button, which will take you to the Pricing site. Please read through the FAQs before committing to any of the subscription plans because they do provide useful information.

Here is how the pricing model works. Basically, after your 30-day free trial period expires, Microsoft will bill you based on your hourly usage of UI testing on actual devices. I will use a simple example to explain. If you run a 10-minute suite of UI tests on three iPhone devices and three Android devices, your consumption will be 60 minutes (1 hour).

$$10 \text{ X } (3 + 3) = 60 \text{ minutes}$$

Microsoft will not bill you based on time spent downloading your app, taking screenshots, or generating test reports. Billed time is actual time spent running your test suites.

You can visit the sites below to learn more about pricing. These pages have more information on how Microsoft bills you if you want to use concurrent builds.

```
https://docs.microsoft.com/en-us/appcenter/general/pricing
https://visualstudio.microsoft.com/app-center/pricing/
```

Migration

Several important events occurred in 2018. If you were a Xamarin mobile developer before 2018, you may have used Xamarin's important services and applications as part of your DevOps pipeline, such as Xamarin Test Cloud and the Xamarin Test Recorder. After Microsoft's acquisition of Xamarin, the company slowly integrated Test Cloud into App Center so now it longer exists on its own. It is all part of the App Center ecosystem of services. In fact, if any of your former apps hit `https://testcloud.xamarin.com/`, you will get redirected to the App Center site. This migration includes all calls to the Test Cloud CLI because those calls will now get rerouted to the App Center CLI. And this migration includes migration of all existing data in Test Cloud into App Center.

On a sad note, Microsoft discontinued development and support for Xamarin Test Recorder, including the Visual Studio extension on Windows. If you remember what this extension was about, it watched and recorded all your actions on the app so you could paste them as actions for your UI tests. This app made the process of creating UI tests effortless. As one of the most loved tools among Xamarin developers, it is also one of the most missed. App Center does provide another tool called Repl, which I will cover later in this chapter. Honestly, if you ask me, it does not do justice to Test Recorder because Test Recorder was easier to use since it offered a GUI. But don't get me wrong. The Repl tool is handy tool in its own right because you can still do most of the operations of Test Recorder, just through a console interface.

You can read more about Microsoft's events and important notices about their migration from older frameworks to App Center at `https://docs.microsoft.com/en-us/appcenter/migration/test-cloud/`.

Configuring Projects for Xamarin.UITest

As mentioned at the start, this book is not about teaching you how to write a Xamarin app. Similarly, this chapter is not about teaching you how to write UI tests. You should have a basic understanding of UI testing coming into this chapter.

Keep in mind that App Center supports a number of test frameworks for running tests. Here is a list of the supported test frameworks:

- Appium

- Espresso

- Calabash (future deprecation)

- Xamarin.UITest

- XCUITest

Please visit `https://docs.microsoft.com/en-us/appcenter/test-cloud/preparing-for-upload/` to learn more about each framework.

Testing on every framework gets redundant and is out of scope for this chapter, so I will show you how to write, integrate, and run UI tests using the Xamarin UITest framework.

Furthermore, if you are coming from another mobile development background like React Native, Cordova, or Unity, even though this book is about App Center using Xamarin Forms, I will show you the steps to run UI tests using the App Center CLI. Developers from other platforms should get value from this chapter because the CLI commands are identical on every platform.

Since you have been following along using the sample app from my GitHub repository, refer to the GoGoGiphy.UITest project in the Visual Studio solution. This project has multiple sample UI tests and some tests that you will run in App Center.

Installing the Necessary NuGet Packages

The first action you must perform is to install the Xamarin.UITest NuGet package for the GoGoGiphy.UITest project. Since you pulled the source code from the repository, these references should already be set up for you. But in the event that you set up your own test project, it is important to know the basic steps.

- Right-click the project and select Manage NuGet Packages.

- Go to Browse and search for Xamarin.UITest. Install the package.

- Return to Browse, search for NUnit, and install version **2.6.4**, since at the time of this writing, version 2.6.4 is the latest version of NUnit that is compatible with Xamarin.UITest. If you install a later version of NUnit, your UI tests in later sections will fail because Xamarin.UITest will ask for this version. In the future, the Xamarin team may update Xamarin.UITest to reference a later version of NUnit.

- Return to Browse, search for NUnitTestAdapter, and install the latest version.

- Your NuGet packages and their versions should be similar to Figure 6-2.

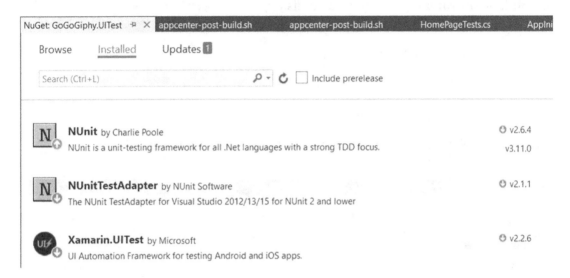

Figure 6-2. *NuGet packages*

Or if you prefer doing the same actions from the command line, open the Package Manager Console and run the following commands with their specified versions:

```
Install-Package NUnit -Version 2.6.4
Install-Package NUnitTestAdapter -Version 2.1.1
Install-Package Xamarin.UITest -Version 2.2.6
```

Setting Up Android

You need to disable the Use Shared Runtime setting in Android before running tests. What is this setting? This setting and its child setting, Use Fast Deployment, help manage and optimize the application size when deploying a Debug version of the app. A Debug version of the app deploys two large packages, Shared Runtime and Shared Platform, to the physical device. This setting allows you to deploy the Shared Runtime package once and every subsequent Debug version of the app reuses the package. In summary, it speeds up your deployment. You can find more information about this setting at https://docs. microsoft.com/en-us/xamarin/android/deploy-test/app-package-size.

But if this setting is enabled when the code is committed before running the Android build in App Center, it will prevent any UI tests from running. Therefore, you need to disable it before running any Android builds.

Follow these steps:

- Right-click the Android project.

- Go to Properties.

- Go to the Android Options tab.

- Unselect the Use Shared Runtime option, as shown in Figure 6-3.

Figure 6-3. *Disabling the Use Shared Runtime option in Android properties*

You can find more information about this setting at `https://docs.microsoft.com/en-us/appcenter/test-cloud/preparing-for-upload/uitest`.

Setting Up iOS

Setting up your iOS project is a little more involved than with Android. The first step is to download and install the Xamarin Test Cloud NuGet package. The Test Cloud agent runs an HTTP server that exposes the iOS user interface so you can interact with it from your UI tests.

Follow these steps in iOS:

- Right-click the iOS project and select Manage NuGet Packages.

- Go to Browse, search for Xamarin.TestCloud.Agent, and install the latest version.

Your installed NuGet package should appear like Figure 6-4.

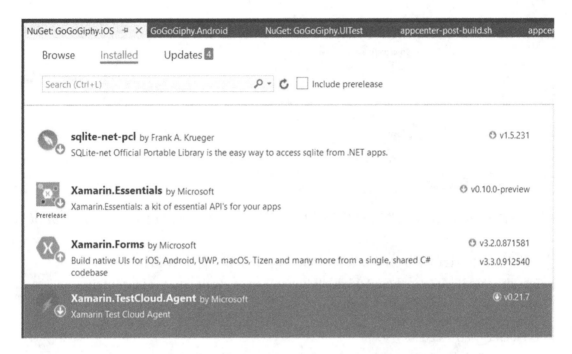

Figure 6-4. *Xamarin.TestCloud.Agent NuGet package*

Or you can install the package from the Package Manager Console as follows:

```
Install-Package Xamarin.TestCloud.Agent -Version 0.21.7
```

The second step is to add a new conditional compilation symbol named ENABLE_
TEST_CLOUD in the Build properties for the iOS project. This symbol instructs the iOS
project to look for this additional symbol during the build when it creates the .IPA
artifact according to the active build configuration. You will launch the Test Cloud Agent
in the next section. You want to encapsulate this launching code within a condition so it
only launches the agent for a debug build and not a release build.

Follow these steps:

- Right-click iOS project.

- Go to Properties.

- Go to Build tab.

- Add ENABLE_TEST_CLOUD to the end of the text in the compilation
  symbols textbox, as shown in Figure 6-5.

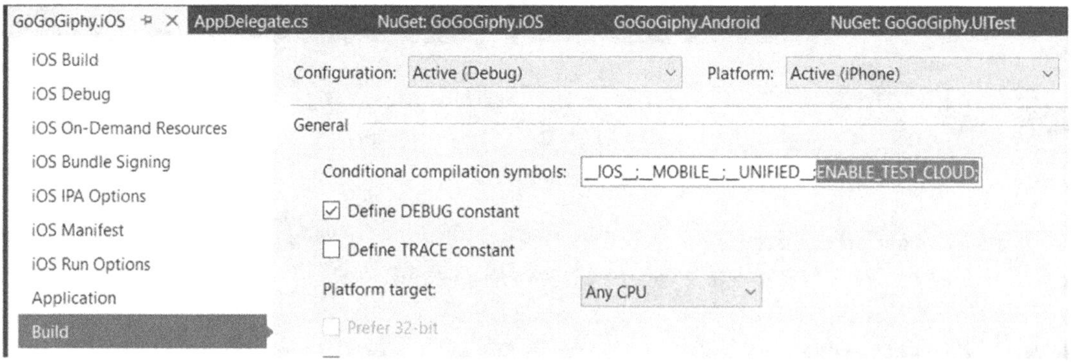

Figure 6-5. *Adding the ENABLE_TEST_CLOUD conditional compilation symbol*

The last step is to launch the Test Cloud Agent in the `AppDelegate` class before the app itself launches. Add the following code section to the start of the `FinishedLaunching(..)` function in the `AppDelegate.cs` file:

```
#if ENABLE_TEST_CLOUD
  Xamarin.Calabash.Start();
#endif
```

The conditional compilation symbol ensures that the Test Cloud Agent only launches for Debug builds. The Test Cloud Agent only works on apps that are signed with a development provisioning profile. When running a UI test on your iOS app in App Center, the service will use one of their preexisting development provisioning profiles to sign your app before running. The above `#if` statement ensures that the Test Cloud Agent will launch when an App Center provisioning profile is used to sign your app before running a UI test.

> **Note**   Remember that you cannot execute and run UI tests locally on Windows using the iOS Simulator. But you can run them locally on a Mac. From a Windows machine, you need to upload your UI tests to App Center to run your iOS tests. The best workflow tip is to run your Android tests locally on Windows against the Android simulator, upload your tests, run both Android and iOS builds in App Center, and verify that your iOS tests run as expected. The UI tests themselves will be identical for both platforms. The only difference is the attributes you apply to each UI test function to differentiate between the platforms. You will see this attribute later.

Installing the App Center CLI Locally

This section is not a mandatory section to run your UI tests. It is optional because you will run your UI tests using build scripts in App Center servers later in this chapter, but the commands are the same CLI commands described in this section. However, your UI tests will not work locally against App Center because the UI test commands use path references on the server and not your local system.

But this section is important because the CLI gives you the ability to query and execute multiple actions in App Center from a terminal window and not logging into the website. If you ever want to automate App Center from a PowerShell script or a .NET application, CLI is the answer. At the time of this writing, not all services that you can perform on the website are supported on the CLI, but the App Center team is adding more and more commands to the CLI all the time, which is part of the reason why I devote a small section to this topic.

You can read more about the CLI documentation and its commands at `https://github.com/Microsoft/appcenter-cli` and `https://docs.microsoft.com/en-us/appcenter/cli/index`.

Follow these steps to get the CLI installed on your local system:

- Verify you have Node.js 8+ installed from Chapter 1. Remember to install Version 8.0 or higher. If not, please download and install the latest version from `https://nodejs.org/en/`.

- After installing NodeJS, use the following command to install the AppCenter CLI locally:

  npm install -g appcenter-cli

Setting Up Device Sets in App Center

App Center lets you set up your own device sets where you can organize what devices your tests will run on. For example, one device set may be called Tier 1 and it may contain the most recently released phones on the market. A device set called iPhoneX may include all the iPhone X devices and the separate iOS versions. Remember to name them something descriptive. At the time of this writing, iPhone X was the biggest cat in the jungle in the Apple family of phone products.

Now you will learn how to set up a device set for iPhone X phones (Figure 6-6).

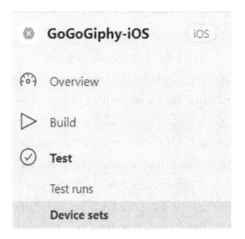

Figure 6-6. *Test device sets*

Enter a name for the device set. Search for iPhone x in the search bar (Figure 6-7).

Figure 6-7. *New device set*

Note that App Center does a wonderful job of giving you the same device but running different iOS versions, as shown in Figure 6-8.

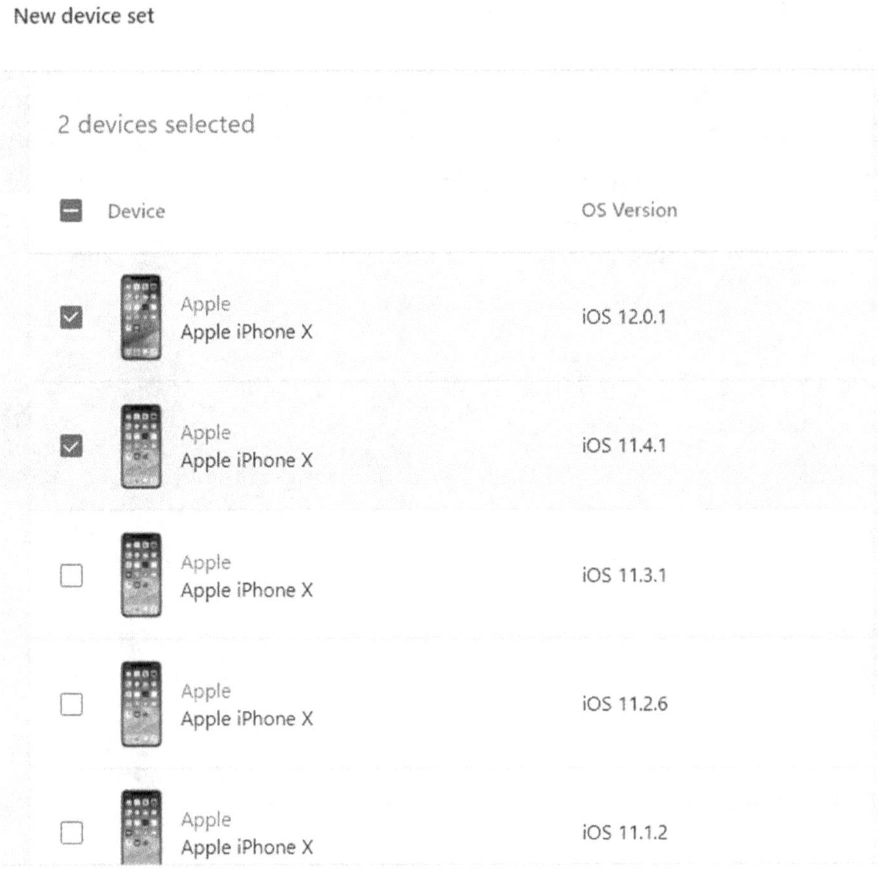

New device set

Figure 6-8. *Selecting devices in a device set*

Select the latest two OS versions of the iPhone X. iOS 12.0.1 and 11.4.1 were the latest two OS versions at the time of this writing. Click the New Device Set button at the bottom right. You should then see your new device set (Figure 6-9).

Figure 6-9. *New device set for iOS*

In Figure 6-9, you can see another device set for iPhone 8 devices. I will leave it to you set one up for yourself.

Now let's set up a device set for Android. Figure 6-10 shows the setting of a name, searching for pixel 3, finding two devices matching the search, and selecting both devices. Note that I use the latest device using the latest Android version here, which is Android 9 at the time of this writing.

Figure 6-10. *Selecting Android devices*

Your new device set should appear like Figure 6-11.

Figure 6-11. *New device set for Android*

You can see the complete list of supported physical devices at `https://docs.`
`microsoft.com/en-us/appcenter/test-cloud/devices`.

About App Center Variables

As mentioned, the App Center CLI commands will run within Bash scripts on the App
Center server. The commands will be included in the post-build script because you want
the UI tests to run after the projects have been built.

The first important concept to understand before writing any CLI commands in your
post-builds scripts is the concept of App Center variables because these variables will
expose network locations on the App Center server. Fortunately, the App Center team
has created these variables to utilize in your Bash or PowerShell script files. The most
relevant App Center variables are the following:

`APPCENTER_SOURCE_DIRECTORY:`	Location of the source code on the build machine
`APPCENTER_OUTPUT_DIRECTORY:`	Location where the build results are stored

App Center provides more system variables that you can read about at
`https://docs.microsoft.com/en-us/appcenter/build/custom/scripts/#app-`
`center-variables`.

Setting Up Post-Build Scripts

Let's learn a few things about build scripts first before jumping into them. App Center gives you the option of providing three different Bash scripts:

- Post-clone: This script runs after the code repository is cloned but before the build runs

- Pre-build: This script runs before the build starts but after dependencies like NuGet packages are installed

- Post-build: This script runs after the build finishes and the artifacts are copied to the output folder

You can find more information about build scripts at `https://docs.microsoft.com/en-us/appcenter/build/custom/scripts/`.

Microsoft also maintains a public GitHub repository offering helpful examples of build scripts at `https://github.com/Microsoft/appcenter-build-scripts-examples`.

For the purpose of UI testing, you will set up two post-build scripts, one for iOS and one for Android. You will return later to these scripts and enter your commands to run in App Center, recommit, and repeat. Trust me. You will find yourself testing these commands repeatedly to see the output in App Center.

Keep in mind that the commands in these scripts are written in the Bash language. Don't worry if you do not know Bash because the commands that you will use in this chapter are simple and easy to follow.

Open the Start sub-folder in your Git folder. Open the solution file in Visual Studio. In the Solution Explorer, you will find two files replicated in two places, one in the root location and the second in the Android project. The first file is called `appcenter-post-clone.rename` for the Post-Clone script and the second file is named `appcenter-post-build.rename` for the Post-Build script. Later in this chapter, you will rename the file extension to "`.sh`" so App Center can recognize the Bash script.

If you want to understand the steps involved in creating the build scripts from scratch, create two files with the name of `appcenter-post-build.sh` because App Center looks for a file with this name. Paste in the commands in Listing 6-1. These three commands basically list the contents of each folder recursively, hence the `-R` parameter and the path to the folder. As a result, they will display the contents of the parent folder, list every child folder, display the contents of each child folder, and so on. The `echo` command simply outputs the string message to the output window.

Listing 6-1. Add Caption

```
echo "APPCENTER_SOURCE_DIRECTORY Contents"
ls -R $APPCENTER_SOURCE_DIRECTORY

echo "APPCENTER_OUTPUT_DIRECTORY Contents"
ls -R $APPCENTER_OUTPUT_DIRECTORY

echo "xamarin.uitest Contents"
ls -R /Users/vsts/.nuget/packages/xamarin.uitest
```

Create the file in the same location as the solution file, as shown in Figure 6-12.

Figure 6-12. *Post-build script for iOS*

Copy the above file. Navigate to the GoGoGiphy.Android folder. Paste the file into the location shown in Figure 6-13.

Figure 6-13. *Post-build script for Android*

Note   Verify that the filename is exactly `appcenter-post-build.sh`. Otherwise, the App Center build will not detect the file.

Commit the two files into your repository. Return to App Center. Select either the Android or the iOS build. I show the Android build definition in Figure 6-14. Open the build definition. You should see the Post-Build icon indicating that App Center sees the post-build script. Save the build definition just once and not Save & Build so App Center can retain the script as part of the build process. Open the build definition again and now click on Save & Build.

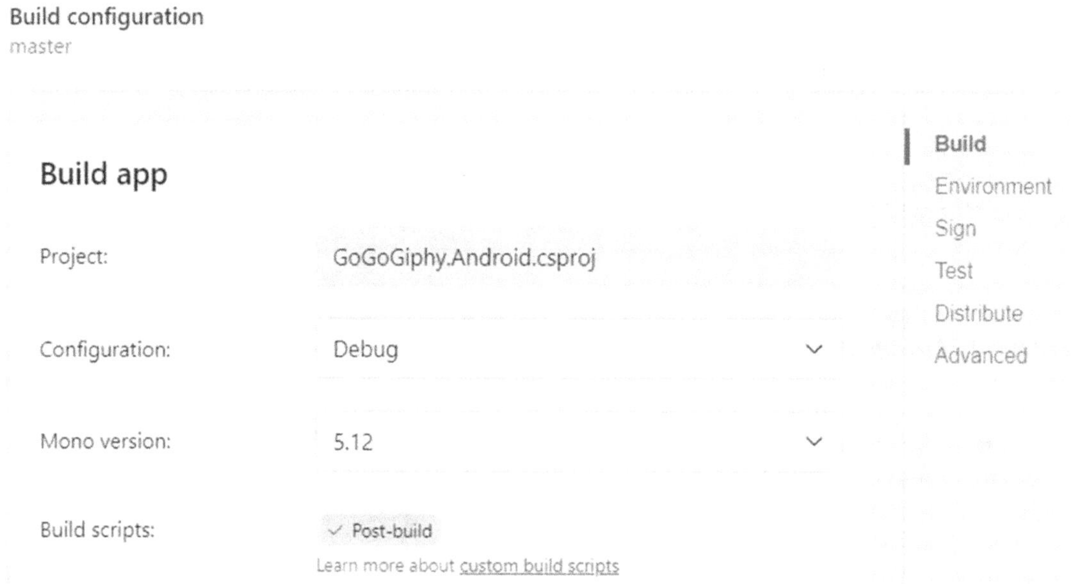

Build configuration
master

Build app

Project:	GoGoGiphy.Android.csproj
Configuration:	Debug
Mono version:	5.12
Build scripts:	✓ Post-build

Learn more about custom build scripts

Build
Environment
Sign
Test
Distribute
Advanced

Figure 6-14. *Android build definition showing the post-build label*

Note   After App Center detects the build script, save both the Android and iOS build definitions. If you simply run the build without saving, the build will not include the script as part of the build.

After saving and running the build, your build output will list the contents of the three folders you included in the script. However, the build output window on the website has a character limit count, so it will truncate the output after a certain point. It is not reliable if you want to inspect the entire output. The best approach to take is to download the logs and inspect the files (Figure 6-15).

Figure 6-15. *Downloading the logs*

Therefore, click the Download logs button, save the zip file, unzip it, and view the Post Build Script.txt file, as selected in Figure 6-16.

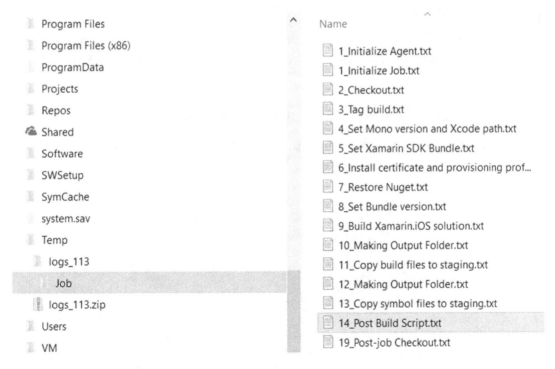

Figure 6-16. *The Post Build Script.txt log file*

Saving the Access Token into an Environment Variable

Since every call to the UITest command will require a login from App Center for security purposes, you need to authenticate yourself with App Center first to prove that you are an authorized user of the service. As a result, you need to automate this step by saving the access token as an environment variable and passing in the access token when invoking the UITest command.

I covered the steps of saving the access token back in Chapter 4. If you forgot the steps or if you forgot to save the value of the token, please revisit the chapter again.

Please refer to Figure 6-17 for the following steps.

- Open either the Android or the iOS build definition.

- Toggle the Environment variables section to On.

- Give the variable a name like AppCenterToken.

- Paste the value of the token.

- Click the lock icon to redact the value because you do not want other members of your team to see this value when they open the build definition.

- Click Save.

- Repeat the above steps for the other build definition, iOS or Android.

You can always click the environment variables link in App Center, shown in Figure 6-17, to learn more about them.

Figure 6-17. *Saving the token as an environment variable*

In a later section, you will reference this environment variable in the Bash script like the following:

```
$AppCenterToken
```

Note the use of the $ before the name of the variable.

Testing on a Real Device

I know, I know. You want to get UI testing already. But you have one last topic to get out of the way so you know what it is about and how it is different from UI testing. App Center gives you the option of launching your app on various devices just to verify it launches successfully.

Keep in mind a couple of things about this step. First, it will not run your post-build script and has nothing to do with running UI tests in App Center. Second, it will add about 10 minutes to your normal build time. This step is helpful when you build an app for the first time and you want to know quickly if it launches on various preconfigured devices.

Return to either your Android or iOS build definition and toggle the command shown in Figure 6-18.

Figure 6-18. *Testing on a real device*

Click the Save & Build option. Wait for the build output. You should see the output shown in Figure 6-19.

Figure 6-19.   Test run in build output

Notice that your build output will show links to your test run. You can navigate to these links or go to Test Runs in App Center to view the test runs. But I will show you later in more detail the layout of the Test Runs section.

If only running UI tests were as easy as toggling an option and clicking a button, this chapter would just be a few pages long! Maybe the App Center team will make UI testing easier for developers in the future.

Getting the UITest Command Template

You are finally here: your first step in a long list of steps to get UI tests up and running! Be prepared because the journey is only beginning. In order to make the journey easier, you will let App Center do most of the work for you by using the UITest command template and then returning to the command template by adding new parameters and modifying the parameters App Center provides for you. In this way, you will make fewer mistakes with syntax errors or misspellings.

Return to App Center, toggle the Test tab open, and find Test runs, as shown in Figure 6-20.

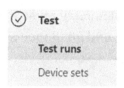

Figure 6-20. *Test runs*

You should see the Start testing your app button if you have never run a test before. Since you launched your app on a test device in the prior section, you will see your test run on this page. If you have never executed a test run, click the Start testing your app option (Figure 6-21). If you have launched your app before on a test device, click the New test run button at the top right.

You don't have any test runs yet.

App Center is waiting for you to run your tests on any of our 400+ device configurations.

Start testing your app

Figure 6-21. *Start testing your app*

Figure 6-22 shows the iOS app. Remember how you set up two device sets before, one for iPhone 8 devices and the second for iPhone X devices. You can select one of the preconfigured device sets or the Choose other device configuration option.

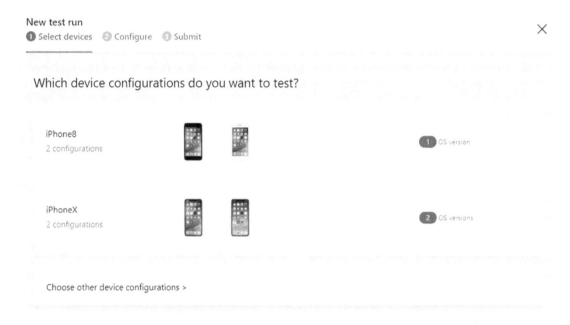

Figure 6-22.   *Selecting the existing device configuration or selecting new devices*

You will see a list of test series. If you enabled the test on a real device option in the build and ran it in the section before, you will see a test series like launch-tests, as shown in Figure 6-18. You can always define a new test series. A test series is a way for App Center to organize your test runs after your UI tests have completed. For example, you can use HomePageTests. But for now, keep it as the default master. And select Xamarin. UITest. Click Next. See Figure 6-23.

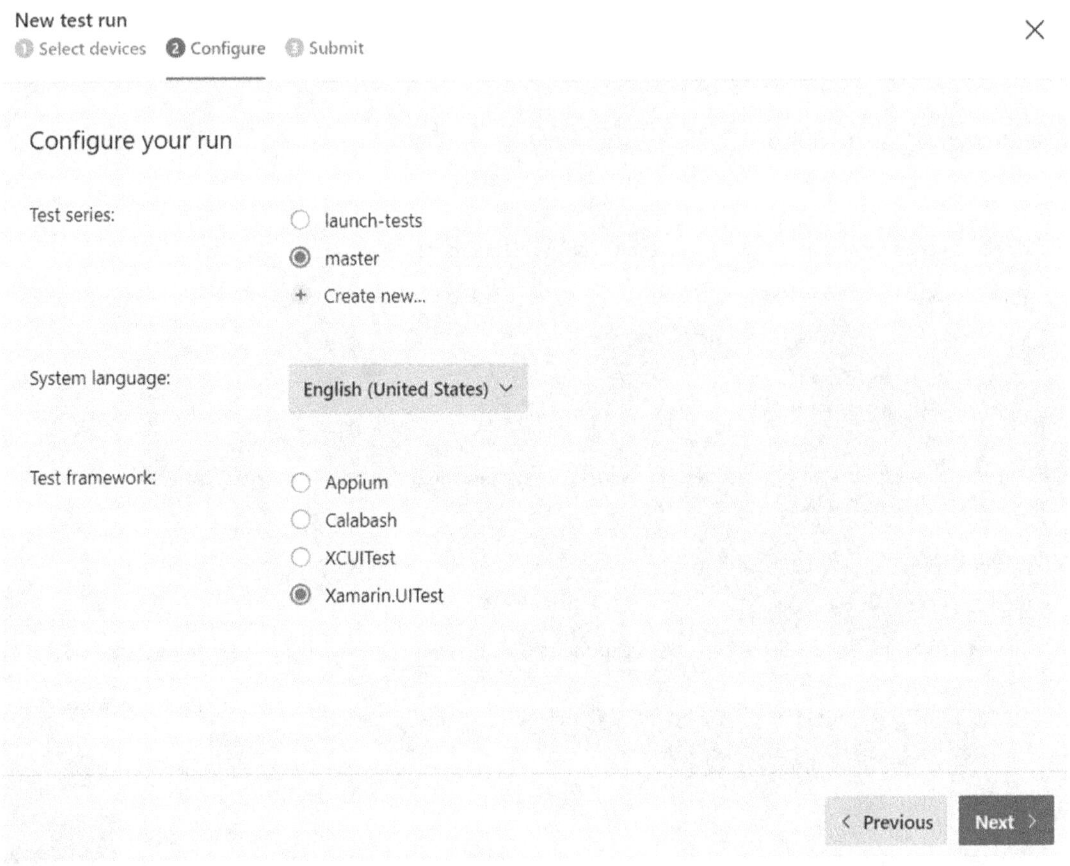

New test run   ✕
① Select devices   ② Configure   ③ Submit
_____

Configure your run

Test series: ○ launch-tests
                                ● master
                                + Create new...

System language: [English (United States) ∨]

Test framework: ○ Appium
                                ○ Calabash
                                ○ XCUITest
                                ● Xamarin.UITest

                                                          ‹ Previous   Next ›

Figure 6-23. *Configuring a test run*

The third and final page shows a lot of relevant and useful information. First, it shows you instructions on how to install NodeJS and the App Center CLI. You completed both steps in a prior section, so you can skip them. Let's focus on the section called Running tests. You are interested in the template for running your UI tests at the bottom of this page.

Please note that the template App Center gives you by default will **not** run as it currently exists. The remainder of this chapter is devoted to customizing this single command. Do not feel discouraged if you get stuck or if you find yourself customizing and repeating multiple times. Failure is the best teacher. This is the part when you get to try 100 times, fail 100 times, and succeed on the 101st! See Figure 6-24.

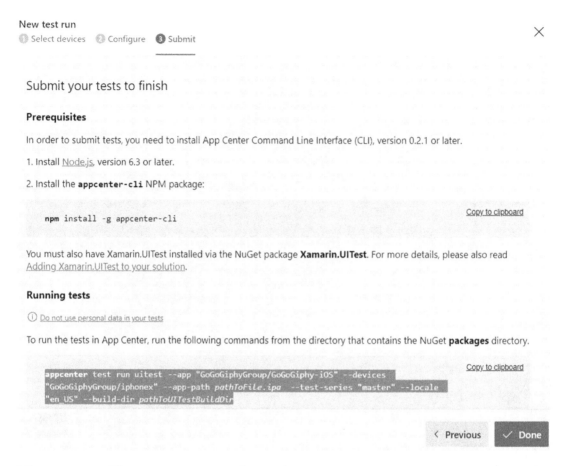

Figure 6-24. *The UITest command template*

Let's break down the command template and understand the purpose of each of the command arguments before moving ahead to customize the command.

The `test run uitest` argument instructs the App Center CLI to run a UI test:

```
appcenter test run uitest
```

The `--app` argument supplies the CLI command with the organization name and the app name so the App Center CLI can locate your app:

```
--app "GoGoGiphyGroup/GoGoGiphy-iOS"
```

The `--devices` argument instructs the CLI to run the UI tests on the specified device set, in this case, the iPhoneX device set that I picked earlier:

```
--devices "GoGoGiphyGroup/iphonex"
```

The `--app-path` argument instructs the CLI to locate either your iOS `.ipa` file or your Android `.apk` file at the specified location. I will show you the steps to get this path in a following section.

```
--app-path pathToFile.ipa
```

The `--test-series` argument instructs the CLI to organize this test run as a master test run for viewing purposes:

```
--test-series "master"
```

The `--locale` argument instructs the CLI that this test run will run in the specified region:

```
--locale "en_US"
```

The `--build-dir` argument instructs the CLI to locate the output or the assemblies containing your UI tests in the Xamarin.UITest project at the specified location:

```
--build-dir pathToUITestBuildDir
```

The coming sections will focus more specifically on the `--app-path` and `--build-dir` arguments because those are the arguments that will require the most trial-and-error attention while the other arguments can be left to their default values. In addition, you will need to supply the CLI with more arguments because the above template will not work as it currently exists. I will explain soon.

Configuring the iOS UITest Command

Let's begin by modifying the `appcenter-post-build.sh.rename` file for iOS first. Rename the existing file extension from `.rename` to `.sh`. If you created the Bash script on your own, locate the file next to the solution file. Open the bash script in either Visual Studio or your favorite text editor.

You need to remember a couple of important points to help you customize the command template. First, every file path will reference paths in the App Center server environment and not your local machine. Second, you will make use of the App Center variables that I presented in a prior section because they will allow you to reference key locations in the App Center server.

Determining the --app-path Value

This argument is the location of the iOS `.ipa` file. The `APPCENTER_OUTPUT_DIRECTORY` will contain the `.ipa` file itself. Instead of taking my word at face value, I will help you prove it to yourself.

If you followed my instructions in the section titled "How to Set Up Post-Build Scripts," you can begin. Otherwise, please revisit this section on how to set up your post-build scripts for the first time.

- Verify that the `appcenter-post-build.sh` file is saved and committed into the repository.

- Verify that the iOS build definition detects the post-build script.

- Click the Save & Build option.

- Click the Download button and select the Download logs option.

- Save and extract the zip file.

- Go to the extracted subfolder called `Job`.

- Locate and open the `Post Build Script.txt` file.

- Search for `APPCENTER_OUTPUT_DIRECTORY`.

- Verify that the next line shows `GoGoGiphy.iOS.ipa` as the only file content since this file is the only build output.

- Finally, change the `--app-path` argument to the following:

  ```
  --app-path $APPCENTER_OUTPUT_DIRECTORY/GoGoGiphy.iOS.ipa
  ```

This command parameter instructs the CLI to look in the output directory for the `.ipa` file.

Determining --build-dir Value

This argument supplies the location to the output or the assemblies of the Xamarin. UITest project containing your UI tests. In your local machine, this value is the location to your `GoGoGiphy.UITest/bin/Debug` folder. You need to determine the same location on the App Center server.

Follow these steps to understand how you derive the value for `--build-dir`:

- Return to your extracted zip file containing the latest build logs.

- Open the `Post Build Script.txt` file in the `Log` folder.

- Search for `APPCENTER_SOURCE_DIRECTORY`. The lines below the current line will show the contents recursively on a folder-by-folder basis. It will list the parent folder first and its contents. It will then move on to show the contents of each child folder.

- Verify that the contents of the parent folder are similar to the following contents. The first line is what was written to the log file from the bash command. The following lines show the contents of the parent folder. This parent folder is the location of `APPCENTER_SOURCE_DIRECTORY`.

    - `APPCENTER_SOURCE_DIRECTORY` contents

        - `GoGoGiphy`

        - `GoGoGiphy.sln`

        - `appcenter-post-build.sh`

        - `packages`

- Scroll down until you see the path to the first `GoGoGiphy` folder. The path except for `GoGoGiphy` is the location of `APPCENTER_SOURCE_DIRECTORY` as **highlighted**:

    `/Users/vsts/agent/2.141.1/work/1/s/GoGoGiphy`

- Copy the value of the `APPCENTER_SOURCE_DIRECTORY` location:

    `/Users/vsts/agent/2.141.1/work/1/s/`

- Scroll down the log file until you see the following line:

    `/Users/vsts/agent/2.141.1/work/1/s/GoGoGiphy/GoGoGiphy.UITest/bin/Debug`

    - Verify that you see the `GoGoGiphy.UITest.dll` as one of the files within the Debug folder. This assembly contains your UI tests. You need to supply this location.

- Finally, append the path to the `GoGoGiphy.UITest/bin/Debug` folder to the `APPCENTER_SOURCE_DIRECTORY` path, which will be your `-build-dir` argument:

  `--build-dir $APPCENTER_SOURCE_DIRECTORY/GoGoGiphy/GoGoGiphy.UITest/bin/Debug`

Determining the --uitest-tools-dir Value

This argument is missing in the original command template. Why do you need this? If you are not convinced, you can enter the CLI with the values that you have ascertained up until now into the post-build script, commit to the repository, run the build, and see what happens. It will throw an error asking you to provide the location of `test-cloud.exe`.

What is `test-cloud.exe`? Remember that Xamarin Test Cloud used to be the official product that ran UI tests. Microsoft acquired Xamarin, but this is the same application that runs your UI tests with the supplied CLI command and arguments. Microsoft retained the original name of the product.

As a result, App Center asks you to provide the location of `test-cloud.exe` on the server. Personally, at the time of this writing, I think App Center can do a better job of integrating the location of the test-cloud application for you since it is a critical component of running any UI tests. It should at least include the `--uitest-tools-dir` as part of the command template. I only learned about this from App Center Support. Hopefully, you can forego this step in the future. But for now you still need to configure this command argument.

Let's get started! You will go through a similar set of steps as before:

- Go to your extracted log files from the zip file.

- Open the same `Post Build Script.txt` file.

- Search for xamarin.uitest contents. This is the `ls` command that you entered earlier in the post-build script. You want to view the contents of all the subfolders and their files.

- Browse through the list of subfolders that are displayed. They should be in version format. Each of these subfolders contains the same but a different version of the `test-cloud.exe` application. You want the latest version. At the time of this writing, the latest version is 2.2.6. It will sort them as earliest to latest version from top to bottom in the output.

- Copy and search for the latest version number, in this case, 2.2.6.

- Scroll down until you see the `test-cloud.exe` application. The path should be similar to the following. Copy this path:

  `/Users/vsts/.nuget/packages/xamarin.uitest/2.2.6/lib/tools`

- Integrate the above path into the `--uitest-tools-dir` argument:

  `--uitest-tools-dir /Users/vsts/.nuget/packages/xamarin.uitest/2.2.6/lib/tools`

At the time of this writing, App Center does not support a wildcard pattern where you can always use the latest version of the application. Therefore, you will need to supply the version number in the path explicitly.

Logging In Automatically to Run UI Tests

Until now, if you attempted to run the CLI command through the Bash script, it would have thrown an error similar to the following message:

`Error: Command 'appcenter test run uitest' requires a logged in user. Use the 'appcenter login' command to log in.`

App Center wants you to log in first before running the command. You already saved the access token as an environment variable in the section titled "How to Save the Access Token." If you forgot or if you skipped the section, please revisit it since it is a prerequisite to this section.

Add the following CLI argument to the command. The `AppCenterToken` variable contains the value for the token you saved earlier.

`--token $AppCenterToken`

If you changed the name of your environment variable to another name, use your own name preceded by the $. The $ character is needed when referencing from the Bash script.

Final iOS UITest Command

If you completed all of the above steps, you should be close to the finish line! Do not get discouraged if it does not work the first time. Some things may have changed in App Center since the time of this writing. I summarized all the steps that I performed after getting my UI tests to run.

Your full CLI command should now look like Listing 6-2.

Listing 6-2. Full CLI Command

```
appcenter test run uitest
--app "GoGoGiphyGroup/GoGoGiphy-iOS"
--devices "GoGoGiphyGroup/iphonex"
--app-path $APPCENTER_OUTPUT_DIRECTORY/GoGoGiphy.iOS.ipa
--test-series "master"
--locale "en_US"
--build-dir $APPCENTER_SOURCE_DIRECTORY/GoGoGiphy/GoGoGiphy.UITest/bin/
  Debug
--uitest-tools-dir /Users/vsts/.nuget/packages/xamarin.uitest/2.2.6/lib/
  tools
--token $AppCenterToken
```

Feel free to customize the `--devices` argument to point to another device set or the `--test-series` argument if you want to call your test run another name; I used the iPhoneX device set that was customized earlier. Leave the other arguments as they exist now.

- Open the `appcenter-post-build.sh` file (adjacent to the solution file). Remember that this file is the post-build script used for the iOS build definition.

- Paste the above command to the end of the file. You can comment out the other commands with a # character. Personally, I leave earlier commands commented out because you may need them later.

- Save the file and commit it to your repository.

- Run the build if it is set to manual build.

- Wait for the build to reach the end, at which point it will execute the post-build script.

- If you configured the command correctly, you will see the start of your UI tests, similar to Figure 6-25.

BUILD OUTPUT

```
/Users/vsts/agent/2.141.1/work/1/s/../../../../../.nuget/packages/Xamarin.UITest/2.2.6/tools:
test-cloud.exe
Running UITest Command for iOS
Preparing tests... done.
Validating arguments... done.
Creating new test run... done.
Validating application file... done.
Uploading files... done.
Starting test run... done.
Test run id: "399241dc-f87c-4708-8d58-b8300a46af28"
Accepted devices:
  - Apple iPhone X (11.4.1)
  - Apple iPhone X (12.0.1)


Current test status: Validating

Current test status: Validating

Current test status: Validating

Current test status: Validating
```

Figure 6-25. *Build output showing the test run starting*

- Remain patient because this step will take a long time. You will see the Current test status message repeat. This is normal because App Center runs the UI test on a physical device in your device set. App Center continues pinging this physical device to get the status of the UI test on a regular interval, hence the repeated output.

- Eventually, you will see the UI test finish, as shown in Figure 6-26.

BUILD OUTPUT

```
Current test status: Running on 1 device (1 / 2 completed, 0 pending) - Report 50% done

Current test status: Running on 1 device (1 / 2 completed, 0 pending) - Report 50% done

Current test status: Running on 1 device (1 / 2 completed, 0 pending) - Report 50% done

Current test status: Running on 1 device (1 / 2 completed, 0 pending) - Report 50% done

Current test status: Running on 1 device (1 / 2 completed, 0 pending) - Report 50% done

Current test status: Tests completed. Processing data.

Current test status: Tests completed. Processing data.

Current test status: Tests completed. Processing data.

Current test status: Done!
Total scenarios: 1
0 passed
1 failed
Total steps: 1
```

Figure 6-26. *Build output showing completed UI tests*

Notice above how the output shows how many scenarios ran, how many passed, and how many failed. In this test run, my UI test failed. This test run failed because one test function is set up deliberately to fail. I will show you how to fix this test function written with Xamarin.UITest in a later section.

Viewing Test Run Results

Now head over to the Test Run section in App Center. You will view the test that just ran. Keep in mind that this is a real UI test that is set up to fail on purpose. You need to know the important areas of this section so you do not miss out on what may help you in the future when writing your own UI tests. Your Test Runs page should look like Figure 6-27.

Figure 6-27. *Test runs*

Click the Test Run to view the details, as shown in Figure 6-28. Notice how App Center shows on how many devices the UI test ran. In this example, it failed on both devices.

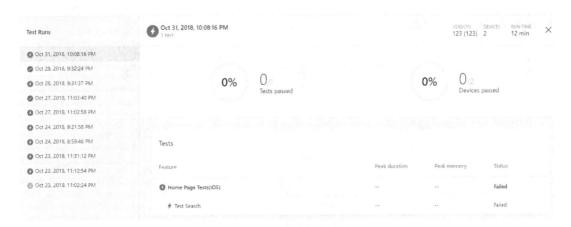

Figure 6-28. *Home page tests*

Click Test Search, which is the name of my UI test. Figure 6-29 shows an actual screenshot of the app that ran on both devices.

Figure 6-29. *UI test called Test Search showing app screenshots*

Click one of the devices. You will see the detailed page, shown in Figure 6-30.

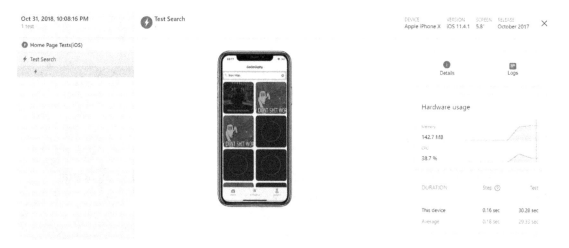

Figure 6-30. *Test search*

You can view the details of the device by clicking Details, in which case you may get a pop-up showing the specifications of the device that ran your test (Figure 6-31).

Figure 6-31. *Device configuration*

Click Logs at the top right. This is the most critical section because you will see three areas, shown in Figure 6-32.

Figure 6-32. *Test failures*

The first section, Test Failures, will show the UI test that ran and what failed. In this example, the Assert command expected a True value but got a False value instead.

The above output is good but not good enough since you want to see why it failed. Click the Test Logs option. You can view the output in the webpage itself or click the Download test logs option (Figure 6-33).

Figure 6-33. *Test logs*

The output may be difficult to see in the image, but the relevant lines that explain the reasons for the failure are as follows:

```
01-11-2018 03:17:24.352 +01:00 - 27335 - Entering text 'Iron Man'
                                         in element matching
                                         Marked("SearchBar") at coordinates
                                         [ 184.5, 113 ].
01-11-2018 03:17:25.019 +01:00 - 28002 - Pressing enter.
01-11-2018 03:17:25.234 +01:00 - 28217 - Query for Marked("CachedImage")
                                         gave 0 results.
```

Notice how the device shows the timestamp, the action that was taken, and the reason for the failure. In this simple example, I entered Iron Man in the search bar, instructed the UITest to press Enter, and instructed the test to search for any image marked with CachedImage from the results. It failed because it didn't find any matching results.

If you do not own an iPhone X device yourself, you have just tested your first UI test on an iPhone X in the cloud! Now you can say you have tested a UI test officially in the cloud!

Configuring the Android UITest Command

Thankfully, you are most of the way through your journey in configuring the CLI command for Android because you can reuse most of the command parameters from iOS. Keep the other argument values the same. I will show only the argument values that you need to change and the one command you need to add.

Determining the --app-path Value

For the iOS command, you determine the --app-path value by finding that the .ipa is located in the APPCENTER_OUTPUT_DIRECTORY folder. The same is true for Android except the name of the file is different, obviously.

Your post-build script should consist of only the lines in Listing 6-3.

Listing 6-3. Post-Build Script

```
echo "APPCENTER_SOURCE_DIRECTORY Contents"
ls -R $APPCENTER_SOURCE_DIRECTORY

echo "APPCENTER_OUTPUT_DIRECTORY Contents"
ls -R $APPCENTER_OUTPUT_DIRECTORY

echo "xamarin.uitest Contents"
ls -R /Users/vsts/.nuget/packages/xamarin.uitest
```

If you already ran the build, your zip file containing the log files should contain a Post Build Script.txt file too. If your zip file does not contain this text file, just save and run the build once. Click Download Logs as before. Extract the zip file and open the Post Build Script.txt.

At this point, search for APPCENTER_OUTPUT_DIRECTORY. Immediately below this line, you will find the name of the Android .apk file to supply to the CLI command.

Your --app-path should be the following:

```
--app-path $APPCENTER_OUTPUT_DIRECTORY/com.companyname.GoGoGiphy.apk
```

Running the MS Build Command

One additional step is required in the post-build script before running the UITest command. If you attempt to copy and paste the Bash commands into the post-build script for Android, the CLI command will fail in App Center with the following error message:

```
/Users/vsts/.nuget/packages/xamarin.uitest/2.2.6/tools:
test-cloud.exe
Running UITest Command
Assembly directory doesn't exist
```

Why would the assembly directory not exist for Android all of a sudden? Remember when you inspected the output of the ls command in the Post Build Script.txt? If you search for APPCENTER_SOURCE_DIRECTORY, it will reveal the contents of all the subfolders in the source directory, including the Bin folders where the build artifacts of each project are created. Then search for GoGoGiphy.UITest in the same file. Look through the subfolders. You will see that the Bin/Debug folder is missing.

Why would the Bin folder not exist? This clue will lead you to uncover how the build definition is originally set up. For iOS, the build definition points to the solution file, meaning that all the projects referenced in the solution are compiled. For Android, only the Android project is referenced, meaning only the Android project is built and not the GoGoGiphy.UITest.

As a result, you need a way to build the GoGoGiphy.UITest project prior to running the UITest CLI command. Therefore, you need to invoke the msbuild application and pass in the path to the .csproj file for the UITest project.

The following is the command:

```
/Library/Frameworks/Mono.framework/Versions/5_12_0/bin/msbuild $APPCENTER_
SOURCE_DIRECTORY/GoGoGiphy/GoGoGiphy.UITest/GoGoGiphy.UITest.csproj
```

The first part of this command is the path to the msbuild executable. If you work with AppCenter support, they can provide you with this path too.

The second part of this command is the argument for the msbuild command. For brevity's sake, I saved you the steps in figuring out how to get the path to the .csproj file for the UITest project. But if you are interested in knowing how to find this path, follow the same steps you performed earlier to inspect the output of the ls command for the APPCENTER_SOURCE_DIRECTORY folder. Scroll through the subfolders and their contents and eventually you will find the location of the .csproj file.

Final Android UITest Command

After following all the above instructions, your final Bash commands should now look like Listing 6-4.

Listing 6-4. Add Caption

```
/Library/Frameworks/Mono.framework/Versions/5_12_0/bin/msbuild $APPCENTER_
SOURCE_DIRECTORY/GoGoGiphy/GoGoGiphy.UITest/GoGoGiphy.UITest.csproj
/t:Build /p:Configuration=Debug

appcenter test run uitest
--app "GoGoGiphyGroup/GoGoGiphy-Android"
--devices "GoGoGiphyGroup/GooglePixel3Android9"
--app-path $APPCENTER_OUTPUT_DIRECTORY/com.companyname.GoGoGiphy.apk
--test-series "master"
--locale "en_US"
--build-dir $APPCENTER_SOURCE_DIRECTORY/GoGoGiphy/GoGoGiphy.UITest/bin/Debug
--uitest-tools-dir /Users/vsts/.nuget/packages/xamarin.uitest/2.2.6/lib/tools
--token $AppCenterToken
```

Similar to how you tested the post-build script, feel free to change a few things in the above command, which may be different in your setup. My device set is called GooglePixel3Android9; change it to your own device set name. If you labeled your test series to another name, change the name as well.

Follow the steps below to save and run your final CLI command:

- Open the appcenter-post-build.sh file next to the Android .csproj file.

- Paste the above msbuild command before the ls commands. You need to paste it before these commands so you can verify that the Bin/Debug folder is created when the project is built.

- Paste the UITest command after the ls commands. You can comment out the ls commands with the # character if you are confident that the UITest command will work. I would leave it uncommented if I were you for troubleshooting purposes.

- Save and commit the file into the repository.

- Run the build.

311

If everything was set up correctly, your build output will look like Figure 6-34.

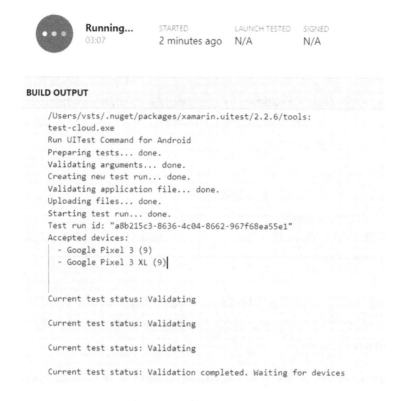

Figure 6-34. *Build output showing Android UI test run*

Notice how the output is similar to the iOS output. The only difference here is the accepted devices where the UI tests are run, in this case, Google Pixel 3 and Pixel 3 XL.

Viewing Test Run Results

Similar to the iOS test runs, return to the Test runs sections for the Android app. Your test run may look like Figure 6-35.

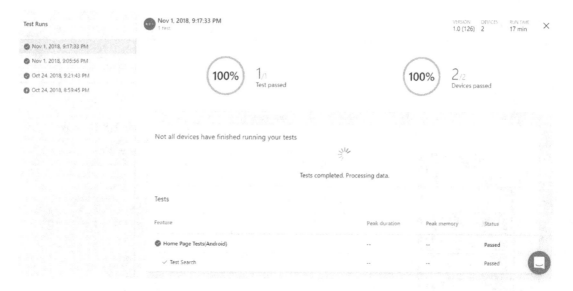

Figure 6-35. *Test runs*

Notice how the same UI test succeeded for both Android devices but failed for iOS. This difference reveals the power of App Center because you have just proven that the same test can yield different results in different devices. If you attempted to reproduce the same result on physical devices, you would need to purchase at least two separate devices, one for iOS and one for Android, to notice that your app behaves differently. Now imagine how much money you can save with App Center!

Follow the same steps you performed for the iOS test run. Click Test Search, click one of the devices, and click Test Logs (Figure 6-36).

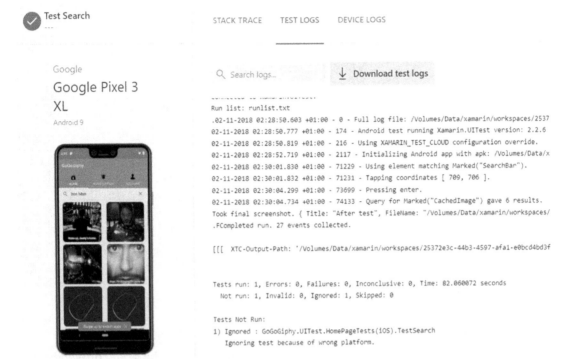

Figure 6-36. *Test logs*

The following are the contents of the log message:

```
Android test running Xamarin.UITest version: 2.2.6
02-11-2018 02:28:50.819 +01:00 - 216 - Using XAMARIN_TEST_CLOUD
                                       configuration override.
02-11-2018 02:28:52.719 +01:00 - 2117 - Initializing Android app with
                                         apk: /Volumes/Data/xamarin/
                                         workspaces/25372e3c-44b3-4597-afa1-
                                         e0bcd4bd3f80/workspace/app.apk
02-11-2018 02:30:01.830 +01:00 - 71229 - Using element matching
                                         Marked("SearchBar").
02-11-2018 02:30:01.832 +01:00 - 71231 - Tapping coordinates [ 709, 706 ].
02-11-2018 02:30:04.299 +01:00 - 73699 - Pressing enter.
02-11-2018 02:30:04.734 +01:00 - 74133 - Query for Marked("CachedImage")
                                         gave 6 results.
```

Notice how the UITest detects six objects with the CachedImage identifier, which is why the test succeeds.

Whew! If you got this far and got both your iOS and Android test runs to execute successfully, congratulate yourself on a spectacular job! Now you hold the crown of officially running UI tests on both iOS and Android in the cloud!

Running UI Tests Asynchronously

One thing you may notice while running your UI tests is that your builds now take a long time to run. You may want to start your build and simply want to see your build finish and trigger the test run instead of waiting for the test runs to finish while holding up the build.

Thankfully, AppCenter provides an --async command that instructs the CLI to run asynchronously. Simply add the --async argument to the command as shown in listing 6-5.

Listing 6-5. Add Caption

```
appcenter test run uitest
--app "GoGoGiphyGroup/GoGoGiphy-iOS"
--async
--devices "GoGoGiphyGroup/iphonex"
--app-path $APPCENTER_OUTPUT_DIRECTORY/GoGoGiphy.iOS.ipa
--test-series "master"
--locale "en_US"
--build-dir $APPCENTER_SOURCE_DIRECTORY/GoGoGiphy/GoGoGiphy.UITest/bin/Debug
--uitest-tools-dir /Users/vsts/.nuget/packages/xamarin.uitest/2.2.6/lib/tools
--token $AppCenterToken
```

Save your post-build script, commit to the repository, run the build, and wait for the build to finish. The output should look like Figure 6-37.

Figure 6-37. *Build Output showing asynchronous test run*

Notice a couple of important details in Figure 6-37. First, it runs your UI tests the same as before. Second, it provides a link to the Test Report that you can follow to view the results of the test run, which is the same webpage I showed you before. Third, the build actually succeeds and finishes a lot sooner than before.

Now your build success is not dependent on the results of your test run. It is a matter of developer preference whether the build should be dependent on the results of the test run. Just keep in mind the trade-off. If the build depends on the test run result, your build will take longer. If you want your builds to finish sooner, your builds will succeed regardless of the outcome of your test run, even a failed test run.

Using REPL (Read-Eval-Print-Loop)

If you remember, the same UI test succeeded for Android devices but not for iOS devices. This difference in results showed you the power of testing in App Center without having to purchase physical devices to run the same tests.

But why did iPhone devices give a different result in the first place? The answer is simple. Return to the solution in Visual Studio. Open HomePage.xaml. Collapse the content. You can press Control+M and Control+L to toggle the expansion and collapsing of all XAML elements. Scroll down the XAML page until you reach a control called `PullToRefreshLayoutControl` and the grid below it. Notice how the `IsVisible` bindable property on this control is bound to `IsTrendingImagesPanelVisible`. This property in the ViewModel collapses the grid and expands the `PullToRefreshLayoutControl` after the user presses Enter on the search bar. On Android, this set of actions completes in time before reaching the `Assert` statement in the UI test. On iOS, this set of actions do not complete in time, which is why the `Assert` statement returns false and the UI test fails.

How can you fix this? First, I will show you a handy little console tool that the App Center team has provided for you. It is called REPL and it stands for Read-Eval-Print-Loop. If you have experience using the C# Interactive tool or the PowerShell Interactive tool within Visual Studio, you know what REPL is about. It allows you to test or read the commands, evaluate them, and print out the results in real time, hence the name REPL. Once you have tested your commands, you can then copy the commands over into your application. Now App Center provides you with this handy tool to make writing UI tests easier by giving you the ability to test out UI test commands, evaluate your commands on your app in the simulator, and print out the results.

You can find more information about the important commands at `https://docs. microsoft.com/en-us/appcenter/test-cloud/uitest/working-with-repl`.

Using app.Repl()

Here are the steps for diagnosing, troubleshooting, and fixing this UI test. Open `HomePageTests.cs` in the UITest project. As mentioned, `TestSearchBroken()` is the intentionally failing UI test function. The working example called `TestSearchWorking()` is below it.

Feel free to create another UI test function or modify `TestSearchBroken()`. But I want to show you how to diagnose the broken example to arrive at the final working result in `TestSearchWorking()`.

See Listing 6-6 and add the command and strip out the existing commands. Verify that your code looks like it now.

Listing 6-6. Add Caption

```
/// <summary>
/// This UITest fails on purpose on iPhone devices to show the working
    example in the next UITest function below.
```

```
/// </summary>
[Test]
public void TestSearchBroken()
{
  app.Repl();
}
```

The call to `app.Repl()` opens the terminal window for the Repl console application and allows you to experiment and play with various UI commands. It will evaluate the console commands and display the results to the user.

Follow these steps in order to run the Repl tool:

- Rebuild the UITest project.

- Go to Test Explorer and verify the tests appear.

- Go to Tools ➤ Android ➤ Android Device Manager.

- Launch one of your preconfigured Android simulators. Wait for it to finish launching.

- Return to Test Explorer. Expand HomePageTests for Android.

- Add the following command either to `TestSearchBroken()` or to your own UI test function:

  app.Repl();

- Right-click TestSearchBroken and either run selected tests or debug selected tests. If you select debug, you can insert breakpoints and step through you UI test functions.

At this point, it will launch the app in the Android simulator and call your selected UI test function. Once it runs `app.Repl()`, it will launch the Repl console application shown in Figure 6-38.

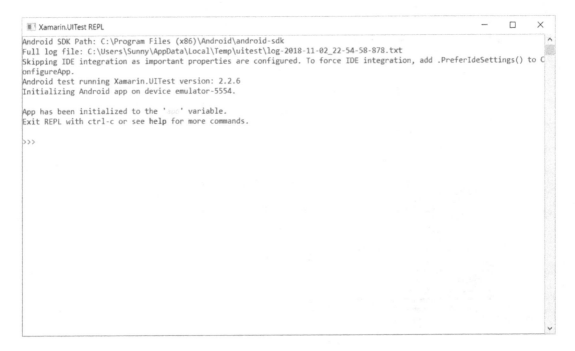

Figure 6-38. *Xamarin.UITest REPL console window*

Using the Tree Command

Type the tree command in the command-line window. The tree command shows you a hierarchical list of all the views visible on the screen. You can use this command to list out all the views. After running this command, scroll down until you see a list of controls with the CachedImage labels, as shown in Figure 6-39.

```
■ Xamarin.UITest REPL                                                    —    □    ×
            [PullToRefreshLayoutRenderer]
              [ScrollViewRenderer > ScrollViewContainer] label: "TrendingImagesScrollView"
                [Platform_DefaultRenderer] label: "TrendingImagesPanel" (center not on screen)
                  [CachedImageRenderer] label: "CachedImage_Container"
                    [CachedImageView] id: "NoResourceEntry-8", label: "CachedImage"
                  [CachedImageRenderer] label: "CachedImage_Container"
                    [CachedImageView] id: "NoResourceEntry-9", label: "CachedImage"
                  [CachedImageRenderer] label: "CachedImage_Container"
                    [CachedImageView] id: "NoResourceEntry-10", label: "CachedImage"
                  [CachedImageRenderer] label: "CachedImage_Container"
                    [CachedImageView] id: "NoResourceEntry-11", label: "CachedImage"
                  [CachedImageRenderer] label: "CachedImage_Container"
                    [CachedImageView] id: "NoResourceEntry-12", label: "CachedImage"
                  [CachedImageRenderer] label: "CachedImage_Container"
                    [CachedImageView] id: "NoResourceEntry-13", label: "CachedImage"
        [Toolbar] id: "toolbar"
          [AppCompatTextView] text: "GoGoGiphy"
      [TabLayout > TabLayout$SlidingTabStrip] id: "sliding_tabs"
        [TabLayout$TabView]
          [AppCompatImageView]
          [AppCompatTextView] text: "Home"
        [TabLayout$TabView]
          [AppCompatImageView]
          [AppCompatTextView] text: "Notification"
        [TabLayout$TabView]
          [AppCompatImageView]
          [AppCompatTextView] text: "Account"
  [View] id: "navigationBarBackground"
  [View] id: "statusBarBackground"
>>>
```

Figure 6-39. Output of the tree command

Using app.Flash(..)

You can see that the control is visible. Now you will flash the actual control inside your app. This command is handy for locating your view visually within your app. Keep your Android simulator visible side-by-side with the Repl tool and type the following command. You will see your control flash.

```
app.Flash("CachedImage")
```

At the end of the flashing, the terminal window will display all the controls that match your command.

Now that you have verified the control is visible with the right label, you will type the rest of your commands in the same order that you will run your UI test. Type the commands in the following order and watch the app in the Android simulator follow your commands:

```
app.EnterText("SearchBar", "Iron Man")
app.PressEnter()
```

At this point, your app should have searched for Iron Man, pressed Enter, and showed all the results for Iron Man. This evidently works great in Android. But you need to account for the delay on iOS now.

Using app.WaitForElement(..)

You will use the WaitForElement(..) function to instruct the UI test to wait for the element with the matching id to be visible on the screen first before proceeding with the rest of the test. This command will wait up to 15 seconds on tests running locally and up to 1 minute on tests running in App Center. Type the following command:

```
app.WaitForElement("CachedImage")
```

Copying Commands into the Clipboard

Now how do you copy all the values you typed up until now? The Repl() application provides the copy command to copy all the commands you typed into the terminal window up until now into the clipboard. I know it does not replace Xamarin Test Recorder, which Microsoft took away from us, but it is the next best thing.

Type copy. Return to the TestSearchBroken() function and paste what is in your clipboard. You should see the following commands:

```
app.Flash("CachedImage");
app.EnterText("SearchBar", "IronMan");
app.PressEnter();
app.WaitForElement("CachedImage")
```

Go ahead and delete the Flash command since it is not relevant for your UI test.

Final UI Test Commands

You are going to perform one final modification to your command before committing these commands as your final test.

.NET provides the ability to provide additional parameters to the `WaitForElement(..)` function. Feel free to play with the parameters. But I am going to use the following command. It instructs `WaitForElement(..)` to display a custom message if the element is not displayed in time. And it instructs the function to wait up to 2 minutes, even though the element will display a lot sooner than 2 minutes.

```
app.WaitForElement("CachedImage", "The CachedImage control was not
available in time", new TimeSpan(0, 0, 2, 0, 0));
```

Your final commands should now look similar to the following:

```
app.EnterText("SearchBar", "IronMan");
app.PressEnter();
app.WaitForElement("CachedImage", "The CachedImage control was not
available in time", new TimeSpan(0, 0, 2, 0, 0));
```

Save your changes to `HomePageTests.cs`. Commit and push your changes to the remote repository.

Once your app finishes building and running the UI tests, both of your test functions will now run successfully for iOS, as shown in Figure 6-40.

 Test Search

Apple iPhone X   Apple iPhone X
iOS 12.0.1   iOS 11.4.1

Figure 6-40. *Test Search result*

Summary

Congratulations on reaching the finish line! If you followed me to the end, you can praise yourself for being patient and persistent and for finishing the most challenging topic in this book. Just look at how much you accomplished and learned in this chapter. You did the following:

- Configured projects for Xamarin.UITest

- Set up device sets in App Center

- Set up build scripts and configured UITest commands

- Learned about App Center variables

- Configured UITest commands for iOS and Android

- Learned about and used REPL to fix a broken UITest function

You can now look back and appreciate what you learned from this book. You did the following:

- Created your mobile builds and linked with your code repository

- Created developer certificates and provisioning profiles

- Configured your builds for distribution

- Handled crashes in your app

- Reported events and analytics from your app

- Sent push notifications on iOS and Android

- Handled push notifications on both platforms

- Sent custom data with notifications

- Set up your build scripts

- Ran UI tests for both platforms using the CLI

This is your accomplishment! Of course, if you jumped around from chapter to chapter instead of going sequentially or if some of the topics are a little hazy, feel free to revisit any chapter and repeat the material.

I structured the topics in this book to be valuable not just to Xamarin Forms developers but developers from other platforms. Most of the topics are platform-agnostic. Xamarin Forms was a nice fit for me given my background with this platform. Also, Xamarin Forms is the most popular cross-platform framework at the time of this writing, but it could have been done just as easily with React Native, Cordova, or Unity.

If you have any outstanding questions, feel free to contact me at my LinkedIn profile at `www.linkedin.com/in/sunnymukherjee/` and I will be happy to answer your questions.

I would like to conclude this chapter and this book with a big thank you to you, the reader, for buying this book. I hope the material in this book has shed light on the next evolution of mobile DevOps using App Center. And I hope this book helps you and your team incorporate App Center into your existing DevOps pipeline.

Congratulations, thank you, and good luck in your journey ahead with App Center!

Index

A

325